ASIAN POLITICAL, ECONOMIC AND SOCIAL ISSUES

THE ROLE OF GOVERNMENT IN ECONOMIC GROWTH AND DEVELOPMENT

THE CASES OF KOREA AND VIETNAM

Asian Political, Economic and Social Issues

Additional books and e-books in this series can be found on Nova's website under the Series tab.

ASIAN POLITICAL, ECONOMIC AND SOCIAL ISSUES

THE ROLE OF GOVERNMENT IN ECONOMIC GROWTH AND DEVELOPMENT

THE CASES OF KOREA AND VIETNAM

SEUNG-HO KWON

nova
science publishers
New York

Library of Congress Cataloging-in-Publication Data
Names: Kwfon, Sfung-ho, 1964- author.
Title: The role of government in economic growth and development: the cases of Korea and Vietnam / Seung-Ho Kwon, Ph. D.
Description: Hauppauge, New York: Nova Science Publishers, Inc., [2019] | Series: Asian political, economic and social issues | Includes bibliographical references.
Identifiers: LCCN 2018055985 (print) | LCCN 2018057365 (ebook) | ISBN 9781536147582 (ebook) | ISBN 9781536147575 | ISBN 9781536147575(hardcover) | ISBN 9781536147582(ebook)
Subjects: LCSH: Korea (South)--Economic policy. | Vietnam--Economic policy. | Economic development--Korea (South) | Economic development--Vietnam.
Classification: LCC HC467.95 (ebook) | LCC HC467.95 .K87 2019 (print) | DDC 338.95195--dc23
LC record available at https://lccn.loc.gov/2018055985

Published by Nova Science Publishers, Inc. † New York

CONTENTS

List of Figures

LIST OF TABLES

PREFACE

The role of government in economic development has been a matter of interest and contention since the early development decades. It was initially thought that big government was needed to ensure rapid economic growth. The private sector in developing countries was inadequate for the task and the only actor that could address market failure was government. Thus, governments were not only involved in determining policies for the economy but were also directly engaged in business through state-owned enterprises (SOEs). This was complemented by faith in central planning brought about by the success of Russian industrialization and the rehabilitation of post Second World War Europe and led politicians, public servants and academics to believe that governments could engineer the desired economic changes that would transform underdeveloped economies and societies. But much disappointment was to come as many developing countries failed to achieve rapid and sustained economic growth. This led to disillusionment with big government and its intervention in the economy. Government was increasingly seen as the problem rather than the solution to economic development. The gradual rise of neoliberalism forced the retreat of the state, the ideology urging governments to attend to core functions and leave economic growth and development to the private sector and the market.

However, there were a few countries that managed to avoid disappointment and record high rates of growth over several decades. These were notably the Asian 'tigers' – South Korea, Singapore, Taiwan and Hong Kong. Most remarkable among these was South Korea. In the 1950s, the country emerged from a highly destructive war with its economy in ruins. Its level of development was below most other countries in the world, less than many in Africa. But out of the ruins of war an economic miracle was born. South Korea experienced sustained high rates of economic growth and steadily improving welfare for its citizens. An authoritarian government made economic development its priority and channeled big business into pursuing state policies using both sticks and carrots. While government involvement in the economy lessened over the years, it was nevertheless ready to intervene whenever it was deemed necessary. In just over three decades South Korea moved from being one of the world's poorest countries to becoming a member of the rich countries club, the Organisation for Economic Cooperation and Development (OECD).

But can this path to success be replicated? One country that seems to be currently on its way to making great socioeconomic gains in a relatively short time is Vietnam. Like South Korea, Vietnam had a mammoth rebuilding task starting in the mid-1970s. In common with South Korea, Vietnam had been devastated by two decades of war and started its journey in economic development from the position of being one of the poorest countries in the world. In both countries the state has undoubtedly played a major role in socioeconomic change. A further similarity with the South Korean experience is that Vietnam has an authoritarian political system as South Korea did in the early decades of development.

The purpose of this book is to explore the economic development trajectories of South Korea and Vietnam focusing on the role of the state in economic success. We are looking for both similarities and differences in their experiences. The central role of the state in generating economic development is certainly evident in both cases but are the paths, the institutions, the policies and the environments the same? These are among the matters that this book explores with its systematic comparative analysis of economic development and the role of the state in South Korea and

Vietnam. The results of this analysis provide lessons that will be useful for other developing countries as well as deepening our understanding of the experiences of South Korea and Vietnam.

In writing this book I have received support from various people. First, I would like to thank my colleagues, Haeyoung Jang and Anne Ke at the Korea Research Institute and Anne Junor and Jason Anthony at the Industrial Relations Research Centre at University of New South Wales for their research assistance and administrative help. Second, I wish to acknowledge the support I received from my family, Eun Hee Han and Zia Kwon, while undertaking this demanding project. This invaluable support maintained my spirits and ensured that I finished the task.

ACKNOWLEDGMENT

This work was supported by the Academy of Korean Studies Grant funded by the Korean Government (MOE) (AKS-2010-DZZ-3101).

ABBREVIATIONS

ADB	Asian Development Bank
AEC	ASEAN Economic Community
AFTA	ASEAN Free Trade Area
APEC	Asia-Pacific Economic Cooperation
ASEAN	Association of Southeast Asian Nations
BTA	Bilateral Trade Agreement
CEIC	Creative Economy Innovation Centre
CMEA	Council for Mutual Economic Assistance
CPI	Corruption Perceptions Index
CPV	Communist Party of Vietnam
EEU	Eurasian Economic Union
EIU	Economist Intelligence Unit
EPB	Economic Planning Board
EU	European Union
FDI	Foreign Direct Investment
FIE	Foreign-invested Enterprise
FYEDP	Five-year Economic Development Plan
FTA	Free Trade Agreement
GATT	General Agreement on Trade and Tariffs
GDD	Grassroots Democracy Decree
GDP	Gross Domestic Product

GER	Gross Enrolment Rate
GNP	Gross National Product
HCI	Heavy and Chemical Industry
ICT	Information and Communications Technology
IMF	International Monetary Fund
ITO	International Trade Organization
IZ	Industrial Zone
KEPCO	Korea Electric Power Corporation
KNOC	Korea National Oil Corporation
KOGAS	Korea Gas Corporation
KORES	Korea Resources Corporation
KOTRA	Korea Trade Promotion Corporation
M&A	Mergers and Acquisitions
MDA	Manufacturing Development Act
MIB	Medium Industry Bank
MNE	Multinational Enterprise
MPS	Material Product System
MoST	Ministry of Science and Technology
MSIP	Ministry of Science, ICT and Future Planning
NATO	North Atlantic Treaty Organization
NGO	Non-governmental Organization
NIC	Newly Industrializing Country
ODA	Official Development Assistance
OECD	Organisation for Economic Co-operation and Development
OPEC	Organization of Petroleum Exporting Countries
PAVN	People's Army of Vietnam
RCA	Real Comparative Advantage
R&D	Research and Development
SEATO	Southeast Asia Treat Organization
SEDP	Socio-economic Development Plan
SEDP	Strategic Economic Development Plan
SEDS	Socio-economic Development Strategy
SIDA	Swedish International Development

	Cooperation Agency
SME	Small and Medium Enterprises
SNA	System of National Accounts
SOE	State-owned Enterprise
TRERA	Tax Reduction and Exemption Regulation Act
UN	United Nations
UNDP	United Nations Development Programme
US	United States
VN	Vietnam Dong (currency)
WTO	World Trade Organization

INTRODUCTION

The role of government in economic growth and development has been a subject of long-standing interest in political economy. East Asia's experience of rapid economic growth since the 1970s has fueled an intense debate over the role of government in that process. The main idea of the East Asian model of economic development is that the rapid industrialization and economic growth in Northeast Asia (including Japan, Korea, and Taiwan) and in Southeast Asia (including Singapore, Malaysia, Thailand and Indonesia) has been in great part attributable to the leading role of government.

South Korea (Korea, hereafter) is a representative example of the EA model of economic development, which, along with Taiwan, Hong Kong and Singapore, led the rise of the Asian "tiger economies." More recently, it has been East Asian countries transitioning from centrally planned economies to market economies. Vietnam, along with China, has shown rapid economic growth, emerging as Asia's next tiger (Fuller 2016). It is proposed that a key factor behind the economic success of these two countries with different political systems is the leading role of government in the promotion of economic development. Based on this proposition, this book begins with the question of whether the East Asian model adopted in Korea is a viable tool for understanding the development experience of Vietnam's transition economy as their experiences could be viewed as country-specific and occurring under differing contextual influences. To find an answer to the question of whether the economic development trajectories of Korea and Vietnam have been similar despite occurring at different times and in different circumstances, the following section reviews the existing scholarly literature on the role of government in economic development and East Asia's development experiences.

THE STATE AND ECONOMIC DEVELOPMENT

Early scholarship in the discipline of development economics highlighted the centrality of government intervention in economic development, in particular its role as the prime mover that would "propel the economy from the uncoordinated, low-income, no-long-run-growth static equilibrium to the coordinated, high-income, dynamic equilibrium, golden-growth path" (Adelman 1999: 1). Government was to play the role of an entrepreneur to fill gaps left by the underdeveloped private sector (Adelman 1999: 1). This model was much criticized during the 1970s for its practical failure in developing countries in Africa, Latin America and Asia. Politicians and bureaucrats instead were found to have abused the power of government to extract rent, bestow favors and manipulate markets for personal and sectional economic gain and political support (Greig, Hulme and Turner 2007). Furthermore, some government policies proved to be wrongheaded, such as import substitution industrialization (ISI) — an approach which established inefficient industries and translated into the provision of low-quality products at higher prices for domestic consumers (Baer 1972; Hirschman 1968).

This led to a growing consensus that government was not solving the problems of development but was in fact the source of the problem, and a different approach was needed. This analysis gave rise to schools of thought such as "getting prices right," "trade is enough" and even" evil government" which focused on market discipline as the way forward for economic development (Adelman 1999: 3). The Reagan and Thatcher governments of the 1980s embodied this faith in neoliberal economics whilst organizations such as the World Bank and International Monetary Fund (IMF) were responsible for exporting it across the globe.

Having been banished to the sidelines for the 1980s and at least the first half of the 1990s, the role of government started to reappear in mainstream development thinking. This was partly as a result of the criticisms of neoliberalism but it was more the realization that a large body of evidence had built up about major state involvement being a key to the economic success stories of East Asian countries (Belassa 1988; Deyo 1987).

The East Asian Model of Economic Development

Labelled by the World Bank as "the East Asian Miracle," the rapid and sustained post-war economic growth and development experiences of East Asian countries were seen as models for others to emulate, starting from Japan, Korea, Taiwan and Singapore in the 1950s-1970s and then spreading to Thailand, Malaysia and Indonesia in the 1980s (World Bank 1997). State intervention was singled out as one of the most important factors that contributed to the East Asian miracle and led to these countries being labelled "developmental states" (Johnson 1982; Haggard and Moon 1983; Koo 1984; Deyo 1987; Lim 2009).

While typically characterized as being based on strong state intervention, the East Asian model of development has variegated economic, institutional and social features. Among them, key economic features include: high growth rates; high investment ratios; state control of finance (such as state-controlled interest rates and bank loans); direct support for particular industrial sectors and selected groups of companies (such as *chaebols* - large business groups - in Korea); emphasis on the manufacturing sector and export expansion (Berger 1988; Boltho and Weber 2009).

Authoritarian governments, although not an essential feature, were also one of the common features of the East Asian model of development. The East Asian countries typically adopted authoritarian developmentalism during the take-off period. The rapid industrialization and economic growth were possible based on powerful leadership, strong commitment to economic development, elite bureaucracy, and performance legitimacy and popularity (Huff, Dewit and Oughton 2001; Ohno 2003). Within East Asian countries, authoritarian government was viewed as necessary because a strong government would enable effective control of resources, personnel investments and policy intervention without power struggles or conflicts of interest between political parties and interest groups (Ohno 2003; Sirowy and Inkeles 1990). Ohno (2003), however, defines authoritarian developmentalism as a temporary political system that disappears automatically once a certain level of development is reached. Sirowy and Inkeles (1990) also hold the view that the authoritarian state is not able to continue further development, but instigates democracy. Ohno (2003) argues that, in East Asian developmental states, authoritarian developmentalism is legitimized as the means for development and that civil society is not necessarily for the installation of democracy.

Although many of the characteristics identified above are shared, there are also many distinct differences between Northeast and Southeast Asia. One of the notable differences is the capacity of state leadership in economic development. Whilst governments of the Northeast Asian developmental states of Japan, Korea and Taiwan implemented, planned and staged approaches to economic development (Beeson 2004), Southeast Asian governments have adopted a more *laissez-faire* perspective, depending more on market based-mechanisms or foreign direct investment (FDI) by multinational enterprises (Jomo 2001; Zysman and Doherty 1995). While the Northeast countries had powerful leading economic development agencies, Southeast Asian equivalents had much less power over other agencies (Doner, Ritchie and Slater 2005). As pointed out by Doner, Ritchie and Slater (2005), the context out of which these characteristics emerged also marks the differences in the regions' capacities. Whilst Northeast Asian developmental states built effective capacities during a period of geopolitical insecurity and scarce resources, Southeast Asian states did not face such "systematic vulnerability"; instead, the ruling elites of countries such as Indonesia, Malaysia and Thailand devoted more attention to securing domination in the political sphere to entrench their power bases. Thus, rapid economic development and industrialization were not as critical in establishing legitimacy of government in Southeast Asia as they were in Northeast Asia.

In addition, whilst North East Asian developmental states prioritized the effective socio-economic transformation of the nation as the goal of economic development, Southeast Asian governments needed to strive for other goals such as inter-ethnic equality in wealth distribution (Booth 1999) or protecting economic and political interests of the ruling class (Woo-Cumings 1999). Furthermore, historical differences and variations in development approaches of the regions exist between the Northeast and Southeast Asian countries. With industrialization in countries such as Japan, Korea and Taiwan occurring earlier than in Southeast Asian nations, governments in faced some different opportunities and obstacles to development according to the time period. As noted by Booth (1999), Southeast Asian states had different colonial legacies; thus, the educational, social and welfare environments necessary for economic development were significantly different from those of Northeast Asian countries (Zysman and Doherty 1995). Regnier (2011) also recognizes that Southeast Asian states have moved towards "pragmatically hybridized" developmental states adopting a mixture of state-guided and market-based systems as a result of the 1997 Asian financial crisis and 2007-2008 global financial crisis, whereas Northeast Asian countries have become more liberalized welfare states.

The divergent paths toward development and growth between Northeast Asia and Southeast Asian countries can be, in part, attributed to regional differences in cultural and social characteristics. While Southeast Asian countries are constantly confronted with internal or interstate conflicts derived from cultural, ethnic and religious diversity (Croissant and Trinn 2009), Northeast Asian countries including Korea have largely homogeneous societies and are prone to exert collective efforts towards growth and development (Song B-N 2003; Stubbs 2009; Suh 1996; Routley 2012).

Despite these differences, many scholars have argued that East Asian countries may be collectively classified as a common group of developmental states that have an interventionist state. Therefore, it has been argued by authors such as Beeson (2004) that all economically successful states in East and Southeast Asia can be viewed as developmentalist states according to their common denominator of having a strong policy focus on promoting economic growth.

Debates on the East Asian Model of Economic Development

During the 1990s, East Asian developmental states began to change or adapt in the face of domestic and external challenges (Stubbs 2009). The combined effect of the conclusion of the Cold War, acceleration of globalization, pressures for political democratization and the 1997 Asian financial crisis led to changes in internal and external environments. The end of the Cold War signaled the end of support from western industrialized countries to reduce economic instability and prevent a communist takeover. As a result, financial and political aid was withdrawn in areas such as: protection of domestic economies; support for industrial policies to promote selected industries; economic aid; and access to western markets. In an environment of strong international competition from western industrialized countries, East Asian states had to adopt new policies as their traditional development approaches were no longer effective. Moreover, the acceleration of globalization and widespread adoption of neoliberal economic policies that dominated in industrialized countries, restricted interventionist policies of East Asian developmental states in terms of finance, government-business relations, industry development and international trade policies.

In this rapidly changing environment, the emerging issue regarding the East Asian development model was that the East Asian developmental states had been "weakened" (Pang 2000), "transformed" (Kwon 2007) or were "evolving" (Cherry, 2005), in line with their political and social democratization following their initial phases of economic growth. As a cause of the change, the correlation between economic growth and democratic transition has been widely examined (Pang 2000; Yeung 2017).

The popular debate is over how far the phenomenal economic growth in East Asian countries could be sustained when faced with the demands of widespread globalization, neoliberalism and democracy. These factors put pressure on authoritarian governments — an important characteristic of the East Asian model — to change to a more inclusive and competitive forms of government and society (Pang 2000; Yeung 2017). It has been explained that the economic success of the East Asian model was accompanied by rising income inequality, which increased social and political instability and thus pressured for political change (Kanbur, Rhee and Zhuang 2014). As a response, governments have undergone a process of becoming more inclusive and democratic. This change has been observed in most developmental states in East Asia, although in different degrees between Northeast and Southeast Asia. The East Asian model of development is thus the process and the policies by which a nation improves the economic, political, and social wellbeing of its people (Wong 2004). But how alike are the different countries of Northeast and Southeast Asia that are tagged with the developmental state label? The answer to this question is sought by a detailed study of the economic development of two countries in East Asia – Korea and Vietnam.

Korea as a Case of the East Asian Model of Economic Development

The remarkable economic growth and development achieved by Korea since the early 1960s is widely recognized as a result of the role of government in leading economic development and becoming a "developmental state" (Haggard and Moon 1993; Koo 1984; Deyo 1987). Although some neoclassical economists and dependency theorists attribute high growth of this period to market-friendly export promotion policies (Frank, Kim and Westphal 1975; Krueger 1982; Koh 2010), others credit the active intervention of government in defiance of free-market principles during the industrialization process (Hong 1979; Cho 1997; Lee 1995;

Haggard and Moon 1993). The success of the developmental state between the 1960s and 1980s was facilitated by favorable international and domestic environments. Externally, initial reliance of Korea on the United States (the US, hereafter)'s generous support in terms of aid and access to western markets in the Cold War contributed to the success of the Korean developmental state (Song B-N 2003; Suh 1996). In the domestic sphere, the threat of the communist north provided legitimacy to the military dictatorship in the south. As a result, the government was able to orchestrate development policies arbitrarily and coercively without obstruction, while the Confucian and nationalist culture in Korea facilitated a domestic national consensus supporting the drive for growth and industrialization (Deyo 1987; Song B-N 2003; Stubbs 2009; Suh 1996; Routley 2012).

However, the political environment, both domestically and internationally, began to change from the 1980s. The ending of military rule and re-establishment of the popular presidential election system in 1987 signaled the start of political democratization. Thus, the extent of authoritarian control by government was significantly reduced. Internationally, the western movement of adopting neoliberal policies, deregulation and downsizing of the public sector had taken hold. Following the 1997 Asian financial crisis, the IMF provided the Korean government a rescue package as quid pro quo for a series of restructuring measures for the Korean economy. At the same time, economic growth rates decreased, signaling the need for reforms in Korean government and private sector growth strategies. With previous military governments enforcing policies arbitrarily, any move away from authoritarian rule was considered by the public to be a step towards a more democratic society. Consequently, neoliberalism was well-received with little domestic resistance by the public as an expression of anti-authoritarian and pro-democratic policy change, thus significantly reducing government intervention in economic development (Kang 2012). From the 1990s onward, drivers of growth and development therefore shifted to factors such as political democratization, the rise of the *chaebols*, increasing openness of the economy and the presence of multinational enterprises (MNEs). Hence, Korea was no longer a developmental state as in the past (Peng and Wong 2004).

Variations in policies echoing different economic regimes and philosophical stances have prompted debates on the role of the Korean government from the 1990s, in particular whether and to what extent Korea has transitioned from a strong authoritarian developmental state to a neoliberal or welfare state. One argument is that, since the 1990s, government has maintained strong control, but its role has shifted from that of a "commander-in-chief" to that of a "senior partner" in economic development policies (Cherry 2005). The concept of a developmental state model seemed no longer applicable to countries in Northeast Asia and thus led to the identification of transformed developmental states as "adaptive" (Wong 2004), "flexible" (Riain 2000), "effective" (Azulai et al. 2014) or "hybrid" developmental states (Hayashi 2010). Alternatively, despite the emergence of neoliberal and welfare policies, some scholars argue that the Korean developmental state has not been entirely replaced but has been merely reconfigured to reflect and respond to changes in the political environment. Some argue that Korea has maintained some developmental state characteristics to generate growth, although they acknowledge that its goals, styles and extent of intervention vary from the old model (Cherry 2005; Chu 2009; Hayashi 2010; Wong 2004). Others argue that the goal of intervention has incorporated the enhancement of welfare on top of the original goal of economic development (Kwon 2007; Routley 2012). There have been persisting debates amongst political economists as to whether each Korean government involved in the democratizing period should be regarded as a developmental, neoliberal, or welfare state or even varying combination of all three.

In governments of most developed countries, neoliberal and welfare policies are widely adopted against anti-cyclical demand management policies to further economic growth alongside socio-economic equality and standards of living. In Korea, however, a combination of three stances — developmental, neoliberal, and welfare state — coexists. Despite the introduction of neoliberal and welfare policies over 20 years, the Korean government has retained its interventionist role in orchestrating industrial policies for socioeconomic development. As Stubbs (2009) has argued, while convergence between the developmental state and the neoliberal model found in Western economies is not likely to take place in the foreseeable future, the transformed developmental state has survived in Korea.

However, economic globalization and liberalization increasingly require the role of the government to change in Korea. A shift to a more inclusive and democratic government became preferable for sustainable growth. Inclusive social movements like the 2016 candlelight protests in Korea (as will be discussed later) have contributed to the functioning of democracy and are expected to assist in putting Korea on a new path toward more inclusive and democratic government.

VIETNAM AS A MODEL OF THE SOCIALIST MARKET ECONOMY

Vietnam has one of the world's fastest growing economies with an average annual Gross Domestic Product (GDP) growth rate of 6.42 percent between 1985 and 2016 and annual export growth exceeding 15.9 percent between 1990 and 2016 (World Bank 2017a). This is a remarkable achievement, attributable to the country's shift to a market economy since the *Doi Moi* (renovation) reform policy launched in 1986. The *Doi Moi* reform was initiated after the failure of the centrally planned economy in post-war Vietnam. Facing a severe social and economic crisis, the Communist Party of Vietnam (CPV) government was pressured to bring in fundamental changes in the economy for its survival and growth. The death of the powerful communist leader, Le Duan, in 1986 was followed by the emergence of new leadership (Nguyen Van Linh as Secretary-General of the Party and Do Muoi as Prime Minister) with more pragmatic views and stronger senses of the urgency for reform (Vu 2015). The new government abandoned the centrally planned economy and adopted a new economic model specific to Vietnam namely the socialist-oriented market economy.

Under *Doi Moi*, the government steered Vietnam's economic transition and played a leading role in economic development. It re-introduced the concept of private enterprise while forming laws and policy for the business sector, paving the way for developing the domestic economy. Its early industrialization was empowered by abundant labor and capital. The liberalization of agriculture freed up labor, while a series of "open door" economic policies increased the flow of FDI into Vietnam (Malesky and London 2014). Generating important achievements in terms of GDP growth, macroeconomic stabilization and export expansion, the government-led reforms laid firm foundations for the country to continue to develop. In addition, normalizing its relations with the US in 1995, was indicative of the government playing an active role in integrating the country into the global economy. Vietnam's accession to the World Trade Organization (WTO) in early 2007 formally was another initiative to further integrate the country into a globalized economy. With the policy of economic openness, Vietnam's economy achieved faster growth with increased trade, although, like many others, its fortunes dipped temporarily in the aftermath of the 2008 global financial crisis.

In contrast to the radical economic changes, the country remains solidly authoritarian, governed by a single party that has absolute power over political and economic governance. Even three decades since the inception of *Doi Moi*, the CPV continues to advocate a socialist-oriented market economy and supports the strong role of government in pursuing the reform process.

For transition countries, Vietnam's economic development has been often compared with China (Malesky and London 2014; Ren, Collins and Zhu 2014; Vu 2015). Combining its socialist goal with free market capitalism, Vietnam's socialist-oriented market economy is similar to that of China, in that it entails transition to a multi-sectoral economy with many ownership types, but different in that the state-owned economy played the most vital role in Vietnam. Although the private sector emerged and was allowed to expand, the state sector remained a pervasive feature of the economy in Vietnam. State-owned enterprises (SOEs) were protected to serve as national champions, although they eventually proved to be too inefficient to compete in the new globalized economy in Vietnam.

The research on Vietnam's growth and development highlights the need for adequate theoretical explanations of Vietnam's success. Some authors assert that Vietnam's development has been a "gradual process" driven by internal and external factors rather than the government's program of reform (Fforde and De Vylder 1996). Others however suggest that the Vietnamese experience, despite the lack of state capacity and frequently ad hoc project management, approximates to the state-led developmentalist model associated with East Asian countries like Japan and Korea. Masina (2012), for example, states that Vietnam government's attempt to reorganize the large SOEs into conglomerates, the establishment of the Ministry of Planning and Investment and the Ministry of Trade and Industry, and selective policies for attracting FDI to strategic industrial sectors all followed Northeast Asian (particularly Korean) exemplars. Others point out the leading role of the Vietnamese government in controlling the market and economic growth (Dixon 2003) and the reform of the country's SOEs (Beeson and Pham 2012) as evidence of following the East Asian model. There is even a suggestion that Vietnam conforms to an East Asian model of development not only economically but also politically. As argued by Pike (1994), economic success since the adoption of *Doi Moi* has led to political changes as seen by the Vietnamese leadership softening its authoritarian grip, more or less following the pattern of Korea or Taiwan, albeit to a much lesser extent. Despite these general insights, however, how the development model adopted by East Asian countries has been interpreted and employed in Vietnam has not been empirically explored, but remains as a topic under-studied and outside the main discussion, which suggests the need for further research (Beeson and Pham 2012).

SIMILARITIES AND DIFFERENCES BETWEEN KOREA AND VIETNAM

Historical and Social Background

Korea and Vietnam have had similar historical paths. Both share long-standing cultural heritages, colonial histories, experiences of a divided nation, and a painful and destructive fratricidal war followed by rapid industrialization and modernization. In both countries, Buddhism and Confucianism have had a profound influence on society and culture. When the quest for colonies started in Asia at the end of the nineteenth century, both countries experienced colonial rule. Korea was under Japanese rule from 1910 until the end of the Second World War in 1945. Vietnam had an even longer history of colonial rule. Vietnam was under Chinese rule for almost 10 centuries (111BC-939AD) before it was occupied by the French colonial power for nearly a century (1858-1954). When the French were defeated by Germany during the Second World War (1939-1945), Vietnam was invaded and occupied by Japan until Japan's surrender in 1945.

Two of the major Cold War conflicts took place in Korea (1950-1953) and Vietnam (1955-1975). After the devastation of war, both countries emerged as being among the world's poorest countries, with millions of people living in extreme poverty. They both benefited from foreign aid. Although, during the Vietnam War, more than 320,000 Korean troops served in the war alongside the US, Korea and Vietnam established formal diplomatic relations in 1992 (Lee 2011). The two countries are now close allies in East Asia.

Despite these notable similarities, however, the socio-economic and institutional disparities between the two countries are also very large. After the Cold War conflicts, the two countries have been run under two very different political systems. Korea has become a republic where communism is outlawed, while Vietnam has been a socialist republic with a one-party system led by the CPV. Compared to Vietnam, Korea has a smaller population (92.7 million as against 51.25 million) while Korea has a land area only a third of the size of Vietnam (see Table 1-1). However, Vietnam and Korea are the world's 14th and 27th most-crowded nations respectively. With 13.6 percent of its population being aged 65 or above, Korea is a rapidly ageing society while Vietnam has a relatively young population with only 6.01 percent of its population being aged 65 years and over (Knoema 2017). These social, political and historical differences have contributed to differences in the paths of economic and political development between the two countries.

Economic Development

Korea is a leading example of the East Asian model that achieved remarkable economic growth and development even before Vietnam started its developmental journey. Although they are at different stages of development, Korea and Vietnam have steadily operated their own economic policies, both representing cases of government-led economic development. They also share some characteristics of open-door and liberalization policies underpinned by export-oriented growth. However, development came at a price for Korea, namely political corruption and growing economic inequality. Decades of suffering and sacrifice were endured in the name of economic growth. With external military threats, economic growth became a national priority that provided motivation for authoritarian developmentalism in both countries. Since the late 1980s, Korea has transformed from the authoritarian developmental state to a more democratic form of government.

Since the radical market reform in 1986 following the launch of *Doi Moi*, Vietnam has undergone rapid economic growth and development, being transformed from one of the world's poorest countries into a lower middle-income country in 2008 and the 47th-largest economy. Under strong government intervention, the Vietnamese economy has grown continuously between 1989 and 2016. The GDP in Vietnam has increased 32-fold, from a low of US$6.30 billion in 1989 to US$205.276 billion in 2016 (see Figure 1-1) – but still far below Korea's US$1.411 trillion GDP in 2016 (World

Bank 2017a). High GDP growth has been particularly apparent in Vietnam since 2000, driven export-oriented manufacturing and FDI inflows (Nguyen 2006; Nguyen 2015). The growth of Vietnam's GDP per capita has also been among the fastest in the world. It has increased 22 times over, from US$97.16 in 1989 to US$2,185 in 2016 (current US$) while reducing the proportion of the population living below the national poverty line from 60 percent in 1993 to 13.5 percent in 2014 (World Bank 2017b).

Table 1-1. An overview of Korea and Vietnam in 2016

Characteristics	Korea	Vietnam
Population	51.25 million	92.7 million
Population aged 65 and over (%)	13.6	6.01
Land size	100,210km²	331,210km²
Main religions	No formal religion (including Confucianism), Christianity and Buddhism	Buddhism, Taoism, and Confucianism
GDP	US$ 1.411 trillion	US$ 205.276 billion
GDP per capita	US$ 27,538	US$ 2,185

Source: World Bank 2017b.

Vietnam's growth since *Doi Moi* has been export-led, with its exports accounting for more than 93 percent of GDP in 2016 (World Bank 2017b). One-third of exports are labor-intensive, low-value-added manufactured products such as textiles and footwear (Breu et al. 2012), similar to the characteristics of export-led industrialization during the Park Jung-hee era (1962-1979) in Korea. Vietnam, however, is now exporting more higher value products. In 2016, mobile phones and phone accessories topped the list of exports, followed by textile products and then computers, electronic devices and accessories (*Vietnamnet* 2017a). WTO accession and the government's acknowledgement of the benefits of integration into the world economy enabled Vietnam to swiftly become a country with high openness. Although the number of SOEs in Vietnam has fallen as part of economic reforms, as of 2016, Vietnam still has 718 SOEs in 19 key sectors, mostly big or medium-sized and still having the lion's share of the economy (*Viet*

Nam News 2016a). The ineffectiveness and corruption in SOEs have weakened Vietnam's competitiveness in recent years.

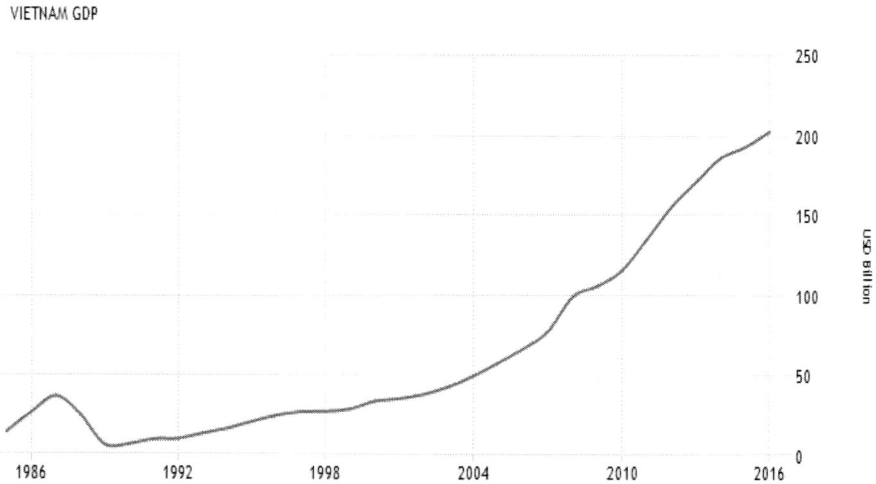

Source: Trading Economics (2017).

Figure 1-1. Vietnam Gross Domestic Product (GDP) 1985-2016

Economic growth in Korea over the past decades has been even more impressive. Korea, also war-torn and the world's poorest country, now has the world's 15th largest economy, attaining "developed country" status in 2009. As will be seen later, large inflows of foreign technology and capital enabled the government to promote an export-oriented manufacturing economy and maintain very close ties with the business sector, (Kim and Hwang 2000). FDI was discouraged in those sectors still protected by the government, but welcomed into the light manufacturing export sector, making Korea a production base for developed countries. The Korean economy grew rapidly after the adoption of the export-led industrialization model. The GDP has increased 588 times from US$2.417 billion in 1961 to US$1.411 trillion in 2016, representing 2.28 percent of the world economy (see Figure 1-2) (Trading Economics 2017; World Bank 2017b). During the same period, GDP per capita increased 293 times from US$93.82 in 1961 to US$27,538 in 2016 (World Bank 2017b). Korea also has an export-oriented economy, the 5th largest in the world with its exports accounting for more than 56 percent of GDP in 2012, although this figure went down to 42 percent in 2016 (World Bank 2017b). The top exports of Korea are manufactures (89 percent in 2015) such as integrated circuits, passenger and cargo ships and vehicle parts, while its top imports are fuels and mining products (30 percent in 2015) such as crude petroleum, petroleum gas and refined petroleum (Observatory of Economic Complexity 2017; WTO 2017). Following decades of sustained economic growth, Korea has transformed from an aid recipient to a donor. Korea became a member of the Organization for Economic Co-operation and Development (OECD) in 1996, and a member of the OECD Development Assistance Committee (DAC) in November 2009.

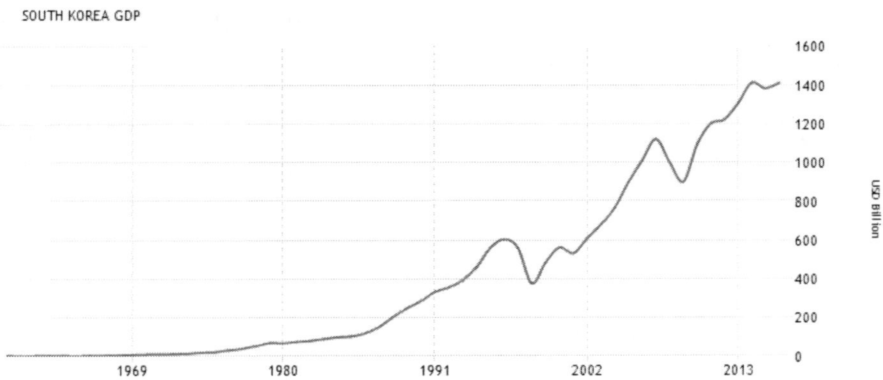

Source: Trading Economics (2017).

Figure 1-2. Korea Gross Domestic Product (GDP) 1960-2016.

Bilateral Exchange Relations

Korea and Vietnam are important partners. In 2017, Korea became Vietnam's second-largest trade partner, after China ("South Korea becomes" 2017). Korea is the fourth biggest export destination of Vietnam, after the US, China and Japan, and second top in terms of import origin, after China (*Customs News* 2016). In 2017, Vietnam's biggest trade deficit was with Korea, followed by China (Minh 2017). Vietnam's imports from Korea have rapidly increased, by 356.7 percent between 2009 and 2016 (Workman 2017). For Korea, Vietnam is the fourth biggest trading partner and the third biggest export destination, after China and the US.

The Vietnam and Korea Free Trade Agreement (VKFTA) was signed on 5 May 2015 and officially came into effect on 20 December 2015. The two countries' bilateral trade and investment have expanded, with trade volume between the two countries amounting to US$45 billion in 2016 (Yonhap News 2017). At the Group of 20 summit meeting in Hamburg in 2017, Korean President Moon Jae-in and Vietnamese Prime Minister Nguyen Xuan Phuc agreed to further expand the countries' bilateral trade and economic relations to achieve a goal of $100 billion in trade by 2020 while also developing their strategic partnership (Yonhap News 2017).

For the past several years, Korea has been the largest investor in Vietnam. Recent data from the Vietnam government suggest that cumulative Korean FDI in the period from 1988 to 2016 exceeded US$50 billion, compared to US$42.1 billion for Japan and US$39 billion for Singapore (Jung 2017; Wright and Blomenhofer 2017). Many Korean companies, especially Samsung, began to move their production plants to Vietnam for cheaper labor. Vietnam emerged as the main production base for Korea's component manufacturers as an alternative to China (*ETNEWS* 2017). Korea's outward FDI in Vietnam led to economic growth, employment generation and technology transfers in Vietnam (Oh and Mah 2017).

Korea is also Vietnam's second biggest donor country after Japan. Vietnam received around US$2.8 billion in Official Development Assistance (ODA) from Korea from 1992 to 2015 ("RoK to provide US$1.5 bln" 2016). A large slice of Korean ODA to Vietnam has been used for infrastructure and humanitarian support, including transport infrastructure, urban development, healthcare, education and the environment (Stallings and Kim 2017). Although Vietnam became a middle-income country in 2010, Korea is still willing to support Vietnam's economic and social development through ODA and international cooperation, as well as exporting its own experience of development unlike traditional donors (Asia Centre 2014). Particularly through the Knowledge Sharing Program (KSP), Korea has taught the developmental state model to Vietnam. Unlike the traditional forms of ODA projects focusing on financial support, material donation and technical support, KSP has provided continuous policy research and consultation on many crucial policy issues regarding Vietnam's economic development, such as WTO accession, SOE reform, macroeconomic stabilization, FDI, the ten-year development strategy and five-year implementation plans (Kim P 2015).

THE QUESTIONS AND APPROACH

Based on the relative lack of adequate theoretical explanations of Vietnam's economic success, this book examines whether the East Asian model adopted in Korea is a viable tool for understanding the development experience of Vietnam's transition economy. To find empirical evidence, two research questions are proposed. First, this book asks whether there is convergence or divergence of economic development between Korea and Vietnam while taking note of the differences in political and social systems between the two countries. To answer this question, the book compares the level of government involvement in the domestic economy between the countries, and explores if strong government intervention has been the source of economic growth in Vietnam. Secondly, the book asks whether Vietnam, as with Korea, has experienced political transition at a certain stage in economic development and whether it has led to changes in the direct role of government in the economy. The book seeks to elucidate how far the socialist market economy in Vietnam and the East Asian capitalist economy in Korea show converging or diverging patterns, and if Vietnam has learned from East Asian experiences or simply forged a unique path of its own.

This book does not aim to offer studies of the full economic intervention policies by either country's government and their impacts, but provides broad and qualitative perspectives on how these policies have been selected, implemented and changed at different stages of economic development and in different social and political contexts. The purpose of this study is to revisit the debate on the efficacy of the East Asian model of development by tracing the historical trajectories of both the impact of government involvement in economic development in Korea and Vietnam and the changes that have taken place along the way. The comparison between two countries with different social, economic and political systems and at different stages of development can be instructive to show whether the state-led East Asian model has changed, evolved, diminished, or is in terminal decline.

The book uses a comparative historical analysis to seek empirical evidence to determine the efficacy of the East Asian model for understanding the development experience of Vietnam. First, in order to understand the role of the government, it is necessary to examine how the governments have adapted to changes in environmental conditions during the process of development and industrialization. A historical perspective, therefore, is indispensable for this task. The development trajectories of each country have been examined according to three key stages to see how the role of the government has changed according to each stage of development. Secondly, a comparative method is essential. The study cannot determine anything of practical usefulness without comparing a wide range of economic, social and political development indicators between the two countries. The comparative historical analysis has been widely used to generate useful knowledge about various aspects of political economy (Clift 2014; Kim and Heo 2017). Finally, the book uses a qualitative method to generate detailed country case studies that are essential to uncover the specific dynamics underlying different development trajectories and outcomes.

PLAN OF THE BOOK

After this introductory chapter, the book is divided into two major parts, each providing a historical overview of the roles played by the governments of Korea and Vietnam in guiding and implementing national economic development. Part 1 includes Chapter 2, 3 and 4, and chronicles Korea's economic development process after the Korean War (1950-1953). Each of these chapters examines a different stage of development: the period of the authoritarian developmental state and rapid industrialization (1962-1979); the period of the adaptive developmental state and the challenges of economic liberalism (1980–1997); and the period of the "capable" state and globalized economy (1998–2016). Part 2 includes Chapter 5, 6 and 7, summarizing the process of Vietnam's economic development after the Vietnam War. Each chapter deals with one of three key periods: the period of the authoritarian socialist state with a centrally planned economy (1976-1985); the period of the socialist developmental state and the transition to a socialist-oriented market economy (1986-2005); and the period of the advanced socialist developmental state and challenges of integration into the global economy (2006-2016).

Each period is again divided into three sections: an overview of the environments for economic development; an analysis of economic policies; and an analysis of outcomes. The first section is devoted to the outline of the domestic and international environmental factors during the reporting period, the opportunities and threats to each country, and the responses as reflected in changes in government policies. The second section presents a detailed analysis of the key economic intervention policies during the reporting period and then sets out key issues and their implications. The third section presents the policy outcomes, taking into account the implications and consequences for economic growth and development as well as for social and political development. In this section, consideration is given to the causal connections between political and social conditions and the government's choice of economic policies and directions.

In the final chapter, Chapter 8, the case studies are analyzed, similarities and differences identified, and conclusions are presented.

Part 1. The Role of the Korean State in Economic Development: From Authoritarian Developmental State to Capable State (1960 – 2017)

Chapter 1

The Authoritarian Developmental State and Rapid Industrialization (1962 – 1979)

This chapter examines the important role of government in South Korea's economic transformation from an underdeveloped agricultural economy to a newly industrialized nation between 1966 and 1979. This period began in the context of the Cold War and the aftermath of the Korean War (1950-1953) from which Korea emerged as one of the poorest countries in the world. With the scarcity of capital and natural resources, foreign aid and a cheap (but educated) workforce were the major sources of foreign income.

Korea's transformation to a newly industrialized nation took place with the emergence of the military authoritarian government under Park Jung-hee, an army general, who seized power through a military coup in 1961 and led the country until the end of 1979. To enhance his regime's political legitimacy, Park committed himself to a comprehensive economic development project based on a series of Five-Year Economic Development Plans (FYEDPs), which led a take-off of the Korean economy from an agrarian economy to one based on manufacturing. With central economic planning and government intervention in the market, Park's government was the driving force behind Korea's economic growth during the 1960s and 1970s. As a repressive and authoritarian ruler, he transformed the country from a weak state into an authoritarian developmental state, which produced remarkable outcomes in economic growth during this period.

This chapter focuses on the background to economic policies, their implementation and their outcomes during his regime. It first discusses how international and domestic environments remained favorable for the Korean authoritarian developmental state during this period. It then provides an overview of how the national economic development plans were prepared and implemented to engineer an economic take-off under the authoritarian government. Finally, it assesses the economic, social and political consequences, including a critical impact on structural imbalances in the Korean econ.

INTERNATIONAL ENVIRONMENT

Cold War Conflicts

After the Second World War, international communities were divided in three groups, according to a country's allegiance. Democratic capitalist countries aligned with the North Atlantic Treaty Organization (NATO) and the US represented the First World; communist states led by the Soviet Union represented the Second World; and other countries that remained non-aligned with either of these formed the Third World. Many of the Third World countries were poor and non-industrialized.

The tensions and rivalry between the First and Second Worlds was called the Cold War; this had significant impacts on the global economy until the 1990s when the Soviet Union collapsed. Both groups struggled to woo developing countries to their side and tried to entice them with aid.

The Korean War (1950-1953) was the first ideological war of the Cold War era. When the Second World War ended in 1945 and Korea was decolonized from Japanese imperial rule, the two superpowers divided the Korean peninsula into two: the southern part managed by the UN Allied

Force and the northern part under the control of the Soviet Union. After its declaration of independence, the pro-Western government in the South established the Republic of Korea in 1948 whilst the Communist-inspired government in the North established the Democratic People's Republic of Korea (North Korea). As negotiations on reunification failed, the entire peninsula became embroiled in turmoil and devastation due to North Korea's invasion of Korea. After much destruction and loss of life, a truce was signed in 1953. After the war, Korea remained an important and democratic ally of the US. The stability and economic prosperity of Korea was of great importance to the US and the allies in their fight against communism. Thus, significant amounts of aid from the US alliance arrived in Korea. The then-government under the first president Rhee Syngman heavily relied on this aid for the execution of the government budget (Haggard and Moon 1993).

As aid decreased in the 1960s, the new president, Park Jung-hee, who seized power through a military coup in 1961, focused on economic development as a means to enhance his regime's political legitimacy and establish a strong independent economy. Cold War tensions and the North Korean threat continued to offer legitimation to Park's authoritarian approach to development and his repression of anti-government movements (Cho 2004). In addition, given the growing importance of Northeast Asia to global stability and prosperity, the US government supported Korea's industrial development and pressed its government and that of Japan to normalize their relations. Between 1946 and 1978, the US provided Korea a total of US$ 60 billion in aid — nearly the same amount provided to all African countries (US$69) (Tran 2011). The US pursued the establishment of an anti-communist bloc in the Northeast Asian region, based on strong bilateral alliances with Japan and later Korea and Taiwan. With the 1965 normalization treaty between Korea and Japan, the Korea-Japan-US triangle trading structure was set up; it provided capital, technology, market access, and political support that supported Korea's rapid industrial development (Shin and Ciccantell 2009: 174).

In the latter years of the Cold War, Korea benefited from another Cold War conflict. Between 1964 and 1973, Korea participated in the Vietnam War to assist US forces. Korea's involvement in the Vietnam War offered an opportunity to modernize Korea's armed forces and strengthen its national defense capabilities through supplying services and products to the US armed forces in Vietnam (Kim and Koh 2010). Between 1965 and 1970, Korea received from the US about US$ 1 billion in foreign currency in return for sending military troops to Vietnam, which provided much needed funds for Korea's economic development during the second FYEDP (1967-1971) (Kim 2004).

The US involvement in the Vietnam War cost the US a great deal and changed US policy toward Northeast Asia. To reduce the burden on the US of upholding regional peace and security, President Nixon announced in 1970 the Nixon Doctrine which demanded that Asian countries increase their self-defense capabilities, saying that "Asian hands must shape the Asian future" (Nixon 1971: 143). This policy change had a profound impact on Korea's economic development strategy during the 1970s. As will be discussed later, Korea promoted self-reliance for national defense through developing the heavy chemical industry, and attracting foreign investment and technology from the US and Japan. Between 1966 and 1978, the US and Japan accounted for 83 percent of public loans to Korea and Japan accounted for 70 percent of Korea's total technology imports (Jung 2014).

Stability in International Trade and Financial Environments

Following the Second World War, leadership of the western countries was transferred to the US. This was partly because post-war economic recovery in many European countries was assisted by the Marshall Plan of the US. Also, in the early 1960s, nearly 35 percent of the world GDP was produced in the US (Kapur, Lewis and Webb 2010: 210). To help administer the Marshall Plan, the Organization for European Economic Co-operation (OEEC), an intergovernmental economic organization, was established in 1948. Later, in 1960, it was reformed into the OECD as a forum for 35 developed countries that advocated democracy and the market economy. During this period, the international monetary system known as the Bretton Woods System was also established under the United Nations (UN) system and with strong US backing. The US dollar became the global currency. At the Bretton Woods conference, three organizations were conceived by the United Nations: IMF, the International Bank for Reconstruction and Development (IBRD, which later became the World Bank) and the International Trade Organization (ITO). However, as the US Congress did not ratify the establishment of the ITO, an alternative arrangement, based on the General Agreements on Tariffs and Trade (GATT), operated until 1993, when the WTO was established.

These changes in the international economic environment were favorable towards the development of emerging countries. The Bretton Woods system provided stability in foreign exchange rates, while the GATT provided significant concessions and some preferential treatment to developing and least developed countries in order for them to meet any required dismantling of trade barriers. For example, greater market access, reduced tariffs and trade barriers, concessions and technical assistance were given to developing countries when trading with rich countries. Korea's export-driven industrialization between 1962 and 1979 greatly benefited from these concessions and preferential treatment, as well as from the stability in international trade and financial environment.

In the first half of 1970s, however, there were several major events in the international economy which began to change trade and investment conditions significantly. First, the Bretton Woods agreement of fixed exchange rates ended in 1971, leading to the instability of exchange rates during the 1970s and 1980s. Shocks in the international finance market were no longer automatically absorbed by the US. Second, the first international energy crisis broke out, disrupting the international economy. Third, as the growing trade surplus between Japan and the US and European countries created trade conflicts, and the US and other developed countries became concerned about the large volume of exports from East Asian countries.

Nonetheless, in order to stimulate economic progress and world trade, OECD countries did not reduce their support for developing countries substantially until the mid-1990s. With Cold War competition still lingering, the need to support developing countries increased, especially because of increased instabilities in the international economy. Until 1989, Korea remained one of the beneficiaries of US trade preference programs, such as the Generalized System of Preferences (GSP) program, which lowered tariffs for the least developed countries, while keeping them in place for rich countries. Despite the disturbances in the international economy, the US and the leading OECD countries were able to absorb exports from developing countries, including Korea, without any major difficulties. These international political and economic environments were very conducive to Korea's adoption of export-driven economic development in the 1970s and 1980s.

Impacts of Oil Price Shocks and Middle Eastern Construction Boom

The world economic boom after the Second World War was led by cheap oil that stayed at US $2 per barrel between 1945 and 1974. In 1973, when the fourth Arab-Israeli War broke out, the twelve members of the Organization of Petroleum Exporting Countries (OPEC) imposed an embargo against the US that supported Israel. Soon, the price of oil began to soar. In the spring of 1974, it became US $15 per barrel resulting in the first oil shock. This shock, however, provided important opportunities for the Korean economy. With the experience of building large-scale physical infrastructure since the 1960s, many Korean companies entered the Middle Eastern countries, which had accumulated vast finances from rising oil prices and conducted various construction projects, contributing greatly to Korea's foreign currency earning in the 1970s (Kim and Koh 2010).

In 1980, a war broke out between Iran and Iraq after a long history of political and territorial disputes. Oil production in the two countries nearly stopped, leading to the second oil shock. In the wake of both oil shocks, the world economy was trapped in a cycle of low growth and inflation, experiencing recession with high inflation, unemployment and weakening growth. The second oil shock also had a major impact on Korea, whose rapid industrialization was accompanied by a rapid growth in energy consumption (KDI School of Public Policy and Management 2017). It caused economic depression in Korea for the first time since 1957 when Korea struggled with difficulties generated by overinvestment in heavy and chemical industries.

DOMESTIC ENVIRONMENT

Rising Out of the Ashes: The Legacy of the Korean War

Korea was known as the "Land of the Morning Calm" while it was ruled by the *Chosun* Dynasty for more than 500 years (1392–1910) until the Japanese occupation of Korea in 1910. During Japanese colonial rule, the Korean economy was used as a source of agricultural products and other resources for Japan and was exploited to supplement Japanese economic needs. During this period, Korea's GDP increased (at an annual rate of 4 percent), but Gross National Product (GNP) decreased. In other words, agricultural and industrial production increased, but the standard of living of Korean people did not improve correspondingly. This reflected the colonial nature of the economic relationship between Korea and Japan — for example, importing more consumer goods than capital goods into Japan (Song B-N 2003). Japan's investment particularly focused on northern Korea. From the late 1930s to the early 1940s, the Japanese imperial government built a vast industrial complex and several hydroelectric power plants in northern Korea to prepare for war with China, while the economy in the south was predominantly agricultural. As a result, North Korea had a higher per capita income than South Korea until 1969, which provided the impetus for Park Jung-hee's commitment to economic development (Kim 1995: 97).

After the defeat of Japan in the Second World War, Korea was divided in half as the US and the Soviet Union failed to agree on a single system of governance for all of Korea. Despite numerous demonstrations against this division, the Republic of Korea (South Korea) was established as an independent country in 1948, only embracing the southern part of the peninsula. Rhee Syngman, a nationalist and a Christian educated in the US, became the first president in 1948 and served three terms until 1960. He was chosen by the US military authorities as a local partner, which facilitated the close relationship between the US and Korea. Meanwhile, in the northern part of the peninsula, the Soviets appointed Kim Il-sung, who was the head of the Korean Communist Party, as the new leader of the country and established the socialist Democratic People's Republic of Korea (North Korea) in 1948. In 1950, North Korea initiated an invasion of South Korea which led to the Korean War (1950–1953).

During the three-year war, one and half million people were killed and millions of families were separated or uprooted and relocated. The country was devastated and depleted of capital, infrastructure and natural resources. When the truce was signed in 1953, South Korea was hard-pressed to feed its population, which had been growing due to the substantial migration from north to south since 1945. With everything destroyed, Korea turned into an egalitarian society where everyone was equally poor.

The rest of the 1950s was devoted to recovering from the war and the beginning of industrialization, which was initially promoted through an import substitution policy. Although real GNP increased at an annual rate of 5 percent between 1953 and 1957, it was largely propped up by substantial injections of foreign aid as the value of commodity exports declined by over 50 percent in dollar terms during this period (Frank et al. 1975). Until the first FYEDP started in 1962, Korea remained one of the poorest countries in the world.

Early Achievements in Education

Education was an early priority for Korea due to high educational aspirations embedded in Korean culture. Through the six-year national plan for compulsory primary education (1945-1959) conducted as part of the FYEDP, primary enrolments increased rapidly. The Gross Enrolment Rate (GER) for children of primary school age, which was below 54 percent in 1945 shot up to 95.3 percent in 1960 (Kim, Shim and Kim 1995). Secondary enrolment rapidly expanded in the 1960s and 1970s, achieving universalization of lower secondary education (95.1 percent) in 1980 from only 41.4 percent in 1965 (Kim et al. 2015). Higher education enrolment also increased, with the number of students enrolled in four-year university degrees growing nine-fold between 1950 and 1960, from 11,358 to 101,014 (Kim 2008: 233).

Despite being one of the poorest countries in the world in the early 1960s, Korea's literacy rate was far higher than other countries with similar GDPs per capita. The literacy rate in 1945 was only 22 percent, but increased to 87.6 percent in 1970 (Seekins 1997: 115). The continued efforts of the government in the 1950s and 1960s produced an inexpensive but highly-educated workforce which provided a strong base for economic development from the 1960s onwards.

Park Jung-Hee Government, the Authoritarian State

Korea in the 1950s was characterized by the combination of weak government and strong society (Haggard and Moon 1993). Although President Rhee had an authoritarian leadership style, his government proved too weak to control the business sector. The labor movement, first organized to fight against the Japanese colonial government, participated in demonstrations that led to the fall of the Rhee government.

Park Jung-hee's military coup in 1961 replaced the previous chaotic leadership with a more orderly military dictatorship, providing the basis for an authoritarian developmental state in Korea (Kim 2010). While his government gained its legitimacy from the Kennedy government in the US based on its commitment to anti-communism, the public's willing acceptance and/or support for his government was believed to come from its ability to deliver economic success (Kim 2004). President Park's focus on economic growth during this period was regarded as timely, considering the social and political contexts of that time. In the aftermath of the war, the country was left with a small industrial base and an agricultural sector struggling to feed its population. Under the previous Rhee Syngman government, the national priority was placed on the reunification issue and not economic development.

Park Jung-hee was an authoritarian dictator, determined to develop Korea's economy. After seizing political power in 1961, Park established the Economic Planning Board (EPB) comprised of western-educated economic officers to formulate a coherent economic strategy. With foreign aid decreasing in the 1960s, President Park signed a treaty in 1965 to normalize the country's relations with Japan and secured the capital supply to achieve the industrialization of Korea. In addition, his government nationalized most of the banks to extend its control over business and push large conglomerates to work toward his development goals. The rent-seeking attitude previously widespread in the private sector was reduced under the Park government. His developmental dictatorship was useful at the beginning of state-led economic development. His high-growth economic strategy, however, was pursued at the expense of human rights and democracy. Most of the population had to endure decades of suppression and suffering. Park's decision to amend the national constitution in 1972 to allow him to remain in power for a third term also created significant opposition in the country, and was challenged by activists such as religious leaders, social activists, and college students. Park suppressed these protests by force, which led to the rise of pro-democracy movement in the late 1970s (as discussed later).

ECONOMIC POLICIES

The Five-Year Economic Development Plans

With economic development as its prime goal, the Park government began instituting economic development plans and commenced a policy of industrialization. In 1962, the first Five-Year Economic Development Plan (FYEDP) was formulated by the EPB with an aim to establish a self-reliant industrial economy through building the foundations necessary for industrialization during the period of 1962 through 1966. The overall target was 7.2 percent annual economic growth by boosting exports, substituting imports, and increasing the influx of foreign currency (Khaled 2007:6). For a self-reliant industrial economy, the government decided not to rely on foreign capital and managerial expertise. The major issue was how to find resources other than US aid. With restrictions on inward FDIs, Korean companies had to rely largely on domestic loans with lesser amounts of foreign capital—hardly sufficient for economic growth. To provide long-term capital to medium and small enterprise industries, the Park government established the Medium Industry Bank (MIB) in 1961. Over 36 percent of investment was devoted to infrastructure (Kwon and O'Donnell 2001: 20). With purchasing power within Korea hardly sufficient to generate economic growth, it was export demand that functioned as an indispensable factor for growth and development. Without full awareness of the importance of exporting, Korea experienced a rapid increase in exports of labor-intensive goods such as clothing, shoes and wigs between 1960 and 1962. In 1964, the Korean government announced a new measure in which export became the central pillar of economic planning. A comprehensive set of export promotion policies was introduced; from 1965, the president himself chaired monthly export promotion conferences with cabinet members, executives of large conglomerates and bureaucrats, which played a decisive role in export growth.

With additional goals of modernizing the industrial structure and maintaining overall sustained growth, the Park government established the second FYEDP for the period of 1967-1971, strongly promoting export-led industries with an emphasis on steel, machinery, and chemical industries. The government encouraged the large conglomerates to invest in these industries and provided easy access to low-interest loans through the state-controlled banking sector (Kwon and O'Donnell 2001: 21). During this period, international economic conditions remained favorable and the economic opportunities offered by participation in the Vietnam War (1964-73) offered an opportunity for Korea's economic take-off. In return for sending more than 300,000 troops to Vietnam, the Korean government received economic aid as well as military and political assistance from the US. Industrialization could proceed without agricultural transformation. The agricultural sector was protected from foreign competition and provided with price support. In addition, the agricultural sector functioned as a major source of additional labor supply.

Realizing that the manufacturing industry, despite its significant contribution to economic growth during the 1960s, also increased imports, the Park government embarked on a new policy of supporting selected heavy and chemical industries at the start of the third FYEDP (1972-1976). This new initiative was known as the Heavy Chemical Industrialization Plan (HCI Plan), or the 'Big Push into HCI'. A number of laws were enacted to promote steel, machinery, shipbuilding, electronics, and petrochemical and nonferrous metal industries. The heavy and chemical industries greatly benefited from the government policy and support. This was provided by government through building specialized industrial complexes, and by offering tax exemptions and subsidized policy loans (Kim and Koh 2010). The government also created and sponsored the system of general trading companies to expand exports for these industries (Kim and Koh 2010). In parallel with the HCI Big Push, the Park government also initiated the *Saemaul Undong* (New Village Movement), a community-based integrated rural development program, in order to reduce the widening income gap between the urban and rural areas. This was a movement not only for economic and social improvement, but also for attitudinal changes in rural areas. Various village projects to accelerate rural modernization were initiated and given to village residents/farmers to participate. In the mid-

1970s, about 10 percent of the total national investment was directed to the rural sector (Yousefi 1997: 60).

The Big Push into HCI continued with the fourth FYEDP (1977-81), focusing on large heavy and chemical industries, such as iron and steel, petrochemicals, and nonferrous metal. To support the development of HCI and improve the country's export competitiveness, the plan fostered the development of technology-intensive and skilled labor-intensive industries such as machinery, electronics, and shipbuilding. With an understanding that securing the energy supply was essential, large-scale investment was made in electric power generation, integrated machinery, diesel engines, and heavy construction equipment (Metraux 1997:145). For advanced technology, the government focused on building an educated and skilled workforce and expanding domestic RD capacity, and many state research institutes were established during this period.

KEY ISSUES

Government-Led Industrialization and Partnership with Private Business

During his presidency, Park Jung-hee pursued a strong industrialization policy and restructured the financial sector. Through the ensuing FYEDPs over the period of twenty years, the Park government played a leading role in economic development. Government-business relationships were established as the Confucian hierarchical "master-student" relationship (Khaled 2007), in which the government led and controlled the private sector through various combinations of support and restraint. From the very early phase of the junta government, various measures were adopted to tame the large companies (*chaebols*) and force them into supporting government initiatives (Kim 2004). The banking system was nationalized in 1961, which gave the government direct control over investment finance for the business sector. Although required to follow the direction and leadership of the government, big business *chaebols* in Korea were strong and took initiatives in expanding their market shares overseas as well as in the domestically.

Park believed that this guided capitalism was the best system of economic management that would lead to the equalization of income and public benefit. He thought that private businesses or other sectors of the society were prone to corruption and inappropriate to lead (Kim 2004). With domestic purchasing power insufficient to drive economic growth, the private sector was inadequate on its own for the planned growth and significant support from the US was available to the authoritarian state for economic development (Suh 1996).

The Park government intervened in the economy in an authoritarian and repressive manner. The EPB controlled resource allocation and the flow of credit, and formulated economic plans and policies. The government nationalized all private banks to ensure adequate financial support was provided to exporting companies. Exporters were granted unrestricted and tariff-free access to imported intermediate inputs and could avail of low interest bank loans. Government-led industrialization also had a significant impact on human capital accumulation. Government policies and assistance fostered the diversification of the industrial structure in a timely manner, which enabled the learning process to continue at the company and individual levels. Social emphasis on education in Korea that contributed to the creation of a high-quality skilled work force was not only culturally supported, but also the result of government emphasis on human capital investment in education (Kim 1991).

Export-Oriented Industrialization

Export-led industrialization was an important development paradigm under the state-guided industrialization strategy of the Park government. This route to development was selected because domestic purchasing power was insufficient to drive economic growth, the private sector on its own could not generate the planned growth while significant support from the US was available to the authoritarian government (Suh 1996). The export promotion policy adopted by the Park government was far from the free market economic model, but was basically mercantilist policy of promoting export and restricting imports.

The government established the Korea Trade Promotion Corporation (KOTRA) in 1962 to promote and support various trade activities. KOTRA took charge of building overseas networks, helping the marketing activities of domestic firms, and collecting market information (Jung 2012). The government also subsidized projects to improve the wrapping and design of products, the expansion of inspection facilities for export goods, the opening of foreign-language training centers, and payment of travel expenses for delegations to overseas expositions and trade shows (Kim et al. 1995). Besides, President Park himself presided over the monthly export promotion meetings and the monthly briefings of economic trends to facilitate broad discussion of policy direction and implementation amongst government officials and business representatives (Yoon and Hellmann 1993: 12).

The Korean government used various ad hoc measures to support exports including: provision of export credits; exemption of tariffs on imports of intermediate inputs; indirect and direct tax exemptions on exports; and accelerated depreciation of fixed assets in major export industries (Koh 2010). Any exporters who received letters of credit automatically gained access to heavily subsidized bank loans. The average interest rate on export credit was 6-10 percent for the period from 1961 to 1981, while the average general interest rate was 17-23 percent for the same period (Kim et al. 1995). Major policy reforms relating to exchange rate, trade controls and the financial sector were also adopted around 1965 to promote exports, following a massive depreciation of the Korean Won against the US dollar from KRW 130 to KRW 255 to a dollar in May 1964 (Kim 1991:15). These incentives were also backed by administrative measures to promote exports.

The Big Push into the Heavy and Chemical Industries

Facing major changes in the domestic and international environments, the Korean government had to change the direction of its economic policy in the 1970s. While North Korea continued to be a threat to Korea, the US appeared to weaken its commitment after the declaration of the Nixon Doctrine in 1970, which led Korea to face a need to ratchet up its defense capacity. It was considered necessary to upgrade the country's industrial structure and find new export industries to maintain a safe lead over other newly industrializing economies. These changes facilitated the introduction of the full-scale HCI drive policy, the Big Push in 1973 during the third FYEDP (1972-1976).

While exports were widely promoted in the 1960s, giving privileges across the board (not to specific industries or companies), the government had more power and control over the execution of export promotion policy in the 1970s. During this period, the Park government targeted specific industries to provide them with virtually unlimited support. Directed credits at very low interest rates and various tax incentives were offered to HCIs. Marginal effective tax rates of HCIs were 30-35 percent lower than those imposed on light industries during the second half of the 1970s (Kwack 1985). General trading companies (GTCs) were established after the Japanese model and granted special privileges, including guaranteed letters of credit, relaxed foreign exchange regulations and further liberalization of import duties (Haggard and Moon 1993).

Economic Outcomes

Growth Outcomes

The developmental state of the 1960s and 1970s was very effective in achieving the goal of economic growth and development. Thanks to strong government-led export-oriented economic strategies, Korea achieved rapid growth in exports and subsequent increases in GDP during the 1960s and the 1970s. Between 1961 and 1981, exports grew about 35-40 percent per annum and their share in GNP increased by more than seven times (Kim et al. 1995: 185). Average annual GDP growth rates rose to 7.5 percent in the 1960s and 8.6 percent in the 1970s (Lee J-W 2016). The key export industries were labor-intensive light industries, such as textiles and footwear, whose contribution to the economic growth rate increased significantly from 1.1 percent in 1960 to the annual average of 7.8 percent during the first FYEDP (Kwon and O'Donnell 2001: 20-21). The rapid expansion of labor-intensive industries also helped to improve the employment situation with a drastic decrease in the unemployment rate from 8.4 percent in 1962 to 4.4 percent in 1971 (Nam 2007: 159). However, as most of the natural resources and intermediates goods were imported, imports grew much faster than exports. Consequently, trade deficits continued to increase until the mid-1980s. Nevertheless, the rapid growth during this period facilitated Korea's stunning transformation from one of the world's poorest countries to one of Asia's Newly Industrialized Economies (NIEs).

Thanks to the Middle Eastern construction boom, Korea also achieved rapid growth in the construction industry. With strong governmental support, the Middle East construction boom created strong currency flows and generated many jobs in a short period of time. The current account surplus was largely driven by foreign currency income from the Middle East's construction boom. Agricultural productivity also greatly improved thanks to the introduction of new farming methods and machinery.

The Big Push into HCI changed the industry structure of Korea significantly. Light consumer goods accounted for 59.5 percent of total manufacturing value added and 86.3 percent of total merchandise exports in 1971, but fell to 43.7 percent and 60.1 percent respectively in 1980; and the proportions declined further in the 1980s (Committee for the Sixty-Year History of the Korean Economy 2010: 216). In contrast, the share of heavy manufactured goods increased from 40 percent of manufacturing output in 1972 to 62 percent in 1984 and from 21 percent of commodity exports to 60 percent in the same period (Committee for the Sixty-Year History of the Korean Economy 2010: 216). Steel, cement and shipbuilding were the fastest growing industries. Korea became the third largest cement exporting country in the world; second largest shipbuilding nation in terms of orders by 1979 (Kwong, Chau, Lui and Qiu 2001:186); and had one of the largest and most efficient steel companies in the world (Encyclopedia of Korean Culture 2015; Kwong et al. 2001:186).

However, the HCI drives in the 1970s were not all successful. They failed to develop some target industries and huge loans given to firms engaged in the drive caused massive inflation and economic distortion in the 1970s. In addition, the government initiatives to create and expand the HCI (including unlimited financial support with low interest) resulted in over-expansion of the HCI production facilities at the expense of neglecting light industries which still had international competitiveness. In 1979, the average capacity utilization rates reached only 35 percent for transport equipment, 60 percent for machinery and 69 percent for electrical appliances whereas it was 82 percent for manufacturing industries (Nam 2007: 162). These excess capacities indicate serious misallocation of scarce resources, although they later enabled Korea to gain international competitiveness and grow faster than other competitors in Asia during the second half of 1980s, when the international environment was favorable. The high rate of growth led to a rapid build-up of foreign debt and stimulated inflation, with widening disparities between industries as well as between rural and urban sectors (Kim 1991). In response to this worsening economic situation, President Park initiated a number of measures to stabilize the economy, but without success. With the impact of the 1979 oil price shock, the Korean economy became even more destabilized.

The Rise of Government-Business Associations

From the beginning, government-business relations formed the cornerstone of the economic development plan adopted by the Korean government. The strong government under Park determined the direction of the economy by applying market-violating administrative measures in the name of development (Shim and Lee 2016). To control the corporate sector and orchestrate export promotion policies, all financial institutions were nationalized, and access to both domestic and foreign credit was totally controlled by the government. By controlling the banking sector, the government was able to control almost all the decisions taken by the companies.

The government-business relationship was very important in all developmental East Asian economies, including Japan, Korea and Taiwan. Although similar in their adoption of a government-led industrialization policy, the role of the government was different in each of these economies. The relationship between the government and business in Japan was more consultative, whereas that in Korea was more vertical top-down. In Taiwan, the government took an even more passive and supportive role, compared with the former two economies.

Apart from disciplined labor availability as a result of the Rhee government's top priority on education, Korea lacked many essential elements for a developing economy to achieve economic growth: stock of capital; adequate technology; and entrepreneurship. Although there was some accumulation of capital during the Japanese colonial period, much of it was destroyed during the war. As the source of capital, Korea initially relied on aid and then on international loans. In the beginning stage of industrialization, high quality capital-saving technology needed for labor-intensive industry was greatly lacking. While other developing countries in East Asia had more open policies towards MNEs which had superior technology, management expertise and capital investment, Korea's market remained closed to foreign direct investment. There was no clear and explicit government policy established for technology transfer. Companies relied on turnkey projects, licensing and informal channels for the transfer of technology during the first stage of industrialization (Kim 1997). Entrepreneurship was important but scarce. The government played an important role in promoting innovation for entrepreneurship. Consequently, it was the government who took on the task of orchestrating the corporate sector and expanding the production and export to form Korea Inc. (Shim 2011).

The Emergence and Expansion of the Chaebols

One of the major characteristics of the postwar economic development in Korea was the dominant role of the large business groups called *chaebols*, family-owned conglomerates of affiliated companies. Most of the Korean *chaebols* were formed before the Park government. For example, five of the 50 largest chaebols in 1985 were founded before the end of the Japanese colonial period in 1945, and 35 were established between 1945 and 1960 (Lee 1997: 21). During the Rhee regime, many companies grew in size through processing raw materials imported as foreign aid to Korea, such as sugar, flour and fertilizer, and selling them in the domestic market (Haggard and Moon 1993). Most of these companies had rent-seeking attitudes and maintained close relationships with the government to sustain their privileges of processing the imported raw materials.

In the 1970s, more power was given to *chaebols,* with help from the state-led industrialization policy that resulted in a strong coalition between the government and *chaebols*. During the first FYEDP, many companies were involved in light industries, which constituted the key export sector. The export-led growth strategy since the second FYEDP utilized Korea's comparative advantage in labor-intensive industries. Most of the then-largest *chaebols* — Samsung, Daewoo, Ssangyong, Hanil, Hyoseong, Lucky Goldstar, Sunkyung, Samhwa, Kumho and Hyundai — were licensed as general trading companies, entering export markets to lift the Korean economy (Kwon and O'Donnell 2001: 21). The government provided generous support to the large companies, but only to those which supported government initiatives and performed well in exporting. Big business became the companions and subordinates of strong government.

The Big Push into HCI in the 1970s facilitated industrial deepening in Korea, although it took more than two decades before excess capacity disappeared and these industries could be competitive internationally. Boosted by the government policy, the number of *chaebols* involved in heavy and chemical industries increased from 30 in 1972 to 122 in 1981 (Kwon and O'Donnell 2001: 21). The involvement in the Vietnam War (1964-73) facilitated business success for *chaebols* and many other Korean companies involved in war-related products or construction. This industrial deepening in the 1970s certainly favored big business. One of the most important outcomes of the Big Push into HCI in the 1970s was the economic ascendance of *chaebols*. In order to achieve this HCI drive, *chaebols* received enormous support from the government which also took on many of the investment risks (Kwon and O'Donnell 2001). During the HCI drive, risks associated with new investments were virtually all borne by the government, which bailed out companies facing financial difficulties. This underwriting encouraged the large companies to expand whenever and wherever opportunities were seen to be available, thus encouraging the reckless expansion of *chaebols* and the underdevelopment of small and medium-sized enterprises (SMEs). Top *chaebols* wielded considerable economic and political power, despite their lack of transparency in management structure and their association with corruption. They were the leading actors in Korea's economic development, but they also became sources of longstanding problems in the Korean development model, including crony capitalism (Kang 2002).

Emergence of Structural Imbalances

After two decades of rapid growth in the 1960s and 1970s, a number of structural imbalances emerged in the Korean economy in the late 1970s. First, the Big Push into HCI under the Park regime resulted in a high concentration of economic power within a small number of very large *chaebols*. Most of these large conglomerates with a considerable degree of excess capacity received preferential support from the government. Substantial loans were granted to the heavy-chemical industry, resulting in the creation of excess capacity in many industries — particularly those relating to power generation, transport equipment and heavy machinery (Aghevli and Marguez-Ruarte 1985). In contrast, SMEs specializing in light and labor-intensive industries (such as the textile industry) were largely neglected and fast losing competitiveness in the international market due to the lack of investment and technical improvement. In 1960, 99.1 percent of companies were SMEs, which accounted for 68.8 percent of sales and 66.3 percent of total value-added. However, in 1979, 96.5 percent of enterprises were SMEs, with their shares in sales and value-added decreasing to 31.8 percent and 35.2 percent respectively (Lee 1997: 33). These figures were much lower than in neighboring countries. In Japan, SMEs were 99.5 percent of total establishments, 52.7 percent of sales and 57.1 percent of total value-added. In Taiwan, 99.0 percent of all firms were SMEs with the shares of sales and value-added of 92.8 percent and 56.8 percent respectively in 1977 (Lee 1997: 33).

Secondly, exports increased throughout the 1960s and 1970s, but imports increased faster, leading to the accumulated current account deficits. With few natural resources and diminutive domestic savings, the Korean government relied heavily on foreign loans and natural resource imports to finance and support the Big Push into HCI. The increase in foreign loans led to the accumulation of current account deficits and continuing devaluation of the Korean Won, all of which contributed to an emerging debt burden in the early 1980s.

Thirdly, the growth in GDP and domestic credit expansion, accompanied by a rapid expansion of the housing market and a construction boom, resulted in an acceleration of inflation. In addition, previously abundant rural surplus labor was exhausted, raising real wages rapidly. Gradually, external competitiveness was eroded and exports were on track to decline. Although a series of stabilization measures was introduced in April 1979 to overcome these difficulties, it did not have any significant effect.

As the 1970s ended with the second international energy crisis and huge inflation, stability became the priority of economic policy in 1979 for the first time since the commencement of industrialization. Various measures were put in place to control inflation and to rectify structural imbalances in the economy. However, before those measures could be fully implemented, Korea entered a period of political instability and turmoil, beginning with the assassination of President Park followed by a military coup by Major General Chun Doo-hwan.

Social and Political Outcomes

Emerging Income Inequality

With the focus of government support on manufacturing companies and the HCI drive, there was widespread dissatisfaction that the benefits of rapid economic growth were very narrowly concentrated. In addition, the progress in industrial development widened the income gap between the urban and rural areas significantly. The average income of rural areas, which was roughly equal to that of urban areas in 1965, was only 67 percent of the urban income by 1970 (Song B-N 2003: 169). The rural sector remained as a source of labor supply until the mid-1970s. As the labor supply from the rural sector dwindled in the mid-1970s, rural-urban migration slowed down after 1980. The rural development program of *Saemaul Undong* was partly successful in reducing poverty and improving living standards in rural areas, and contributed to narrowing the developmental gap between urban and rural communities. Statistics show that income levels in farm and non-farm households became nearly equal in 1975 (Amsden 1986; Song B-N 2003). Despite such a positive effect, however, general income inequality worsened during the 1970s. In Korea, the Gini co-efficient, which indicates the level of social inequality, rose from 0.33-0.34 in the second half of the 1960s to 0.39 in the second half of the 1970s before it showed a slight decline to 0.36 in 1985 (Ahn 1997: 34). In addition, rapid economic growth caused upward pressure on prices and wages and led to high inflation, with the average annual inflation rate of 16 percent in the 1970s (inflation.eu 2017). Due to high inflation, the real rate of interest fell from 5.3 percent in 1973 to -19.3 percent in 1974 and real estate emerged as a preferred form of investment. The Seoul land value index increased at an annual rate of 29 percent in the 1970s, contributing to growing income inequality (Kim 2007).

Park's government also pursued growth-friendly labor market policies throughout his tenure (Khaled 2007). His government and police resorted to violence and other repressive measures to deal with conflict and differences among social groups. As soon as he seized power, Park placed a ban on trade unions and launched a new trade union federation. The Park government tightly controlled labor markets, forbidding the emergence of labor union movements. Although the level of real wages continued to increase during the 1960s and 1970s, the labor market was repressed. In 1971, he issued an Emergency Decree on National Security. As a result, all collective labor actions were suspended, replaced by direct government intervention. Although there were a number of illegal labor protests, often led by liberal groups from Protestant and Catholic churches, they were harshly repressed by government authorities. The growing power of the business sector combined with increasing income inequality and tight control over the labor movement posed considerable burdens to the governments that followed the Park regime.

The Sacrifice of Democracy and Human Rights for Economic Development

Following his military coup in 1962, Park Jung-hee assumed dictatorial powers for 18 years, serving five terms as president between 1963 and 1979, having forced through the necessary amendment of the constitution. His authoritarian rule hindered Korea's transition to democracy. President Park believed that economics preceded politics or culture (Das 1991: 147). He thought that western-style democracy did not fit underdeveloped countries like Korea, and instead developed the notion of "Korean (or nationalistic) democracy" that prioritized results over processes (Kim and Vogel 2011: 380; Moon 2009: 26). In Korean democracy, civil society was largely neglected. People lived under an enormous amount of control and influence by the government, with mandatory curfews and regulations on attire and music.

Political rights were also greatly restricted. Illegal intervention by state agencies in the presidential and general elections continued throughout Park's authoritarian regime. Political influence-peddling and bribery became widespread during election campaigns. Despite that, the silent resistance of the people managed to achieve the victory of the opposition party in a small number of elections. Then civil protests became stronger towards the end of the 1970s with the assassination of President Park and the abrupt ending of his regime in October 1979.

Numerous democratization protests took place between October 1979 and May 1980, the period which was later called “the Seoul Spring” (named after Czechoslovakia's “Prague Spring” of 1968). The Seoul Spring was quickly suppressed under martial law imposed throughout the nation by General Chun Doo-hwan as the chairman of the National Statesman Committee. It finally ended with the Kwangju Massacre on 18 May 1980 that left many citizens dead, missing and wounded.

CONCLUSION

This chapter has examined the growth of the authoritarian developmental state in Korea during the Park Jung-hee era (1962-1979). During this period, various environmental forces, such as the Vietnam War demands, the normalization of relations with Japan, Cold War tensions and the Middle Eastern construction boom, offered a variety of challenges as well as opportunities for Korea’s economic development.

Taking office via a military coup in 1961, Park pursued economic development as a means to enhance his regime's political legitimacy and promote economic independence. Implementing a series of FYEDPs, the Park government played a pivotal role in economic planning and programming and was the dominant agent in the nation’s economic development. With few resources, skills and scant experience, the government focused on export-driven growth and worked to develop Korea’s industrial capacity through its support of *chaebols*. Park controlled the banking system and used it to force the *chaebols* to work toward his development goals. Korea’s economic development during this period can be characterized by the following three key aspects: (i) government-led industrialization; (ii) export-oriented industrialization; and (iii) a big push into heavy and chemical industries.

As a result of central planning and government direct intervention, between 1962 and 1979, Korea's real GNP and exports rapidly grew at the average annual rates of 9.3 and 33.7 percent respectively (Kim 1991: 6). Park's government-led and export-oriented economic growth strategy, although successful in generating rapid economic growth in the short term, began to generate adverse economic effects in his regime's later years. High growth and increased exports during this period not only saved the country from poverty, but also paved the way for continued domination of the Korean economy by *chaebols*, increasing imbalance in industrial development, income inequality, the suppression of unions and human rights, and real estate issues. The goal of rapid economic growth under Park's authoritarian developmental state greatly suppressed human rights and democracy. In this context, the major oil crisis in 1979 had a significant negative impact on the Korean economy, resulting in substantial economic deterioration between the late 1970s and the early 1980s. More significantly, these economic and social consequences of the authoritarian developmental state remained as challenges for the future of the economy and impediments to the development of democracy.

Chapter 2

The Adaptive Developmental State and the Challenges of Economic Liberalism (1980 – 1997)

This chapter explores the changing characteristics of Korea's developmental state between 1980 and 1997. With the negative side effects of Park Jung-hee's authoritarian developmental state and the assassination of Park, Korea underwent enormous economic, social and political turmoil in the early 1980s. Economic growth began to fall as a result of high inflation, the debt burden and overinvestment in heavy and chemical industry, while the long repressed pro-democracy movement brought the masses onto the streets. Amid internal turmoil, the oil crises in the late 1970s also had severe consequences for the Korean economy. In the 1990s, following the end of the Cold War, the global environment became more favorable for the Korean economy. Many developing countries in Asia that used export-oriented strategies experienced an economic boom based on three lows (low international energy prices, low exchange rates and low interest rates) while recession swept the US and Western Europe.

Following the death of Park, another military government emerged in Korea via the 1980 military coup of General Chun Doo-hwan. The major challenges facing the Chun government were to maintain internal political stability and to resolve the economic insolvency caused by the government-led economic growth strategy of the previous regime. Chun's authoritarian government adopted "Comprehensive Policy Measures of Economic Stabilization" in 1979 while continuing the FYEDP, the core planning tool of the previous developmental state, under the new name of the Five-Year Economic and Social Development Plan (FYESDP). FYESDPs were in place from 1982-1986, 1987-1991 and 1992-1997 (until Chun was succeeded by Roh Tae-woo). This enabled government's direct intervention in the economy to continue into the 1980s and 1990s. In the FYESDPs, Korea's developmental state continued to pursue optimal economic growth but went into a transition process, with the focus moving toward stability, efficiency and restructuring of the heavy-chemical industrial sector. The leading role of government also became less authoritarian, partly owing to growing public demands for democracy and emerging economic liberalism. The transition of Korea's developmental state became more evident during the following government under Kim Young-sam, the first elected civilian president since 1962, who launched a new Five-Year Plan (1993–97) for economic, social and political reforms. Unlike previous development plans, his plan drew attention to the role of the private sector in economic growth, and adopting globalization as a nationalist goal. With a view that membership in the WTO would be an important driver of economic growth, the Kim government abandoned the developmentalist view in formulating economic policies and carried out a series of reforms in trade and related policies. His reform efforts, however, were confronted with the outbreak of the 1997-1998 Asian financial crisis in Korea.

Providing a brief review of the economic development during this transitional period between 1980 and 1997, this chapter aims to shed light on how Korea coped with changing domestic and international environments, their impact on domestic economic policy and contribution to rapid economic growth and social change, followed by the economic crisis.

INTERNATIONAL ENVIRONMENT

Economic Reforms in the Communist Bloc and the End of the Cold War

It is instructive to compare Korea with other states that were reliant on central planning and authoritarian regimes to foster rapid economic development, and to note the impact of the gradual shift away from this model. Centralized state planning and administrative decision making had some success in the Soviet Union's economy, when the government controlled land, labor, and capital, and effectively achieved rapid industrial growth from the 1930s to the 1950s. While western economies continued to grow and underwent a post-Second World War thirty-year golden era until 1975, the growth rate of the Soviet Union and other communist countries of Eastern Europe began to decline. Central planning caused poor information flows, poor resource allocation and lack of incentives, leading to stagnation in technology and agricultural development, and a widening gap with capitalist countries (Cummings 2008). The collapse of crude oil prices in 1986 placed additional pressure on the economy of the Soviet Union, which was at the time a major supplier of oil and gas. Economic reforms emerged as a pressing need.

When Mikhail Gorbachev became the new leader of the Soviet Union in March 1985, his primary domestic goal was to revive the stagnant Soviet economy. He initiated a process of political liberalization. Before his efforts became fruitful, however, long-repressed nationalist movements and ethnic disputes led to the collapse of the Soviet Union in December 1991. In this context, Boris Yeltsin emerged as Russia's leader. Economic reforms failed in other eastern European countries including Poland, Hungary and Czechoslovakia. Experiencing great economic problems with hyperinflation, these countries were pushed towards a painful transformation, along a pathway of macroeconomic stabilization, liberalization and privatization, as laid out in the Washington Consensus in 1989 as standard prescriptions for economic crisis recovery (Dallago and Rosefielde 2016).

The collapse of the Soviet Union ended the Cold War and transformed the world's geopolitical balance. Politically, the military tension between the West and East ended. In the absence of the security threat, the Cold War alliance weakened, with the emergence of a US-centered international order. Economically, there was a growing trend toward globalization, with increased world trade and connectedness among people and places, including in communist countries in Indochina. Many MNEs entered the newly open markets in Russia and former Eastern Bloc countries to take advantage of the new opportunities.

During the post-Cold War period, while security tensions eased, bilateral trade issues became a core concern of US policy towards the Northeast Asia region (Campbell 2012). Japan became one of the world's largest economies, creating huge trade surpluses with the US. Korea also followed Japan along the path of state-led and export-oriented economic growth, emerging as an important trading partner of the US. The rise of China's economic power in the 1990s also emerged as an enormous threat as well as offering opportunities to North America and Europe, which were experiencing recessions.

After the collapse of the communist bloc, the Korean government promptly expanded diplomatic relations with Eastern Europe and China during the Roh Tae-woo government. With the end of the Sino-Soviet split after the Cold War, Korea established official diplomatic relations with China in 1992, a move which led to rapid expansion of economic and social exchanges between the two countries. Many export-related Korean companies shifted their production facilities to China to use cheap local labor. They also utilized China as their export platform. In this context, North Korea's nuclear threat solidified the Korea-US alliance, enabling Korea to develop a strategic cooperative partnership with the US for economic development.

The "Three Lows" Period in the 1980s

In the second half of the 1980s, developing countries in Asia benefited from the era of the "three lows": low international energy prices; low exchange rates; and low interest rates. After the Plaza Accord in September 1985, Japan agreed to appreciate the Yen, while the US and other European countries depreciated their currencies. This gave Korea new opportunities to grow exports and catch up with Japan to assume an increasing share of international exports.

In the 1990s, recessions began in the US and Western Europe, and the momentum for economic growth shifted to Asia. In the early 1990s, East Asia (including Korea) was the only region in the world that experienced an economic boom and continued on the path of economic growth. As the standard of living improved in the region, the entire Asian region emerged as the world's most important region as both a market and an investment destination (BRINK 2016).

Alarmed by the nation's growing trade deficit, the US government began to pressure the Asian NIEs to liberalize trade and decrease protectionism by implementing several measures such as realignment of major currencies. Exacerbating the trade friction between Korea and the US, US protectionism in the US threatened Korea's export expansion. Given the important role of trade in Korea's economic growth, the spread of protectionism provided enormous challenges for the country's future economic development.

The Emergence of Neoliberalism

During the Great Depression, Second World War and the ensuing post-war economic expansion (1945-1973), the standard economic model in the developed nations was Keynesian economics that advocated the role of government intervention in economic stabilization. As economic conditions worsened significantly in the later 1970s, however, a significant change began to emerge and grow in strength from the early 1980s. Sustained stagflation combining high levels of inflation and unemployment undermined faith in the recommendations of Keynesian economics and western countries began to take a new stance: the so-called neoliberalism (Centeno and Cohen 2012).

Neoliberalism was based on the belief that a free market would lead to higher efficiency and higher growth and therefore, government intervention in the economy should be limited (or abolished) and tax rates should be lowered along with welfare assistance. The Prime Minister of the United Kingdom (the UK), Margaret Thatcher, was the first head of the state who adopted strong policies based on neo-liberalism. The US President Ronald Reagan similarly promoted "supply-side (or trickle-down) economics," based on a belief that economic growth can be most effectively achieved by increasing incentives and lowering barriers to the production and exchange of goods and services. Since then, almost all OECD economies joined in the campaign for "small government" and commenced extensive economic liberalization policies such as free trade, deregulation and privatization (Scholte 2005).

Neoliberalism was accepted as the panacea for economic growth and development in North America and EU countries for over 30 years. Fueled by the integration of China and the former Soviet Bloc into global capitalism and the supply of new technologies, neoliberalism continued to gain international recognition and support. The adoption of neoliberal economic policies (such as opening doors to direct foreign investment) created favorable conditions for economic booms worldwide during the 1990s and capitalist development in many Asian countries. This was the background to the IMF's support for neoliberal reforms in Korea after the 1997 Asian financial crisis. The introduction of neoliberal ideas and policies had a profound impact on the direction of Korean economic development, leading to the reform of the Korean developmental state.

Globalization and WTO Accession

The post-Second World War international trading environment among the western economies was very favorable. The GATT negotiations continued to reduce or eliminate various trade impediments over subsequent decades. During the GATT negotiation rounds, most of the discussion aimed to reduce trade barriers to manufactured goods. Under these negotiations, developing countries were given concessions and the US and European economies absorbed the exports from developing countries (Finger 1974).

By the mid-1970s, however, the international trading system began to show signs of strain. As the internal economic conditions of the US and Europe worsened and trade deficits began to accumulate, the OECD countries were less open to the needs of developing countries. With remarkable growth among developing countries in the service sector (including business, communication, construction, education, energy, environment, financial, health, tourism, transport and other related services), liberalization of service trade emerged as a hot issue. As a result, during the Uruguay GATT negotiation round between 1986 and 1994, 123 countries agreed on the comprehensive reform of the world's trading system, allowing further liberalization and expansion of international trade (Schenk 2011). Liberalization of the agricultural sector and international protection of intellectual property rights were also included in discussions and negotiations.

After the signing of the Uruguay Round agreements, GATT was replaced by the WTO, a new intergovernmental entity regulating international trade from 1 January 1995. The WTO incorporated all the agreements of the Uruguay Round. The establishment of the WTO was certainly an important achievement for freer trade and investment. However, for a developing country, it was questionable whether free trade with neoliberalism could provide the necessary conditions for the country's economic take-off and further development.

In January 1995, Korea obtained full membership of the newly established WTO, under the Kim Young Sam government. In preparation for this, the government abandoned the developmentalist view in formulating economic policies and carried out a series of reforms in trade and related policies. In the era of rapid economic globalization, Korea needed to make a timely and appropriate response.

The Asian Financial Crisis in 1997

Many countries in East Asia and South Asia had achieved remarkable economic growth during the several decades after the Second World War. The golden years, however, ended in the late 1990s when the devaluation and collapse of the Thai baht in July 1997 initiated the spread of financial crises in East and Southeast Asia. Capital inflows slowed sharply or reversed direction and economies exhibited negative or very low growth. Thailand, Indonesia, Malaysia and Korea were the countries most affected by the crisis. With slumping currencies, stock market crashes, and rising private debt, these economies entered deep recessions whose spillover effects reached Latin America and Eastern Europe in 1998. Although the causes of the crises varied in each country, critics argued that it was because economic growth in emerging markets was unstable, as it was formed and maintained not necessarily with improvement of efficiency, but mainly based on plentiful supplies of cheap labor and capital (Krugman 1994).

In 1996, Korea became a member of the OECD, a group of 30 wealthy developed countries. Less than a year after this, Korea was hit by the 1997 Asian financial crisis, which caused a sudden stop in capital flow and decline of capital reserves. As a result, Korea underwent the nation's worst recession since the Korean War. The Kim Young-sam accepted an IMF bailout program requiring financial sector restructuring in Korea. As a result, the opening of the Korean economy took place, much earlier and more rapidly than expected.

The IMF offered rescue packages to Korea, Thailand, Malaysia and Indonesia under the conditions of implementing structural reforms in line with the neoliberal policies of the US and other OECD countries. Korea, Thailand and Indonesia accepted the conditions and the rescue package, whereas Malaysia declined it and designed its own policy solution (Sato 2004). The need for structural reforms was emphasized in order to address the root causes of the crisis that included weaknesses in the financial and corporate sectors. To improve the efficiency of markets and increase competition, the markets of Korea, Thailand and Indonesia were required to become more open and integrated into the world economy (Sato 2004).

DOMESTIC ENVIRONMENT

Economic Crisis in the Early 1980s

The two decades of rapid growth in the 1960s and 1970s were followed by a worsened economic situation in the 1980s. The adverse effects of Park Jung-hee's government-led economic growth strategy became apparent towards the end of the 1970s, exacerbated by domestic political turmoil and an unfavorable international economic environment including the 1979 oil price shock. In 1980, the Korean economy was on the verge of collapse, with a negative GDP growth (-5.2 percent) for the first time since the launch of the FYEDP in 1962, inflation soaring to 38.2 percent and wholesale inflation reaching 42.3 percent (Kim Y 2015). Exports greatly declined owing to a prolonged global recession and foreign debt became unsustainably high due to depreciation of the Korean Won and increases in international interest rate.

During this period, the external environment was not favorable to Korea either. High international interest rates initiated by Reaganomics and the deterioration of the country's terms of trade alone increased the debt burden by approximately 13 percent of GNP during 1979–1980 (Collins and Park 1989). The worldwide recession after the oil price shocks also contributed to the slowdown of Korea's economic growth. As a result, real GDP decreased by 5.2 percent for the first time since 1953, while the Consumer Price Index (CPI) and the Wholesale Price Index (WPI) increased by 34.6 percent and 38.9 percent respectively (Suh 1996: 580). In order to fill the gap in the current account, the government borrowed heavily abroad between 1980 and 1981, as it had in the past. Consequently, the ratio of debt to GNP that had steadily risen since 1964 reached 53.5 percent in 1982 (Collins and Park 1989: 129). The growth rate of GNP started to recover in 1982 so that the saving ratio increased gradually and the current account deficit decreased (Suh 1996). In the face of such an unfavorable environment, the Korean government was saddled with the need to adjust the existing growth-oriented and export-oriented development strategies.

Social and Political Conflicts

Following his military coup in May 1980, Chun Doo-hwan was elected president by indirect election in September 1980, ushering in the Fifth Republic (1980-1988) under the new constitution. The beginning of the Chun government initiated a new military regime and signified an extended postponement of democracy. Amid the Seoul Spring, Chun expanded martial law to the entire country to close universities, ban political activities and further curtail the press. Pro-democracy movements were brutally suppressed, especially in the city of Kwangju by firing at, killing, beating and arresting thousands of civilians, which left deep scars on the psyche of the Korean people (Plunk 1985).

As Roh Tae-woo, a former military general and Chun's right-hand man, was announced successor to the presidency in June 1987, the democracy movements peaked and became nationwide with the rising support of the general public including young urban citizens.

Chun and Roh, through the June 29th Declaration, finally acceded to public pressure and agreed to constitutional revisions that essentially included direct presidential elections. Due to divisions within the opposition party that split the vote, Roh was elected president in December 1987 with only 36 percent of the vote. However, as the opposition party won the general election, becoming the absolute majority in the National Assembly, his government had reduced power and its capacity to carry out contentious policies was significantly limited. Roh had to work with a minority ruling party and regularly respond to requests of the opposition parties and street demonstrators. During the Roh government (1988-1993), political activism remained strong. The rural sector and labor movement began to attain stronger voices. Between 1987 and 1989, thousands of industrial disputes and strikes, large and small, occurred. Initially, Roh wanted to distinguish himself from his predecessor by controlling the large companies, but soon changed his policy and took a pro-business stance. As the Soviet Union collapsed and Germany was reunited, Korea officially began political dialogues with North Korea and much attention was paid to the prospects of reunification.

In 1990, after 30 years of being the opposition leader suppressed by military governments, Kim Young Sam led his party to merge with president Roh's military-backed governing party and became the head of ruling party. He was elected president in 1992 to serve between 1993 and 1997, becoming the first elected civilian president since 1962. His immediate agenda was to clear the legacy of military regimes and create the image of the civilian government. He identified his government as a "*Mun-min*" (civilian) government to differentiate it from the previous military rulers. However, his government could not break from the legacies of the military government completely and many politicians who served under the previous governments remained his allies. As a means to show divergence from the previous governments, "globalization" was appropriated as a national goal. The Kim government also offered an optimistic view on inter-Korean relations. However, after the sudden death of Kim Il-Sung, the Kim Jong-Il government retreated from the unification dialogues and the progress on inter-Korean relations was halted for a while.

Economic Policies

The National Five-Year Economic Development Plans

In 1980, the incoming government under president Chun Doo-hwan faced the major challenge of stabilizing the internal political situation and resolving the economic difficulties created by high inflation, high foreign debt and high excess capacities created in the late 1970s. A suite of Comprehensive Policy Measures of Economic Stabilization was announced in 1979. Various measures to control inflation and stabilize the current account balance were adopted as the highest priorities, while the focus of investment was transferred from heavy and chemical industries to technology-intensive industries such as precision machinery, electronics and information, which were at that time in great demand on the world market.

Reliance on government-led national economic development plans also continued into the 1980s under the Chun Doo-hwan and Roh Tae-woo governments. The fifth FYESDP (1982-86) was launched by the Chun government to address structural problems resulting from the government-led economic growth strategy of the past. Under this plan, the government tried to switch to a market-led growth strategy and to decrease reliance on foreign borrowing, which sharply contrasted with the policies from the 1960s and 1970s. The plan incorporated policy measures to stabilize the economy and new directions for industrial policy while implementing extremely tight fiscal and monetary policies to reduce the public-sector deficit and monetary expansion. Preferential interest rates for priority sectors were eliminated in 1982, but directed loans remained an important feature of Korea’s financial system, though its share in total loans showed a decreasing trend, from 20 percent in 1980 to 16 percent in 1982 (Aghevli and Márquez-Ruarte 1985: 12).

Recording the largest current account surplus in the country’s history due to the economic boom based on the “three lows (low international energy prices, low exchange rates and low interest rates),” the Roh government promoted the internationalization of the capital market to improve Korea's position internationally and to open up capital markets.

During the Sixth FYESDP (1987-91), the Roh government made a shift in its development strategies towards liberalization in investment as well as external trade to effectively respond to changes in internal and external conditions, including sluggish domestic economy and the global move towards neoliberalism. Priority was given to the removal of restrictions and barriers on imports in order to enhance the country's industrial competitiveness. Also noticeable was that the Sixth FYESDP sought to move towards more balanced growth. Owing to a massive current account surplus during the three-lows period in the late 1980s, the debt burden was no longer a major concern and previously neglected areas began to receive greater attention. These areas included: the agricultural sector; SMEs in the manufacturing sector; income inequality; the labor market; the social welfare system; and research and development (R&D) programs. Despite the initial intention, however, attention to these sectors quickly waned. Soon after, the Seventh FYESDP (1992-96) was formulated by the Roh government with a goal to establish an advanced industrialized economy by the year 2000. This plan continued to stress import liberalization and improved export competitiveness, and the development of high-technology industries, but began to reduce government intervention. This plan, however, was not continued by the subsequent government.

Discarding the existing FYEDP, the new government under president Kim Young Sam (1993-1998) introduced a New Economy Five-Year Plan (1993–97) that initiated rapid and daring state reforms. With a clear statement of its vision and the goal of the "creation of a New Korea," the Kim government had three major priorities: social welfare enhancement; economic revitalization; and political reform through the eradication of social injustice and corruption (Cha 1993: 851). To revitalize the declining economy, the New Economy Plan aimed in particular at reducing the role of government role in economic growth while expanding that of the private sector. Through measures based on economic liberalization and deregulation Kim vowed to end the cozy relationship between government and business (Graham 2003: 91) and adopted globalization as a new policy for diplomatic and trade relations and also in order to break away from US dominance (Saxer 2013). However, the major goal of government's reform drive was to revitalize the economy. Joining the OECD, the developed nations' club, was a goal that symbolized economic success and its international recognition. With growing protests for wage increases, a nationwide trade union was officially established in 1995 under the name of the Korean Confederation of Trade Unions (KCTU).

KEY ISSUES

Structural Reforms for an Advanced Industrialized Economy

Starting from 1980, in the aftermath of the oil price shocks and negative growth rates, the Chun Doo-hwan government began to restructure the heavy-chemical industrial sector. The Heavy and Chemical Industry Promotion Committee was dismantled and wage growth was curbed in a complete budget freeze in 1983. In the process of restructuring, mergers and acquisitions of companies were carried out in low profit sectors.

In response to the excess capacities and worsening profitability created during the heavy-chemical industry drive, the government initiated three rounds of "investment coordination" from 1979 until 1983, designed to ensure the efficient allocation of investment in line with shifts in comparative advantages in the world market (Kim 1991). The first round was initiated in May 1979 by the Park government, following its first-ever economic stabilization program and continued by the new government under Chun. Investments and financial assistance were concentrated on nine companies in three industries including power generation, automobile and construction machinery (Koh 2010: 44-45). In October 1980, the second round of restructuring was imposed on three more industries (heavy electrical instruments, electronic switchboard and copper smelting). The restructuring was completed in 1983 with some modifications. The government provided rescue packages, including loans from state-controlled banks, to troubled companies being restructured (Koh 2010: 44-45).

In 1985, to carry out restructuring programs in a systematic way, the government laid out the legal basis by revising the Tax Reduction and Exemption Regulation Act (TRERA), abolished the promotion laws for individual industries and introduced the Manufacturing Development Act (MDA). Based on these laws, the government provided financial support and tax benefits to existing companies subject to rationalization and restricted market entry and investment in rationalized industries, bailing out firms that made losses. A number of insolvent firms were designated for restructuring between 1986–1988. Their liabilities in excess of assets were rescheduled or written off and new loans were given. In this way, *chaebols* were able to increase their size in the process of restructuring and rationalization, which contributed over time to the growth of corporate debts and non-performing loans held by banks and was to exacerbate the damage incurred by the 1997 Asian financial crisis (Koh 2010: 46-47).

Policies for Economic Liberalization and Globalization

With the end of the Cold War in 1991, leading western countries were competing to benefit their own national economic interests. As Korea's trade surplus sharply increased in response to government intervention to protect domestic industries and to expand exports, there was growing international pressure, especially from the US pushing for market liberalization in Korea (Park 2008: 35).

With the recognition of the limitations of the developmental state, the South Korean government also realized the need to pursue the global trend towards a more open and market-oriented economy. Although financial markets were still strongly affected by government regulations, there was a movement towards a more market-oriented system. In 1982, the government abolished the direct control over bank lending through credit ceilings and quotas, relying more on open market operations, reserve requirements and the re-discount mechanism. The rationale was that too many regulations imposed on corporations would repel foreign capital from Korea.

Deregulation was conceived as a necessary step towards expanding Korea's exports and creating an open and market-oriented economy.

Following several more failed attempts at domestic market deregulation in the early 1980s during the period of the Chun government, deregulation began to emerge as an important priority in the late 1980s (Koh 2010: 54). In 1988 and 1989, the new administration under President Roh established the Administrative Deregulation Committee within the Prime Minister's office and designated eighteen industries, including alcoholic beverages, refineries, shipping, and passenger transport, as targets for deregulation. However, the market liberalization and deregulation process proceeded slowly until the 1990s. The main goal of regulatory reform changed quickly as the economy dipped into a downturn in 1989. Instead of moving to a more market-oriented structure, it was proposed that government should assist the corporate sector to stimulate their investment. Consequently, deregulation was postponed until the next government.

Under increasing foreign and domestic pressures for liberalization and deregulation, the Kim Young Sam government adopted policies of economic liberalization and deregulation as a new engine for economic growth (Cha 1993). The financial liberalization began sporadically in the 1980s, albeit without significant achievements. The liberalization of interest rates and lending began officially in 1991 under the Roh government, but progress was slow and the actual implementation differed from the plan. Full implementation began during the Kim government and was completed only in 1996-1997. Although the privatization of commercial banks began in the early 1980s, government interventions continued. In 1993, the Office for Bank Supervision introduced a rule for more open selection of bank presidents, but the government's influence on the nomination processes remained. From the 1980s until the early 1990s, non-bank financial intermediaries (NBFIs) flourished due to restrictions in the banking sector. The constant creation, conversion, merger and diversification of banks and NBFIs were inevitable and desirable phenomena. However, as prudential regulation was not strengthened simultaneously, financial deregulation increased the instability of the system. Most direct industrial policies disappeared and the control of the government decreased during this period.

However, alternative measures to provide a transparent and conducive environment were not provided. The Kim government introduced a radical reform aimed at transparency in financial transactions. This was a requirement for public disclosure of the real names of parties to financial transactions which commenced in 1993 as the first step towards a transparent society. From that time, secret financial dealings became far more difficult.

In 1994, Kim Young Sam announced his globalization policy as a new political and economic goal for Korea. He envisaged that the new competitiveness of Korea would come from globalization. Kim's policy paved the way for the opening of the Korean economy and its integration with the neoliberal global economy. In effect, this was a prelude to the adoption of neoliberalism in Korea. Following the opening of the rice import market in 1993, Korea joined the WTO in 1995 and the OECD in 1996 and achieved a level of liberalization of the manufacturing sector comparable to those in the OECD countries (OECD 1994). However, the opening of the capital market was passive in nature. Liberalization plans followed a positive list approach, permitting the trade only of commodities evaluated and approved by government, until major changes took place after the 1997 Asian financial crisis (OECD 1996).

Economic Outcomes

Growth Outcomes Achieved during the 80s and 90s

With the focus on stabilization, the economic policies adopted by the Chun government were largely successful. The Chun government regulated excess investment policy for the heavy-chemical industry in the 1970s, and initiated the opening of the financial market to improve economic stability. After this restructuring, although the share of large firms and *chaebols* in the national economy expanded, the economy stabilized. By 1983, the economy regained its momentum for growth and inflation was completely controlled. Inflation and wholesale inflation declined to 3.4 percent and 0.2 percent respectively (Kim Y 2015).

As international interest rates decreased and export performance improved, the debt burden decreased. As the world economy started to show signs of recovery in 1983, the Korean economy also entered a recovery period. Furthermore, with the help of a flexible exchange rate policy, external competitiveness was restored. In the late 1980s, the economy recorded rapid growth, with an average annual growth rate of over 12 percent between 1986 and 1988, compared to 9 percent between 1980 and 1985 (Lee K 2016). The economy boasted a massive current account surplus for three consecutive years from 1986. In addition, after the establishment of diplomatic relations, China emerged as Korea's main export market, providing a major contribution to Korea's economy from the 1990s. A large surplus of funds led to massive monetary expansion, which rather reduced economic vitality. In addition, during the Roh government, wage rates increased significantly following the democratization movement.

The surge of the current account surplus after 1987 caused many side effects such as rising prices (including that of real estate) and skyrocketing stock prices. Although growth rates stayed high, the economy was already showing signs of problems ahead during the Roh government. Economic instability increased along with growing political instability, social inequality, labor problems, a foreign exchange rate policy failure, coupled with huge economic and social costs of hosting the 1986 Asian Games and 1988 Olympic Games. As the growth of the economy became increasingly dependent on export performance, the fluctuation of the business cycle increased and most of the government policies were devoted to the controlling of export and domestic demand in order to sustain high growth. The hope of reunification assisted in providing legitimacy for the economic policies adopted by the government (Kil 2017).

In general, economic policies were not coherent during this period and the rapid growth was attributed to the favorable international economic environment including the “three lows” (low interest rate, low oil prices and low exchange rate). The “three lows” period during the late 1980s provided a unique opportunity for the Korean economy to carry out restructuring of large businesses and strengthen its international competitiveness. However, major restructuring was postponed as the government continued to bail out ailing companies that belonged to large *chaebols*. With a rising democracy movement and the growing complexity and size of the national economy, however, the government‘s direct intervention in the private sector was not as efficient as it had previously been.

Despite the delay in carrying out the necessary financial restructuring, the Korean economy continued to grow under the Kim Young-sam government. The growth rates were favorable at 7.1 percent per year from 1993-1997, while inflation ran at 5.0 percent per year over the same period (Koh 2010). Although the average growth rate decreased from 10.7 percent in the late 1980s to 6.97 percent between 1990 and 1997 (Countryeconomy.com 2016a). This indicated that the Korean economy had entered a medium-growth phase since the late 1980s and that the growth potential had decreased.

However, the Korean economy under the Kim government had to face long-term consequences of the government-led development. Despite the period of lower growth, neither the expansionist spirits of *chaebols* nor the role of the government changed fundamentally. Large chaebols such as Hyundai, Samsung, LG, SK and POSCO established themselves as global brands and began to compete with their Japanese counterparts.

Government policies continued to address short-term and cyclical symptoms without paying serious attention to the long-term structural issues. Instead, globalization was selected as an important goal of the government in all areas of policies including political, economic, social and cultural. To prepare for OECD membership and sustain economic growth, liberalization of capital movement and deregulation of the financial sector proceeded. Industrial policies and the government-business relationships that had prevailed for the previous 30 years began to be dismantled, without establishing effective alternative controls of the large business by transparent and strong government policies (Shin and Chang 2003). A rapid liberalization and deregulation during the Kim government, however, contributed to the conditions that led to the 2007-2008 financial crisis in Korea.

Increased Power and Expansion of Chaebols

From the beginning of industrialization in the early 1960s, the monopoly power of large companies was of public concern in Korea. Various attempts were made to introduce anti-monopoly regulation in the 1970s, but in vain. The Monopoly Regulations and Fair Trade Act (MRFTA) was first legislated in 1980 under the leadership of the Chun Doo-hwan government. However, growth had already taken priority over equity until the end of the 1980s, and many government interventions increased industrial concentration rather than promote market competition. During this period, regulations on *chaebols* were more or less ad hoc and with no coherent strategy. The close relationship between government and *chaebols* continued with increasing collaboration in illegal activities, and workers and SMEs were largely neglected, contributing to massive imbalance in the economy and society.

As a nationwide democracy movement proceeded rapidly from 1987, *chaebols* demanded less oversight and further liberalization. By and large, the control of the government decreased considerably under the Roh and Kim, which resulted in a significant increase in the power of *chaebols*. Although the coalition between big business and government continued until the 1997 Asian financial crisis, *chaebols* became too large for the government to control in the 1990s. They continued to gain more power politically as well as economically and began to influence government decisions often through bribing and corrupting politicians and high-ranking bureaucrats who were willing recipients of this financial largesse (Turner, Kwon and O'Donnell 2017). Chung Ju Young, chairman of Hyundai business group was even a serious contender in the 1993 presidential elections.

Meanwhile, *chaebols* established their reputation in the international community and continued expanding in foreign countries. They established subsidiaries in North America, Europe and Asia simultaneously, whereas SMEs relocated their production plants to low-cost sites in Southeast Asia and China. With increased access to international capital markets, *chaebols* became less dependent on government assistance and support.

The Impact of the Asian Economic Crisis

In the late 1990s, Korea was heavily affected by the Asian financial crisis and entered into the worst recession in decades with severe consequences for unemployment, household debt and SMEs. This crisis situation had its roots in structural weaknesses in the Korean economy, largely attributed to industrial policies during the 1970s, particularly the debt-based and volume-oriented expansion policies of *chaebols*, and the failure of structural reforms during the late 1980s (Koh 2010). The government had a longstanding policy of favoring *chaebols*. Since Park Jung-hee until Kim Young-sam, the government had shared risks and rewards with *chaebols*. Being supplied with subsidized loans and financial bailouts whenever required, *chaebols* had maintained expansionist attitudes for nearly 30 years. Inefficient companies were not closed down but assisted by the government. Structural reforms were attempted in the 1980s but failed to eliminate excess capacity, only accelerating the concentration of economic power in top *chaebols* and strengthening the monopolistic market structure (Koh 2010: 44-45). The heavy-chemical industry continued to experience difficulties, and industrial rationalization (industrial restructuring programs) became necessary in most of the heavy industries until the late 1980s.

Towards the end of the 1980s, the Korean economy entered a medium-growth phase and the growth potential decreased considerably. Despite this, the *chaebols* did not revise their expansion strategy, but continued with new investment in both domestic and international markets. Although the Kim Young Sam government made some attempts to break the government-bank-*chaebol* nexus, the financial liberalization and the reduced intervention by the government actually strengthened the interconnections between *chaebols* and financial institutions. Consequently, *chaebols* continued their debt-based growth strategies, causing financial institutions to be burdened with bad debt. In 1972, the average debt-equity ratio was 300 percent for all industries, increasing to 349 percent in 1987 and 424 percent in 1997 with the top ten *chaebols* showing even higher percentages (Bank of Korea, various years). The bankruptcy of some *chaebols* was followed by the effective bankruptcy of other businesses by the spring of 1997.

The vulnerable financial sector was also responsible for the economic crisis. There was a proliferation of non-bank financial institutions (NBFIs) in the 1990s after financial deregulation, many of which were established by *chaebols*. With continued recessions in North America and Europe in the early 1990s, Asia was the only region that showed robust growth. Lenders were looking for opportunities to invest, while financial companies in Asia including Korea were looking for opportunities to borrow for the expansion of their businesses. As short-term interest rates were much lower than long-term rates, and also long-term borrowing was much more controlled than short-term borrowing, NBFIs in Korea moved out to borrow from the short-term market in amounts that were un-hedged and denominated in US dollars. While short-term debt increased, the country's foreign reserves rapidly deteriorated. From 1994 onwards, short-term debt increasingly exceeded foreign exchange reserves. Despite the government's aggressive intervention in foreign currency markets, the foreign reserves of Korea were almost depleted by mid-December of 1997, when the government announced an emergency loan from the IMF (Coe and Kim 2002).

SOCIAL AND POLITICAL OUTCOMES

Social and Political Request for Democratization and Chaebol Reform

By the mid-1980s, Korea had become a modern industrialized society. Along with economic development, public expectations for an improvement in the quality of life had grown. Demands for democratization had begun to emerge in the 1970s, but were suppressed by governments intent on the ultimate goal of economic development. The pro-democracy movement, however, broke out nationwide in the mid-1980s as the general public, including the educated urban middle class, joined the fray. The eventual outcome was democratization and the consequent addition of welfare issues to the policy agenda of government (Song H 2003). This was especially manifested in the government of Kim Young Sam (1993-1997), who attempted to pursue both political and economic democratization. Policies included reform of *chaebols* and the improvement of human rights for workers. While close government-*chaebol* relations remained, there were challenges to state autonomy through liberalization of government controls, including financial deregulation and privatization (Koh 2007). Political democratization led by economic development was an outstanding achievement, extremely rare in the developing world.

After the end of military dictatorship, democratization made steady, albeit slow, progress. Political successions took place peacefully and all realms of Korean society underwent democratic transitions. Driven by deepening democratization, various anti-corruption measures were introduced under the Kim Young Sam government. Kim purged a clique of politically ambitious army officers named "*Hanahoe,*" which roughly meant "an association of one-for-all, all-for-one." The officers were forced to retire. Even two of his presidential predecessors, Roh Tae-woo and Chun Doo-hwan, were convicted on charges of mutiny and corruption for their roles in the 1979 coup and a bloody crackdown on a pro-democracy uprising the following year, as well as for collecting hundreds of millions of dollars each in bribes from businessmen, although they were eventually pardoned.

President Kim also made pseudonyms on bank accounts illegal. This marked a critical step in Korea's long-running campaign against corruption, as bank accounts under borrowed names were widely used by politicians and businessmen to hide slush funds.

Growth of the Labor Movement

The Seoul Olympics in 1988 put Korea in the international spotlight and provided hope and encouragement for the public. The global event left a lasting impact on people's lives. People became less collectivist and consumerism was encouraged for the first time in the history of the country's industrialization. Workers began to avoid so-called "3-D jobs" (difficult, dangerous and dirty). The younger generations began to display a decreasing preference for jobs in manufacturing.

Between 1987 and 1989, more than 7,100 labor disputes, large and small, broke out and the number of labor unions doubled (Kim 2010: 108). Labor organizations requested higher wages, that were generally accepted by the large companies which had good export performance. As a result, average wage rates in manufacturing increased by 35.5 percent between 1987 and 1989 (Lee K 2016). However, many labor-intensive industries relocated their production bases to Southeast Asian countries and some to China in order to maintain their price competitiveness. Following the emergence of various national and regional trade unions (including those that were *chaebol*-based), the Korean Confederation of Trade Unions (KCTU), also known as *Minju-nochong*, was officially established in 1995. The Kim government abandoned its principle of non-intervention in industrial disputes and changed the labor law to reduce struggles over wages. Following labor reforms that began in rich countries in the latter half of the 1990s, the Kim government announced the New Labor Relations Initiative in April 1996 and set up a plan for a flexible labor market. Despite stubborn opposition from the opposition party and organized labor, Kim's ruling party passed the bill on 16 December 1996. This flexible labor market plan was criticized for contributing to the formation of a dual structure between regular and non-regular workers.

The organized labor movement brought about massive improvements in real wages, especially in heavy industry from the late 1980s. Along with the successful hosting of the Seoul Olympics, it encouraged the public to pay attention to the quality of life and leisure and enjoy the outcomes of economic prosperity. As restrictions on overseas travel and capital outflow decreased, people began to travel freely abroad. Since the mid-1990s, Korea's information and communication technologies (ICT) industry improved significantly and its hardware sector became one of the world's most advanced. Internet usage rates were among the highest in the world, and younger generations rapidly embraced various facets and patterns of western culture.

CONCLUSION

This chapter has examined Korea's transition from an authoritarian developmental state to a more democratic developmental state during the period of rapid economic growth between 1980 and 1997. During this period, global and domestic environments rapidly changed, playing an important role in inducing rapid economic growth. The collapse of the Soviet Union and the end of the Cold War markedly diminished the international security concerns while the new US-led international order was established. In addition, globalization and neo-liberalization in the financial and economic spheres became prominent trends while the international economic environment was greatly enhanced in the mid-1980s with the three-lows economic boom (low oil prices, low exchange rates and low international interest rates). In Korea, growing pro-democracy movements led to the end of the military regime and the establishment of formal democracy. This political transition entailed changes in government roles and characteristics during this period.

Despite political instability, Korea continued as a developmental state and underwent a period of high economic growth during the 1980s. With the policy focus on stabilization, the economy was able to achieve double-digit growth rates by 1983 (Adesnik and Kim 2008). The average annual growth rates were recorded at 9 percent between 1980 and 1985, and over 12 percent between 1986 and 1988 (Lee K 2016). This was a result largely driven by the favorable international environment provided by the "three lows" (as well as the government's industrial restructuring efforts. While the developmental state remained central to economic management, it was also challenged by the global trend towards greater economic liberalization and growing public demand for democracy. For instance, the removal of restrictions and barriers on imports became inevitable to enhance the country's industrial competitiveness. The rise of a civil society and the achievement of democratic political transition also helped to hasten the loosening of government control over the economy. As a result, Korea's developmental state underwent a transition.

The Kim Young Sam government actively tried to remove the legacy of the authoritarian developmental state and create the image of the civilian government. In his Five-Year Plan for the New Economy (1993–97), the policy objectives were announced as social welfare enhancement, economic revitalization, political reform and globalization, reflecting the weakening authoritarian developmentalist state in Korea. Instead, a diminished government role, along with greater private sector participation through economic liberalization and deregulation, were emphasized as new engines for economic growth. In response to challenges from economic liberalism, the Kim government began opening the country's market to greater foreign trade and investment. The process of liberalization and opening up of capital and financial markets and the rice market started in 1993. In addition, Korea joined the WTO in 1995 and the OECD in 1996. The process of financial liberalization and deregulation undertaken during the Kim government, however, strengthened the nexus between *chaebols* and financial institutions, which contributed to the condition that led to the 1997-1998 financial crisis in Korea. Along with economic development, public expectation of improvements in the quality of life and labor rights also grew, necessitating a need for the role and policy agenda of government to change.

Chapter 3

The Capable State in a Globalized Economy (1998 – 2016)

This chapter examines the weakening of the direct role of government in the Korean economy associated with political transition from conservative to progressive governments, as well as economic movement towards neoliberalism between 1998 and 2016. During this period, the international trade environment became increasingly multi-polarized and neoliberal while the world economy was in a low-growth period. As discussed earlier, Korea underwent a severe recession during the 1997 Asian financial crisis as well as political transition between conservative and progressive government. These changes in the global and domestic environments created various opportunities and challenges for Korea's economic policy. In this context, the Korean government responded with a policy mix that incorporated attributes of neoliberalism, developmentalism and welfare statism. This coexistence of seemingly contradictory approaches was necessary and useful as it provided the government with the flexibility and opportunities to further economic and social development.

This co-existence began in the aftermath of the 1997 Asian financial crisis. As part of the IMF's bailout program, the new progressive government under Kim Dae-jung was forced to implement broad neoliberal reforms on the Korean developmental state, including *chaebol* reform and rapid opening up to global markets. Amid the country's neoliberal transformation, however, the progressive regime under Kim and his successor Roh retained some of the fundamental characteristics of a developmental state, maintaining strong state intervention in the economy when seen as necessary. Both leaders adopted state-driven development policies to revive the domestic economy and achieve welfare state expansion. The transition from a developmental state to a neoliberal market economic system, however, intensified under the pro-business conservative governments, and was reinforced by their active participation in free trade agreements (FTAs). Government interventions in the economy were limited while deregulation and privatization were advocated and pursued.

During this period, Korea's developmental state was in a transitional period with an overall weakening of the role of the government and expansion of the private sector (Kim 2010). The acceleration of globalization and neoliberalism in the Korean economy and democratic transition in politics, by which the market and the public gained more power, required a more capable role from government to efficiently manage opportunities and challenges emerging from an evolving environment. Driven by a new focus on the efficiency of government and its role as a provider of welfare, both progressive and conservative governments pursued the idea of a state that was capable of realizing opportunities and managing the challenges of a changing environment efficiently. The creation of such a capable state was the prime objective of this period.

The chapter continues with a brief overview of the international and domestic environments during this period, followed by a review of economic policy responses to the environment, and their outcomes and implications.

INTERNATIONAL ENVIRONMENT

Globalization, Regionalism and Growing Competition in a Multi-Polarized World

In the post-Cold War world, international political leadership had become increasingly multi-polarized, as had the international trade environment. The European Union (EU) strengthened its role as an actor in the international order. Starting from six European countries in 1952, the EU, as of 2017, developed as the largest economic union in the world, comprising 28 European countries, of which 15 joined before 2000 and 13 after 2000. Despite the significant challenges of creating and introducing the common currency named Euro, the process of Europe's postwar political and economic integration was regarded as the most developed model of regional integration (Cameron 2010). Along with North America and the Pacific Rim, the EU formed the triad market, comprised of the most world powerful economies, representing 70-75 percent of world production (Rajagopal 2007: 44).

New economic powers were emerging. China rose as the center of global industrial production and merchandise trade based on cheap labor, rapid industrialization and trade liberalization. Since China's adoption of opening-up policy in 1978, Guangdong province had been a testing ground for economic reform. The success of the economic reform in Guangdong gave much confidence to large western companies to invest in China. From the 1990s, the momentum of economic reform and growth expanded to Shanghai and other coastal regions of China. China was the fastest growing economy in the world during the 1990s, and became one of the world's largest economies by 2000. Russia also re-emerged as a leading country and continued to exercise its power in international politics and economy (Cooper 2009). The economic transition from centrally planned to market economies in Eastern Europe and the Soviet bloc in the 1990s was not as initially successful as it was in China. With extensive socialist social welfare systems remaining in place, rapid economic reforms led to sharp declines in GDP and high inflation in these economies (Sachs 1996). As they recovered, many foreign companies entered the countries of Eastern Europe and the Soviet bloc to take advantage of large untapped markets and to secure natural resources. In addition, since 2000, other large developing countries such as Brazil, India and Indonesia have emerged as important economic powers with high growth potential.

In this multi-polarized world, the WTO was no longer the only international organization dealing with the rules of trade and investment between countries. Since 2000, regional organizations and bilateral FTAs have become as important as multilateral negotiations through the WTO. These changes in the international environment highlighted the increasing importance of both long-term and stable strategic partnership and capacity building to better respond to the changing world economic order. Global and regional economic integration offered the Korean economy new opportunities for exports. They also enabled many Korean companies to establish production facilities in third countries and export the finished products from these locations.

Expansion of Neoliberalism and the 2008 Global Financial Crisis

The limitations of the neoliberal economic order were vividly revealed through the 2007 global financial crisis and the increased public debt in rich countries in Western Europe and North America. The global financial crisis began in 2007 with the collapse of the subprime mortgage market in the US, which turned into a major international banking crisis when the 158-year-old investment bank Lehman Brothers filed for bankruptcy on 15 September 2008. Many other financial institutions in developed countries followed in bankruptcy filing, contributing to the European sovereign-debt crisis in Iceland, Greece, Ireland and Portugal. This led global financial institutions to withdraw US dollars from emerging financial markets, including Korea, in order to secure financial liquidity and de-leveraging (Kim 2014). Eventually, the financial crisis spread globally. Recording a negative growth rate for the first time since the Second World War, the world economy sank into major recession between 2008–2012, although the scale and timing of the recession varied from country to country. The global economy was facing a new period of slowing growth and rising risks (IMF 2011).

Following the crisis, the economic environment became particularly unfavourable for the triad economies, which faced serious structural challenges coupled with massive public debts and decreasing purchasing power. The OECD countries were not able to find any easy way out from the crisis, and an alternative economic regime that would help them to resolve massive public debt and other problems was not suggested. Economic growth and stability was gaining momentum in emerging economies. China, along with other countries deemed to be at a similar stage of economic development (Brazil, Russia, India and South Africa), formed the BRIC club in 2010 and emerged as an alternative power to the ailing OECD economies (Besada and Tok 2014).

Korea was one of the victims of the global crisis. As a result of the economic reform after the 1997 Asian financial crisis, the Korean financial sector became directly linked to the global financial sector, joining the neoliberal global economic order. This increased the vulnerability of the Korean financial market as did its growing dependence on foreign investors. As a high proportion of the country's public debt was international investment liability, the instability in the global financial market infected the domestic economy. The fast growth period ended and growth potential decreased considerably in Korea. The growth strategies and goals needed to be revised both at firm and national levels. However, thanks to broad structural reforms implemented after the previous financial crisis, the Korean economy was more flexible and resilient to changes within a highly globalized economy.

Domestic Environment

Political and Economic Transitions

Between 1998 and 2016, Korea underwent democratic political transitions between conservative and progressive forces, while the role of government changed. Kim Dae-jung became a new president in 1998, when the Korean economy was in deep turmoil in the aftermath of the 1997 Asian financial crisis. For a long time since the Park Chung-Hee era, Kim Dae-jung, along with Kim Young-Sam, had been a leading political activist who fought to achieve democratization in Korea. During the period, the Korean parties and voters were divided based on their regional interests. Unlike Kim Young-Sam, Kim Dae-jung won the presidential election as a leader of the opposition party, enabling the establishment of a new government with new people. During his presidency (1998-2003), one of the marked differences in policies was his promotion of peaceful engagement and rapprochement with North Korea. This approach made significant progress in the inter-Korean dialogue and economic cooperation. For the first time since the division between North and South, the presidential summit was held in Pyongyang in June 2000. Kim received the Nobel Prize for Peace in 2000 for his efforts to restore democracy in Korea and improve relations with North Korea. Kim's approach towards North Korea was called the "sunshine policy," which was inherited and expanded by the following Roh Moo-hyun government. Roh visited Pyongyang for the second presidential summit in 2007 while he kept his distance from the US and Japan in foreign policy.

After Kim Dae-jung, his successor Roh Moo-hyun formed an even more liberal government (2002-2008). His election was greatly supported by young followers using internet and social media, and signified the arrival of a new generation of politicians in Korea. As a human rights lawyer, he had actively participated in the democratization movement and various civil society activities for a long time. When he took office, former leaders of pro-democracy and civil rights movements (representing a progressive younger generation, the so-called "386 generation") were invited into his government. Roh continued to favor democratic reforms and made an effort to stop regional support bases, political factions and strong ties with *chaebols*. However, in the context of slow economic growth and deepening bipolarization, many of his progressive reform policies, coupled with his anti-American and pro-North Korean views, received a tremendous backlash from conservative media and citizens and thus faced strong opposition.

In the context of the growing public discontent resulting from slow growth during the Roh Moo-hyun government, conservative former businessman Lee Myung-bak was elected president in 2007 on the promise that he would become the "economy president" of the country and revive the "old Korea." Upon taking office, he stopped or reversed many of Roh's liberal policies, placing far more emphasis on pro-business policies and relations with the US. Unlike his progressive predecessors, he took a hardline stance on North Korea. His government reversed the Sunshine policy, and promoted greater focus on stopping North Korea's nuclear program and human rights issues (Snyder 2009). His policy toward North Korea was expressed in terms of mutual benefits and common prosperity. In this policy, the priority was on denuclearization and finding a way for both the North and South to achieve mutual benefits and common prosperity (Suh 2009). For this, the government supported a diplomatic relationship and denuclearization talks between North Korea and the US and continued inter-Korean economic cooperation projects as it had done in the past.

Park Geun-hye, his conservative successor, was elected the first female president of Korea in the 2012 election. She began her political career as a member of parliament in 1998 after years of seclusion following her president-father's assassination, and had a popular support base, especially from those aged over 60 who had a sense of nostalgia and sympathy for her and her parents. As the daughter of a former authoritarian strongman, she was an icon of the conservative establishment in Korea. Park Geun-hye inherited Lee's pro-*chaebol* conservatism and continued to take a hard line against North Korea's nuclear provocations. In March 2017, she became the first democratically elected Korean president to be forced out of office over a corruption and cronyism scandal. Moon Jae-in was elected president after a series of candlelight protests participated in by millions of citizens (Turner et al. 2017). Deferring to the people's demands, he promised to restore and stabilize democracy, and eradicate deep-rooted practices. Moon also promised to implement a tailored welfare system guaranteeing basic income corresponding to people's lifecycle ("What Moon Jae-in pledged" 2017).

The Increasing Demand for a Welfare State in Korea Amid Rapid Social Change

Korean society changed considerably following the 1997 Asian financial crisis. Rapid urbanization and industrialization diversified social demands. As the standard of living improved and the population below the poverty line decreased substantially, more importance was given to the quality of life. With a more consolidated democratic political system and improvements in public awareness and education, civil society moved their focus from the general demand for political democracy to other issues, including labor and working conditions as well as the creation of the Korean welfare state. Government policies were expected to address the welfare of individuals in society. The government also made efforts to eliminate political corruption, including the formation of the Independent Commission Against Corruption in 2002.

Korea was also experiencing considerable demographic change, with its fast-ageing population and low fertility rate. The proportion of Korea's population aged 65 and over increased threefold in a single generation, from 3.5 percent in 1975 to 11 percent in 2010 — the fastest rate in OECD countries (*Yonhap News* 2014). By contrast, the total fertility rate — the total number of children that would be born to each woman — recorded the lowest point at 1.08 in 2005 and remained the lowest among OECD countries (*Dong-A Ilbo* 2014). With elderly people over 65 already making up 13.6 percent of the population as of January 2017 (Kim D-S 2017), Korea is expected to follow Japan and become a "super-aged" society by 2030 (that is, 20 percent of the population aged 65 or older). These demographic trends have major fiscal, economic and social implications as they mean a shrinking workforce, limited growth potential and increasing fiscal burdens on the government. In addition, with prolonged high unemployment and slow growth, younger generations have found it much harder to settle in society successfully. There were growing concerns that the performance of large conglomerates no longer created direct benefits to them. Maintaining vitality and vision among the younger generation became important for government to ensure the continued development in Korea while an economic transition to less labor-intensive and more technology-intensive industries emerged as a pressing matter.

Progress in Democracy

The election of President Kim Dae-jung in 1997 marked an important step forward in democracy as it was the first peaceful transfer of power from the ruling to the opposition party. A quick recovery from the 1997 Asian financial crisis under the Kim Dae-jung government strengthened the political consciousness of Koreans (Hahm 2008). People realized that the belief that economic development required the limitation of political rights — the notion that was used to legitimate the authoritarian regimes — was wrong.

Pursuing a non-authoritarian course and embracing a participatory civil society, President Roh Moo-hyun made notable contributions to democracy in Korea (Hahm 2008). Firstly, Roh and his government advocated for civil society involvement in governance and the policy process, actively promoting policy-making participation by all civic groups including labor organizations (Lee and Yun 2011). Secondly, the division of political parties based on regional interests was diluted, with parties beginning to represent different classes and political interests through social integration programs. Thirdly, the transparency of the government improved significantly, and procedures as well as outcomes of government activities came under public scrutiny.

His progressive and unpopular moves (such as reconciliation with North Korea and keeping distance from the US), however, encountered strong opposition from the conservative political groups and media. With his approval ratings hitting rock bottom, he was impeached by parliament in March 2004, ostensibly for breaking election rules. This, however, provoked massive candlelight protests in Seoul, and Roh's approval rating quickly soared from 30 to 50 percent (Hahm 2008: 138). On 14 May, the Constitutional Court ruled in favor of the sanctioned Roh, returning him to office less than a month later. This incident showed that the people in Korea could overcome ideological bias and regional bigotry and act as citizens of a mature democracy (Hahm 2008: 138).

Chaebols in the Globalized World Economy

Globalization of the world economy and the pursuit of neoliberalism signified the expanding role of MNEs. Until the 1980s, most MNEs operating in emerging markets were concentrated in the manufacturing sector, as the service sector was usually tightly controlled. During the GATT negotiations, there were no serious attempts to open the service sectors of emerging markets until the Uruguay Round that began in 1986. When the Uruguay Round negotiations were successfully completed in 1994, elements of the service sectors of emerging markets were rapidly integrated with those of OECD countries. After a short period of open market operations, the service sector of emerging markets was heavily affected by economic crises and instability that started in the developed countries.

New MNEs emerged from Asia as well, creating a new wave of Asian multinational corporations. Japanese companies had established subsidiaries in North America and Europe since the 1970s and 1980s. In keeping with this trend, many Korean *chaebols*, including Samsung, Hyundai and LG, also became global brands from the 1990s, while the domestic market became more dependent on these companies.

ECONOMIC POLICIES

Neoliberal Reform and the Welfare State

It was the 1997 Asian financial crisis and the IMF bailout program that triggered the neoliberal reform of the Korean developmental state (Kim and Park 2004). In the aftermath of the 1997 Asian financial crisis, the Kim Dae-jung government's utmost priority was to recover from the economic crisis. While committed to economic recovery, Kim also faced the difficult task of steering the country's neoliberal economic reform. According to the first IMF agreement signed by his predecessor, Kim was required by the IMF to undertake structural adjustment involving trade liberalization and integration into the international economy. The Korean market was forced to open to the global economy, with many restrictions on imports and foreign investment removed. President Kim's liberal reforms also attempted to deal with the *chaebols* by reducing their debt-equity ratios and ensuring transparency of *chaebol* activities. Despite these major neoliberal reforms, President Kim did not fully abolish government intervention in the economy. In the aftermath of the financial crisis, he emphasized national unity for economic recovery and adopted a number of developmentalist policies including the state-led industrial realignment under the name of "Big Deal" policy. However, unlike in authoritarian and comprehensive developmental states, his government acted as "senior partner" rather than "commander-in-chief" in the economy (Cherry 2005).

Continuing the transition from a developmental state to a neoliberal market economic system, the subsequent Roh Moo-hyun government (2002-2008) more explicitly pursued a mixed policy approach, implementing both neoliberal and developmentalist policies. Under the slogan of "participatory government," Roh took a pro-labor and anti-chaebol stance even more strongly than Kim Dae-jung and placed the priority on equity above growth. His policies were designed to focus on balanced economic growth and social development, and to achieve more equitable distribution rather than rapid growth. In this vein, the Roh government advocated the decentralization of economic, social and political power and promoted the democratization process in both economic and political arenas. A substantial transfer of decision-making power took place from the central government to local governments. President Roh also sought to relocate the capital of the country from Seoul to the mid-west region. Embracing institutional reform and technological innovation, his government aimed to strengthen the fundamental capabilities in government, economy and society as a new source of international competitiveness (Koh 2007). His goal was to reduce the country's dependence on the US military and economy, to redistribute wealth from the rich to the poor through higher taxes, to eradicate corruption in government and business and to curb the power of *chaebols* (Koh 2007). The developmental state approaches continued during the progressive Kim and Roh governments, and were most visible in the role that the government played in the growth of the knowledge industry, the rise of Korea's cultural and entertainment economy, and the transition towards a welfare state.

The conservative Lee government (2008-2013) was a pro-growth and pro-business/*chaebol* government. With economic growth as the key objective, the government prioritized growth over equity (Suh and Kwon 2014). Neoliberal policies were the norm under the Lee government. Many business-friendly policies, including reduction of corporate taxes, a taxation system for job creation and tax reductions plans for the rich, were introduced as responses to the effect of the global financial crisis. Fiscal stimulus and low interest rates were also implemented to boost economic growth. The government expected that benefits from the *chaebols'* economic success would trickle down to SMEs and increase their productivity. Many regulations were relaxed and removed to stimulate business development. Deregulation also took place in the housing sector to spur the private housing market and improve housing availability. However, the Lee government also intervened in the economy by spearheading various demand management projects. These included the Four River Project that commenced in late 2008 with an estimated cost of approximately US$ 20 billion. This construction project was said to resemble a developmental policy combined with a Keynesian demand management project (Thurbon 2016). Developmentalism was also evident in Green Growth policy which involved significant government support to the producers of alternative sources of energy, such as solar energy, and to initiatives for reducing carbon dioxide emission and controlling environmental pollution.

Another conservative government under President Park Geun-hye (2013-2016) continued to embrace pro-business neoliberalism. Its goal was to break out of low growth via creating another venture boom, but many of its economic policies primarily benefited *chaebols*. In 2014, she announced a three-year plan to change chronic problems and abnormal practices in the Korean economy. In this plan, she proposed a so-called "474 vision" targeting a 4 percent GDP growth rate, a 70 percent employment rate and a per capita income of US$40,000. In line with the Park government's pro-growth fiscal policy, the plan provided three main directions for future economic policies: "an economy with strong fundamentals, dynamic innovation and a balance between domestic demand and exports" (OECD 2014: 47). Government's objective was to restructure the economy, with the growth model shifting towards being private-led and domestic market-centered (Song 2014). The government wanted the private sector, especially the service industry, to thrive without excessive government regulations that had squeezed economic growth for the previous few years. Accordingly, Finance Minister Choi Kyung-hwan introduced a US$40 billion stimulus package to support the government's pro-growth fiscal policy. The central bank (the Bank of Korea) cut its key interest rate several times, reaching an historic low of 1.25 percent in June 2016 (*Fox News* 2016). The Park government also reduced regulation primarily within the business sector. Other measures included housing-market deregulation aimed at revitalizing the housing market and stimulating growth. These policies included a relaxation of loan-to-value and debt-to-income ratios (Kalinowski, Rhyu and Croissant 2016).

Driven by a renewed focus on growth, each conservative government sought to formulate a new economic and social development vision and find a new economic growth engine for Korea. President Lee Myung-bak announced "green growth" as the nation's new guiding economic development philosophy, stressing next-generation energy sources and technologies as an engine for economic growth. President Park Geun-hye's solution was to transform Korea into a "creative economy" and end its heavy reliance on *chaebols* by promoting a "venture boom."

KEY ISSUES

State-Led Economic Restructuring

The pressing need to overcome the 1997 Asian financial crisis meant that President Kim Dae-jung (1998-2002) faced no domestic opposition to strong economic intervention by the government. In contrast, there was considerable pressure from the IMF to undertake economic restructuring as a condition of its rescue package. In addition, in the context of social vulnerability, the government faced increasing domestic pressure to transform Korea into a welfare state. Since 1997, progressive governments under Kim Dae-jung and Roh Moo-hyun had been committed to welfare state development. Massive amounts of public funds were injected into welfare services and programs, although the tax revenue to finance welfare expenditure did not increase, resulting in budget blow-outs. Since then, welfare state development has remained as the overriding issue in the presidential elections and was an important policy item of the conservative government of Lee Myung-bak. Despite its pledged commitment to economic growth and tax cuts, the Lee Myung-bak government did not reduce welfare spending. Although many people were not yet willing to exchange higher income tax for welfare benefits, election results and public opinion made it difficult to reduce public services. Thus, the attributes of neoliberal, developmental and welfare states began to co-exist in Korea during this period (Suh and Kwon 2014). This co-existence provided the Kim Dae-jung government with flexibility and opportunities to restructure the economy. In response to the 1997 Asian financial crisis that affected almost all parts of the Korean economy, the Kim Dae-jung government's reform and restructuring efforts were diverse and varied.

The process of economic restructuring during the post-crisis transition period can be summarized in five categories. First were the fiscal and monetary policies introduced for macroeconomic stability. During the first half of 1998, the government adopted tight budgetary and monetary policies to reduce demand and improve the current account. However, these tight policies deepened the recession and increased the criticisms of the IMF program. During the second half of 1998, an expansionary fiscal policy was adopted as both the current account and export performance improved.

Second was corporate sector reform, also known as *chaebol* reform, through two major intervention programs typical of the developmental state model. One was an industrial realignment policy known as the Big Deal, which aimed to trim the operations of major conglomerates so that they could focus on a small number of core businesses and enhance their international competitiveness (Cherry 2005). The other was the adoption of "workout" programs to manage those companies that could not repay their debts. For this, the Kim Dae-jung government and the owners of the four largest *chaebols* made an agreement on corporate reforms, including the reduction of debt-equity ratios from 500 percent to 200 percent in two years, and improving transparency among the large *chaebols* (Kwon and Suh 2003).

Third was the financial sector reform that rationalized the commercial banking sector. Banks with prospects of regaining competitiveness were given rescue funds while banks with poor prospects were closed down. An overriding purpose of the financial reform was to rebuild a consolidated regulatory agency.

Fourth was labor market reform. While he was still the opposition leader, Kim Dae-jung had always sided with labor unions whenever they had conflicts with management. However, after the 1997 Asian financial crisis, the Kim government legalized the massive layoffs resulting from corporate restructuring. Such layoffs had been prohibited since the outbreak of industrial conflicts in the second half of the 1980s.

Fifth was public sector reform. A large-scale privatization program was undertaken in the while employment within privatized companies decreased considerably. This represented the stance of the Kim government, which adopted neoliberal economic policies on a major scale.

During the restructuring of the economy, a large number of companies faced bankruptcy. Government assistance and restructuring were given mostly to the large companies, while SMEs were largely left to make adjustments on their own. Large companies that received assistance from the government survived, but the second and third tier companies were either purchased by other companies or left to go bankrupt. This worsened the gap between large and small companies in terms of size and value. The largest companies continued to expand and excel, while SMEs struggled to survive (Gregory, Harvie and Lee 2002).

President Roh Moo-hyun called for sweeping reforms of the *chaebol*-dominated economic system. His government shifted its attention to SMEs, especially in ICT, which was identified as a new economic growth engine. During the Roh government, *chaebols* had a relatively difficult time doing business. More attention was paid to workers, and trade unions' protests decreased. Execution of his reform program, however, was continuously resisted by conservative opposition parties and criticized by conservative media for not being compatible with country's economic growth.

Despite the controversy, these reform and restructuring efforts contributed to the economy weathering the 2008 global crisis better than most other OECD countries. Learning from the 1997 Asian financial crisis, the Lee Myung-bak government employed more diverse and timely policy responses including expansionary fiscal policy and extended tax exemption and support with an aim to revitalize the Korean economy and boost domestic investment and consumption (Kim 2014). The government lowered the benchmark interest rate and supplied liquidity to financial institutions to extend their credit supply capacity and to relieve the tensions in the financial market. Regarding foreign exchange policy, the government signed a currency swap agreement with the US, China, and Japan, and provided commercial banks with foreign currency to increase liquidity. The government also carried out the restructuring of financial institutions and the business sector. The government established a "restructuring fund" in 2009 to take over the non-performing loans of financial institutions and the assets of insolvent companies, and made financial institutions play a pivotal role in restructuring the business sector (Kim 2014). A key strategy behind these policies was that the growth of the economy would be led by the expansion of the corporate sector — in particular, large companies — so that the benefits would flow to the rest of the economy. The Lee government supported tax cuts and small government as the main strategies for reviving economic growth. The government kept tax rates low for large companies and high-income individuals and emphasized greater liberalization. During his time in office, the corporate tax rate was reduced from 25 percent in 2009 to 20 percent in 2012 (Kim Y 2015). The Lee government also tried to retain employment amid the global financial crisis. The government encouraged companies through subsidies and tax incentives, aiming for job creation in the service industry and for the young, the elderly, the poor, and the disabled (Ministry of Employment and Labor 2012). Employment support measures were also introduced.

The Expansion of Welfare Policies

Amid neoliberal reforms, the Kim Dae-jung government began to expand the national social welfare system, proposing the goal of setting up a Productive Welfare State in Korea. This was inevitable, firstly, because Korea joined OECD with its social standards not yet completely compatible with OECD principles. Secondly, Korea also needed a welfare state as it was facing a new problem of irregular employment after the economic crisis in 1997-1998 and a recovery from the crisis by 2003-2004, which led to the restructuring of labor relations.

Public attitudes to the role of government in the economy, the provision of public services and social security also changed during this period. Equitable distribution was considered more important than overall growth. People were more concerned about inequality and the gap between the rich and poor and between large companies and SMEs. Such attitudinal changes dissipated people's sense of loyalty and willingness to sacrifice individual needs and wellbeing for a national quest for economic growth.

Under the Kim government, the economy started to make a transition to a welfare state and a neoliberal state at the same time. Major improvements were carried out in the areas of medical insurance, national pension system, unemployment benefits and insurance, and industrial accident compensation insurance. Kim Dae-jung's welfare policy was closely followed by the government of Roh Moo-hyun. It acknowledged equitable income and wealth distribution across different social classes as one of the important aims of the government and continued to increase welfare spending (Suh and Kwon 2014).

In terms of welfare policy, the conservative governments under Lee Myung-bak and Park Geun-hye were less active than their progressive predecessors. The Lee government's pro-business policies presented challenges to the developmental welfare state. Aiming for "welfare through work," the Lee government advocated "Active Welfare" seeking to increase social productivity as opposed to a passive consumption-centered welfare (Lee, Lee and Park 2012: 13). As a result, welfare programs declined in scope and there was little change to the employment statistics except an increase in temporary workers (Suh and Kwon 2014). With decentralization, national coordination of policies became much more difficult and the provision of social welfare varied according to the capacity of each region. To appeal to the voters, Park Geun-hye pledged to increase welfare benefits, but abandoned her promises soon after the election due to budget problems. With ever-increasing social welfare needs, however, government welfare expenditures continued to rise even during the conservative governments' tenures.

Reinforcing Neoliberalism through FTAs

Through the post-Asian financial crisis economic restructuring, neoliberalism was making inroads into the Korean economy under the IMF's guidance. Neoliberal influences were most sharply felt in the deregulation of financial markets, such as the removal of import and capital market restrictions and the lifting of the foreign ownership ceiling from 50 percent to 100 percent. As both share prices and the value of the Korean Won were extremely low, foreign investors flooded in to decrease the debt-equity ratios (Shin and Chang 2003). With the increased integration of the world's capital markets, the share prices on the Korean Stock Exchange became very sensitive to the actions of foreign investors. This integration of the domestic capital market into the global market and the increasing size of the government debt owned by foreigners created a vulnerability to external shocks within the Korean economy.

In parallel with its move towards globalization, the government's neoliberal reforms were consolidated by its initiation of FTA negotiations to remove trade barriers such as tariffs and import quotas (Hundt 2015). In the context of an unfavourable foreign business environment and declining FDI, the Roh Moo-hyun government had begun its engagement in bilateral FTAs in the late 1990s. The motivation was both economic and political. FTAs were expected not only to strengthen bilateral economic, trade and investment relations, but also to upgrade the bilateral alliances (Liou 2008). The Korea-US FTA signed on 30 June 2007 was significant for the Korean economy as an attempt to create a Northeast Asia financial hub, and to increase labor market flexibility to enhance international competitiveness. At the same time, it also provided a mechanism for expanding the security alliance between the two countries. Viewed as deepening economic, political and strategic partnerships, FTAs were an emerging trend of world trade preferred over the WTO (Liou 2008). FTAs, however, were unpopular with trade unions, non-governmental organizations (NGOs), academics and the public in Korea, who perceived they would do more harm than good. Amid strong opposition, however, the Roh government concluded FTAs with Chile (April 2004), Singapore (March 2006), EFTA (September 2006), Association of Southeast Asian Nations (ASEAN) (June 2007) and the US (April 2007) (Cheong and Cho 2009: 156).

Neoliberalism was even more strongly reinforced during the Lee Myung-bak government (2008-2012). Adopting a pro-business/*chaebol* approach, Lee himself was a strong supporter of the FTA between Korea and the US. He stated that a closer alliance with the US would help to maintain peace and stability in the Korean peninsula (Worsnip 2008). With the US-Korea FTA that entered into effect in March 2012, the Lee government implemented a massive economic reform that would reduce trade barriers and costs and enhance transparency. Extensive economic liberalization policies were introduced, including privatization, fiscal austerity, deregulation, free trade, reductions in government spending, low interest rates and an undervalued currency, which all greatly assisted the corporate sector and resulted in the increased concentration of power in *chaebols*. As of 2017, Korea had concluded 15 FTAs with 52 countries including the EU, ASEAN, Australia, Canada, China, India and Vietnam, and was negotiating eight FTAs with 24 countries including Japan and six countries in Central America (Korea Customs Service 2017).

The Search for New Growth Engines

Amid the shift toward neoliberalism, the Korean governments of this period retained the attributes of a developmental state and a welfare state, although there was a difference in degree between progressive and conservative governments. Each government tried to develop its economy by reviving government direct intervention and developmental projects while supporting the private sector. Their use of this mixed policy approach was driven by a renewed focus on growth amid global economic difficulties. The following sub-sections provide examples of strong state-driven development policies adopted during this period.

The Knowledge and Culture Industries (Kim Dae-Jung and Roh Moo-Hyun)

As one of the means of overcoming the crisis and reviving the national economy, the Kim Dae-jung government made an all-out effort to promote venture companies in high technology and knowledge-intensive industries, especially in the ICT industry. The government privatized, deregulated and liberalized the ICT markets, but at the same time played a leading role in initiating, supporting and funding them to promote their technological competitiveness (Jin 2017: 184). Similar developmental state approaches continued during the Roh government which identified and supported the growth of the knowledge industry, including the development of IT and biotechnology, and the cultural industry as engines for economic growth (Suh and Kwon 2014). Several long-term policies were set up for the development of nano- and bio-technology and environmental technologies. In addition, with the emergence of the "Korean wave" in the 1990s, referring to an almost viral popularity of Korean culture in the Asian region (Cheng 2008: 76), the Roh government also sought to increase the export of cultural products, including Korean pop music, TV programs, movies and online games.

National Strategy for Green Growth, the Four Rivers Project and Natural Resource Diplomacy (Lee Myung-Bak)

Despite his pro-neoliberalism stance, Lee Myung-bak initiated many economic policies and programs that resembled the government-led developmentalism of Park Jung-hee. The Lee government's intervention in the economy was evident in its launch of the National Strategy for Green Growth 2009-2050. In the context of climate change and growing global interest in environment protection and green energy, the Lee government launched the National Strategy for Green Growth in July 2009. The strategy involved significant support for the alternative sources of energy, such as solar energy, reducing carbon dioxide emissions, and control of environmental pollution. As part of this developmentalist strategy, the Lee government also launched the Four Rivers Project in late 2008 with an estimated cost of approximately US$ 20 billion. The project aimed to provide water management systems in the four major rivers in Korea including the Han, Nakdong, Geum and Yeongsan, and to create multipurpose spaces for local residents and enhance regional development around rivers. It involved extensive construction work on the rivers, including dredging and construction of weirs and dams.

The Lee government's developmental approach was also visible in its foreign policy. Under the vision of a "Global Korea," President Lee pushed the so-called natural resource diplomacy as one of many strategies to reshape the nation's international standing. His government aimed to secure overseas resources, and many state-run energy companies competed for deals with overseas energy businesses using public funds amounting to over KRW26 trillion (US$26 billion) (Kim Y 2015). Korea National Oil Corp. (KNOC), Koreas Resources Corp. (KORES), Korea Electric Power Corp. (KEPCO) and Korea Gas Corp. (KOGAS) signed many ambitious contracts, but had to face mounting net losses due to failed investments. Debt-ratios of these companies soared, exacerbating their financial health. The KNOC's 2009 botched acquisition of Harvest Operations, the Canadian oil refinery was one of the major cases in which taxpayer money was blatantly wasted. As part of restructuring efforts, many subsidiaries of these energy companies were listed on the stock market, which caused controversy about eventual privatization and favoritism of specific conglomerates (Choi 2016).

Creative Economy (Park Geun-Hye)

The Park government (2013-2017) abandoned the Lee government's concept of "green growth." Park instead pledged economic democratization during her presidential campaign, prioritizing government reforms for establishing a fair market and tackling *chaebol* problems. Soon after taking office, however, she held back on her reform plan and instead pursued a new growth model. With slow growth below 4 percent and the need to generate employment, her government needed a new economic growth engine. With China emerging as a powerful competitor to Korea's manufactured exports, it was evident that Korea's traditional growth model based on *chaebols* was no longer sustainable.

President Park's solution was the creative economy. This policy promoted innovation and entrepreneurship within the SME sector. The Park government wanted to foster start-ups and venture businesses to revitalize the economy and generate new jobs, just as ICT had been an important driving force for economic growth during the Kim Dae-jung and Roh Moo-hyun governments.

For the effective implementation of these strategies, in February 2013, a new government ministry was launched under the name of Ministry of Science, ICT and Future Planning (MSIP), after combining the Ministry of Science and Technology (MoST), the Ministry of Information and Communication, and the Korean Broadcasting Commission. The MSIP built Creative Economy Innovation Centers (CEICs) in the 18 local governments and supported the growth and overseas expansion of SMEs through linkage and cooperation with large companies and business groups. In June 2013, the government introduced the Third Basic Plan for Science and Technology 2013-2017, which proposed government investment for R&D across 30 main technologies in five strategic technology areas, covering fields from economic growth to quality of life. The government invested KRW22 trillion over a 3-year period between 2013-2015, nearly the same amount as Lee Myung-bak's Four Rivers Project (Sohn 2015).

Economic Outcomes

Growth Outcomes

Amid the 1997 Asian financial crisis, the Kim Dae-jung government managed to recover the economy quickly due to relatively sound internal fundamentals achieved as a result of the restructuring process (Cho 2010). The rapid growth of IT-based technology-intensive industries provided an engine for growth in the post-crisis period. In addition, there was a consensus amongst the public that they should share the burden of economic recovery. Almost a quarter of the entire country's population participated in a campaign to help pay the nation's IMF debt by selling their gold jewelry (Holmes 2016). Koreans living abroad also sent their foreign funds to Korea to help the government control exchange rates.

As a result, the economic outcomes were extremely favorable. Annual GDP growth rate increased from -5.7 percent to 10.7 percent in just one year (between 1998 and 1999), and the government fully repaid a multi-billion-dollar loan from the IMF in August 2001, three years earlier than expected (Gluck 2001; World Bank 2017a). The unemployment rate was reduced from 7 percent in 1998 to 3.3 percent in 2002. There was a current account surplus for five consecutive years, and an increase of the foreign exchange reserve by US$90.6 billion during the Kim presidency (Koh 2010). Trade and current accounts returned to profitability under the Kim Dae-jung government, achieving successive years of surpluses during the Roh Moo-hyun government (Park 2013). The Korean economy stabilized, and GDP annual growth rate averaged 7 percent between 1999-2003 and 4.5 percent between 2003-2008 (Countryeconomy.com 2016a). Due to its strong currency, Korea exceeded the $20,000 milestone in nominal GDP per capita in 2006 during the Roh government for the first time in history. The ICT industry played a decisive role in the process of recovery from the economic crisis and take-off to a new phase of development. The ICT contribution to GDP growth increased from 34 percent in 1999 to 46 percent in 2000. The ICT component in total exports also grew continuously from the 1990s, reaching 36.9 percent of total exports in 2004 (Kim D 2009).

However, with its financial and export sectors more exposed to the forces of global competition and accumulated short-term foreign debts since 2005, Korea was particularly vulnerable to the global financial crisis of 2007-2008. The global crisis plunged the Korean economy into deep trouble once again. Korea experienced abrupt capital outflows and drastic collapses in export demand and GDP. Foreign investors quickly sold off their investments and considerable capital left the country. With a slowing global economy, demand for Korean exports weakened, as did domestic demand. The Korean foreign exchange market was showing signs of deterioration even before the collapse of Lehman Brothers. The currency continued to slide to 1997 Asian financial crisis levels. At the end of November 2008, the Korean Won had depreciated by 25.4 percent in dollar terms since the collapse of Lehman Brothers in September 2008 — the largest fall among major Asian countries except for Turkey. The stock price also collapsed by 27.2 percent during the same period (Kim K 2009). Banks reduced their lending to low-rating householders and companies, causing a credit crunch in the financial market. The instability in the financial market had a great impact on the real economy. From the fourth quarter of 2008, the Korean financial market plunged in terms of interest rates, stock prices, and exchange rates (Kim 2014). Asset prices plummeted and exports also collapsed at a rapid pace. The year-on-year growth rate of exports declined from 27.6 percent in September to 7.8 percent in October and further to -19.5 percent in November 2008 (Cho 2010). With the deterioration of the export-led economy, the annual GDP growth rate plunged and the GDP per capita income also fell under $20,000 (Kim K 2009). The annual GDP growth rate more than halved between 2007 and 2008, from 5.5 percent to 2.2 percent and was only 0.7 percent in 2009, the lowest figure since -5.7 percent in 1998 (Countryeconomy.com 2016a).

Compared to the 1997 Asian financial crisis, however, the impact of the 2008 global financial crisis on Korea's labor market was less significant (Yang 2012). One reason was the reforms of *chaebols* and financial institutions introduced after the 1997 Asian financial crisis. Another was the government's timely intervention in the economy. The Lee Myung-bak government's post-crisis policy responses were very effective for economic recovery within a very short period. With this active governmental engagement, the Korean economy managed to recover from the global financial crisis faster than other OECD countries (Lee J 2016). The expansionary fiscal policies and low interest rates led to more than 8 percent growth in a mere one-year period after the global financial crisis until the first quarter of 2010 (Cho 2010). By mid-2010, the GDP was restored to its pre-crisis level faster than most of other countries. In addition, the unemployment rate remained at 3.8 percent in the first half of 2009 and dropped to 3.2 percent in May 2012, nearly its pre-crisis level of 3.1 percent in 2007 (it was over 8 percent in 1998 after the 1997 Asian financial crisis) (OECD 2012; Yang 2012). Korea attained global status as a "developed country" in 2009, with an open economy and a mature democracy.

Although it successfully recovered from the global financial crisis, the Korean economy entered a low-growth stage and with rising insecurity and inequality. Neoliberal reforms under the conservative regime left a legacy of socioeconomic polarization, enhanced economic dominance of *chaebols* and increased influence of financial institutions, all of which were challenges to the developmental state. The Lee government's policies including privatization, low interest rates and an undervalued currency greatly assisted the corporate sector. Accordingly, the concentration of power in the *chaebols* increased. Welfare programs, however, declined in scope and the labor force participation rate did not change except for an increase in temporary workers. Despite his promise to create 600,000 new jobs annually, the average number of new employees during the five-year presidency of Lee was only 250,000 (Lee 2014). Nevertheless, the unemployment rate was still low by OECD standards; that of youth (aged 15-29) increased in May 2012 to 8.0 percent from 7.3 percent a year before (OECD 2012). In addition, the relative position of temporary workers also deteriorated. While the average wage of temporary workers in 2003 was 55.7 percent of that of permanent workers doing the same task, this figure declined to 48.5 percent by 2011 (Suh and Kwon 2014: 688).

Many of the policy initiatives after the crisis faced a range of internal and external barriers. For example, China emerged as an economic giant with increasing domestic production capacity, which led to the decline of Korean exports to China in the late 2000s. In addition, in the globalized era, returning to former developmentalist policies did not work as intended. Despite various demand management projects (discussed below), economic growth remained very slow, falling short of government goals. The average growth of GDP remained at 2.8 percent under the Lee government (2008-2012) and 2.9 percent under the Park government (2013-2016), much lower than the previous progressive governments (5.0 percent and 4.3 percent respectively) (Kim 2016). In 2015, the economy suffered from weak exports and low domestic demand partly due to concerns over the outbreak of (Middle East Respiratory Syndrome (MERS) that killed 36 people in Korea. Even after a revival in exports, economic conditions continued to remain fragile. With the economy still relying on exports from *chaebols*, the growth potential decreased compared with the pre-crisis period and household debt increased to a record W1,200 trillion (US$973 billion) at the end of 2015 (Mundy 2016). The economic growth fell far short of political promises made by President Park Geun-hye in the so-called "474 vision" (Kalinowski et al. 2016). Nevertheless, the Korean economy had shown higher growth rates compared to other OECD countries over the previous decade, with a steady increase of GDP per capita that reached an all-time high of US$25,458 in 2016.

The Impact of Economic Restructuring

The restructuring after the 1997 Asian financial crisis resulted in major changes in the Korean economy in areas including corporate strategy, the nature of competition, transparency and the globalization of society. The corporate sector regained strength and continued to grow. The 1997 Asian financial crisis endowed President Kim Dae-jung with the power to discipline and control large *chaebols* and revise labor policy. Many of the reforms following the 1997 Asian financial crisis ensured the quick recovery of *chaebols* but the government-business relationship changed. The vertical and subordinate relationship of *chaebols* to the government ended and the *chaebol*-government nexus became either an alliance-based or mutually contested relationship, depending on the political stance or leverage of the government (Hundt 2005; Kim, Han and Jang 2008).

The *chaebols'* expansionist strategy that prevailed until the 1997 crisis largely disappeared and the debt-equity ratio decreased considerably. Restructuring *chaebols* to be more competitive in the global market led to inefficient companies being sold or closed. *Chaebols* were reorganized into clusters of companies, and the chairman of the *chaebol* and the planning office no longer controlled all the companies. Through the developmental state approach to promote venture companies in technology and knowledge-based industries, the growth of SMEs outpaced that of large companies and the number of venture companies increased from 2000 in 1998 to 10,000 in June 2001 (Suh and Kwon 2014). However, due to rises in the wage rates, Korean companies became less globally competitive in many export products (Kim 2010). After 1997, many large companies began to relocate their production bases to China and Southeast Asia and some even relocated their R&D centers as well. Manufacturing SMEs also had to either relocate their production bases overseas or depend on foreign workers.

As a result of corporate sector reform, the debt-equity ratio of all industries decreased from 424 percent in 1997 to 195 percent in 2001. Among the four conglomerate groups, Samsung was the first that achieved the debt-equity ratio reduction target, and then LG and Hyundai. However, the Daewoo group did not follow the restructuring agreement and was dissolved in 1999 (Bank of Korea, various years). Being forced to reduce the debt-equity ratio within two years, *chaebols* began to sell the assets as they were not allowed to issue new shares or corporate bonds. The exchange rate was unfavourable in 1998 and the share prices in the stock market were low. In order to stay afloat, *chaebols* had to sell shares, mostly to foreign buyers. Corporate transparency was improved as the proportion of foreign ownership among the large Korean companies increased. As part of the reform measures, barriers to foreign ownership of Korean companies were lowered and foreign investors became large shareholders in big companies in Korea. The proportion of foreign-owned shares in all companies listed on the Korean stock exchange (except for KOSDAQ) increased over threefold in 10 years, from 13 percent in 1996 to 37 percent at the end of 2006 (Chew and Gillan 2009: xvii). Transparency with respect to corporate finances improved significantly. *Chaebols* were obligated to provide consolidated financial statements on a regular basis beginning in 1999, and their accounting standards were revised to be more in line with international accounting standards. With their improved financial and governance situation *chaebols* could afford a large amount of R&D investments for innovation and improved competitiveness.

Economic restructuring had unfavourable outcomes as well. The direct intervention of the government, in particular the "Big Deal," was not very effective as it attracted only modest levels of participation from the large *chaebols*. The injection of public funds to rescue private companies proved quite costly, leading to a sizable increase in government debt. There was increasing criticism that the government should focus on restructuring the banking sector, leaving private company restructuring to the market. Globalization also created vulnerability within the Korean economy. As the capital market was forced to open to foreign investors, the share prices in the Korean stock exchange became very sensitive to the actions of these foreign investors. With many companies being sold or closed down, unemployment resulted. Also, the notion of lifetime employment largely disappeared and the proportion of temporary (as opposed to permanent) workers increased. This led the Kim Dae-jung government to improve public welfare and establish a nationwide social safety net (Lee 2004). Major improvements in the welfare system included medical insurance, a national pension system, unemployment benefits and insurance, and industrial accident compensation insurance (Song H 2003). However, due to increased fiscal expenditure, South Korea's national debt in proportion to gross domestic product continued to rise. The national debt to GDP ratio was 11.9 percent in 1997, but almost doubled to 21.6 percent in 2003 and then increased to 31 percent in 2010 (Kim Y-m 2017). The magnitude of public debt more than doubled and the debt to GDP ratio increased by 50 percent during the Kim presidency.

The subsequent neoliberal economic restructuring efforts by the Roh Moo-hyun government were undermined by several factors. Firstly, the continuing expansion of *chaebols* did not create any significant new employment in Korea, because automated production techniques had been adopted in the manufacturing industries and major growth took place in the technology and knowledge-intensive industries such as IT and biotechnology. In addition, many companies continued to relocate their production bases to China and Southeast Asia. Secondly, the restructuring of *chaebols* failed to restrain their market power and expansion. Under the Roh government, the concentration of the economic power in *chaebols* increased along with their shares in national capital and GDP. The Total Investment Limit applied to large companies to put a constraint on their expansion in the domestic economy was raised. Third, the proportion of low-wage temporary workers continued to increase, through the introduction of the flexible labor market policy. Despite the increase in welfare expenditures, income inequality increased. Fourth, rising welfare costs led to an increase in local governments' expenditures and caused further tensions between local and central governments. With more decision-making power transferred as a result of the decentralization policy, the amount of outstanding debt held by each local government significantly increased (Kalinowski et al. 2016).

The Failure of Conservative Governments and Corruption

Despite some positive impacts on the economy and the environment, developmentalist policies — particularly the Green Growth and Creative Economy policies — attracted a lot of criticism. Lacking clear direction and procedures, these policies often focused on specific elements or groups and led to negative outcomes. The Four Major Rivers Project, for example, was one of the most controversial projects that attracted significant criticism for its disastrous results. Opposition parties, provincial leaders, civic and environmental groups, the intellectual community and the media strongly criticized the project for its non-legal and non-democratic decision-making procedures and the environmental degradation it caused and would cause (Park 2011). For this project, small natural weirs were rebuilt into massive concrete weirs capable of keeping water at a depth of 4-6m. The completion of the project, however, reignited controversy as the water quality of the four rivers plummeted and key natural habitats were destroyed, endangering many native species of flora and fauna. It was also followed by the allegations of corruption and mismanagement involving government officials and construction companies. The Lee government had to face lawsuits and protests across the country. Controversies also arose regarding shady deals by President Lee's confidants. Despite resistance and protests, however, the government proceeded with the project and declared its completion in October 2011, right before the 2012 presidential election.

In the creative economy policy of the Park Geun-hye government, the stated goal of ending economic reliance on *chaebols* soon became a distant memory. The country's transformation into a creative economy was heavily dependent on *chaebols*, a situation that invited trouble. The operation of some CCEI centers was impossible without financial support from the large conglomerates. In the end, the creative economy policy was tainted by a corruption scandal involving President Park and the *chaebols*. In October 2016, media reports revealed that president Park allegedly forced some 50 *chaebols* to donate a total of KRW 77.4 billion for the creation of two non-profit foundations, Mi-R Foundation and K-Sports Foundation, that were set up by her long-time friend Choi Soon-sil to assist President Park's creative economy initiatives.

Social and Political Outcomes

Deepening Social Polarization

Income inequality in Korea first gained momentum from the Big Push into HCI during high rates of economic growth during the 1970s and widened in the 1980s. However, the imbalance between industries and the gap between rich and poor, although growing, was not of major concern up until the early 1990s when rapid industrialization was still a policy priority. South Korea's income inequality increased after 1998 when the post-Asian crisis structural reforms were implemented (Lee et al. 2012: 4). Amid financial crisis, the economic adjustment under the IMF-supported program emphasized economic recovery over equitable distribution of wealth and income (Lee 2007: 301). The recovery process, however, was much slower and more painful for irregular, short-tenured or less-educated workers, and caused increases in economic and social inequality and precarious employment (Lee, Kim and Cin 2013). As the workforce shrunk, employment and wage levels deteriorated. While housing prices surged, the purchasing power of average Korean households was reduced due to low wage growth (Kalinowsk et al. 2016). In his 2005 New Year`s speech, President Roh Moo-hyun said that bipolarization was at the heart of Korea`s economic problems, calling for "sharing growth" with less privileged groups and individuals. Nevertheless, his notion of profit share was avoided by many people ("Gap between the rich and poor" 2011).

Pro-business policies under conservative governments intensified social polarization with their policies that mainly benefited businesses and *chaebols*. In the context of a stumbling labor market and soaring house prices, income inequality increased after 2003 and peaked in 2009. In 2009, income inequality in Korea was the second highest (after the US) among 22 OECD countries (Im 2014: 29). During the conservative regime under Lee and Park, inequality deepened, with the basic rights of labor threatened and labor relations worsening (Lee et al. 2013: 105). Wealth inequality also became more pronounced. In 2012, the top 10 percent of the population possessed 46 percent of the country's total wealth, while the bottom 50 percent possessed only 9.5 percent (Koo 2014). Bipolarization in business also deepened due to policies favoring large companies rather than SMEs. There was no trickle-down benefit from the *chaebols'* economic success to SMEs. Despite restructuring, the economy was still divided between export-oriented global conglomerates (*chaebols*) and the SMEs on which the conglomerates relied (Kalinowski et al. 2016: 4). The bipolarization of businesses and the concentration of power in the *chaebols* remained important issues for the next government's policy agenda (Suh and Kwon 2014).

Candle-Light Protests for Transparent and Democratic Government

Despite making steady progress in democratization, Korea experienced a noticeable decline in freedom of expression for both journalists and the general public after the inauguration of President Lee Myung-bak in 2008 (Freedom House 2011).

From the start of his government, President Lee Myung-bak faced several economic and political crises. Firstly, soon after he took office in 2008, the global financial crisis hit Korea. Under the impact of it, the economy shrank rapidly, with virtually no GDP growth in 2009 (Cho 2010). Secondly, in support of the US-Korea FTA, soon after his 2008 inauguration, Lee announced the lifting of the ban on US beef imports which had been in place since the 2003 outbreak of mad cow disease in the US. His decision, however, provoked a series of massive "candlelight" demonstrations across the country for months. He later issued a public apology about his ignorance of public health concerns and his entire cabinet offered to resign. His approval rating fell below 20 percent in the first of his presidency (Yang 2008). Thirdly, he had to face public ire again in the following year, when his presidential predecessor, Roh Moo-hyun committed suicide after being investigated over allegations that his family members received bribes while he was in office. Many of Roh's supporters believed that the bribery allegation was political revenge, which caused political turmoil during Lee's presidency. Finally, due to his hard stance against North Korea, inter-Korean relations rapidly chilled. North Korea not only suspended official inter-Korean dialogue and contacts but also made military moves such as the sinking of Korea's Navy corvette Cheonan and the shelling of Yeonpyeong Island in 2010.

In response to widespread public doubt and criticism, the Lee government (2008-2013) used state power to suppress freedom of speech and to control the media (You 2015). One of the first things Lee did upon taking office in 2008 was to take firm control of media companies under the direct and indirect influence of the government. The government interfered in the management of major broadcast media with allies of President Lee put in high-ranking posts. Many journalists and broadcast workers walked out to demand editorial independence and the resignation of pro-government corporate presidents. Overshadowing the progress in other aspects of democracy since the 2000s, Korea's freedom of the press status declined from "Free" to "Partly Free" in 2010 to reflect an increase in official censorship, particularly of online content, as well as the government's attempts to influence media outlets' news and information content (Freedom House 2011). Government control over free expression continued during the Park Geun-hye government. President Park and the culture ministry allegedly kept a blacklist of nearly 10,000 artists and cultural figures critical of her administration, and excluded them from government-controlled support programs. These behaviors ignited outrage among citizens, civil society and opposition parties as they were reminiscent of past authoritarian dictatorships that controlled mass media as one means of maintaining social control.

Despite the alarming decline in freedom of expression during the Lee government, the trend was maintained by the Park Geun-hye government (2013-2017) after its accession in 2013. It continued efforts to suppress criticism of its policies, invoking the National Security Law and a criminal ban on defamation, making Korea's democracy move backward (Freedom House 2016). Despite democratization, citizens thought their political institutions were not working for the greater good, that they could not be trusted, and that anti-corruption efforts were not achieving success (Turner et al. 2017). The fears and suspicions of many citizens about corruption in high places were realized in October 2016 when a massive corruption scandal involving President Park, her close confidante, and some of the *chaebols* erupted to capture the media and the nation's attention.

This corruption scandal led to a series of weekly mass "candlelight" protests calling for Park to step down, but the protests remained peaceful and non-violent. Citizens were angered by their president's apparent corruption, and presidential decision-making being influenced by her personal confidante. Park's government was also blamed for systemic lapses that led to the Sewol ferry tragedy in 2014, which killed 304 passengers (including 250 high school students).

The largest protest in Seoul's central square comprised an estimated 1.5 million people. On 5 December 2016, three opposition parties agreed to introduce a joint impeachment motion against President Park. The motion was put to a vote on 9 December 2016, and passed with 234 out of 300 votes. On 10 March 2016, the Constitutional Court removed President Park from office in a unanimous 8 to 0 decision. On 31 March 2016, Park was arrested and taken into custody, standing trial on charges including bribery. Choi, her confidante, was accused of using her presidential connections and attempted fraud. Samsung Group chief Jay Y Lee was also arrested for corruption investigation.

Park became the first sitting president to be removed from office by impeachment since the creation of the Republic of Korea. It is notable that it was the people who initiated and maintained an extraordinary wave of civic activism leading to Park's impeachment. Her removal from office therefore represents a significant milestone in South Korea's journey back to "full democracy." In the 2015 Democracy Index among 167 states and territories, Korea was demoted from the "full democracies" category to "flawed democracies," despite being the most democratic nation in Asia (EIU 2015). The Economist Intelligence Unit (EIU) defined flawed democracies as countries where there were "free and fair elections and, even if there are problems (such as infringements on media freedom), basic civil liberties are respected," but democratic weaknesses remain. Such weaknesses included "problems in governance, an underdeveloped political culture, and low levels of political participation." Korea is now facing new challenges in strengthening and sustaining democracy.

Conclusion

This chapter has examined the weakening direct role of government in the Korean economy between 1998 and 2016. Undergoing massive economic and political transitions after the 1997 Asian financial crisis, the period between 1998 and 2016 was a time of hardship, changes and challenges for Korea.

Coming to power amid the country's worst economic recession caused by the 1997 Asian financial crisis, the progressive president, Kim Dae-jung implemented a radical neoliberal transformation of financial markets and *chaebols* following the bailout conditions laid down by the IMF, while also retaining state-driven approaches to overcome the economic crisis. The subsequent Roh Moo-hyun government retained this mixed policy approach making it a significant characteristic of progressive governments. Unlike previous authoritarian developmentalist governments, however, the progressive governments during this period pursued representative and participatory governments and played the role of "senior partner" in the economy.

With the inflow of IMF rescue funds and foreign liquidity and the success of state-led developmentalist policies, the South Korean economy recovered from the crisis during the Kim government. Annual GDP growth rate increased from -5.7 percent to 10.7 percent between 1998 and 1999. The subsequent progressive Roh Moo-hyun government Inherited a relatively stable economy. Accompanying the democratization of political institutions, economic growth continued and Korea succeeded in exceeding the US$ 20,000 milestone in nominal GDP per capita for the first time in 2006. Being increasingly integrated into a global economic system, however, Korea faced both opportunities and challenges. While Korea could expand its trade through FTAs, it was also greatly influenced by changes in the global environment and economy such as the outbreak, in 2007, of the global financial crisis.

After the 2007-2008 global financial crisis, governments switched from progressive to conservative, which led the country back to greater neoliberalism. The new conservative Lee Myung-bak government held a strong pro-business policy stance, supporting greater economic liberalization and deregulation. With many policies that assisted the corporate sector and the reduction of the corporate tax rate, *chaebols* gained more economic power during his presidency. Lee's pro-business policies continued in the form of business-friendly labor policies adopted by the subsequent conservative government under Park Geun-hye. Business-friendly policies under the conservative rule, however, had adverse economic consequences by increasing the gap between regular workers and non-regular workers in the labor market, intensifying economic inequalities and repressing the labor movement. Amid the flurry of unfettered market forces, conservative governments also tried to revive the economy by adopting developmentalist projects.

As a response to greater economic globalization and liberalization, the role of the government was increasingly required to change in Korea. To achieve sustainable development and meet the needs of their citizens, the government was increasingly required to be capable of realizing opportunities and managing the challenges of changing domestic and global environments more efficiently. This led governments during this period to incorporate the attributes of neoliberalism, developmental and welfare states to develop the economy in an era when globalization and liberalization were dominant forces. The coexistence of neoliberalism, developmentalism and welfare statism played a significant role in shaping government response to changes in the political and economic environment. Regardless who was in power, each Korean government retained some faith in a state-driven approach and all sought new economic growth engines to further economic and social development. The knowledge industry and the cultural industry were promoted as new growth engines under the progressive governments while extensive construction projects and SME promotion were evident during the conservative governments. With more emphasis given to the efficiency of government and its role as a provider of welfare, Korea attained global status as a "developed country" in 2009, became the world's eleventh largest economy by the end of 2015 while public expenditure on social and welfare services had rapidly increased since the 1990s (Kim 2010). The effectiveness of government was increasingly seen by citizens in government's ability to correct social inequality and promoting public goods.

Continued reliance on *chaebols*, however, remained a longstanding problem in the Korean economy, clearly exposed by the outbreak of the massive corruption scandal involving President Park Geun-hye. With Park being removed from office in 2017, the burdens of *chaebol* reform and the future of the welfare state were transferred to the new government under Moon Jae-in. This latest governmental change imparts the lesson that capable government in Korea cannot be achieved without reacting effectively to environmental changes yet accommodating democratic transition (Kim 2010).

Part 2. The Role of the State in Economic Development in Vietnam: From Authoritarian Socialist State to Advanced Socialist Developmental State (1960s–2010s)

Chapter 4

THE AUTHORITARIAN SOCIALIST STATE WITH A CENTRALLY PLANNED ECONOMY (1975 – 1985)

This chapter examines how post-war Vietnam transformed into a socialist economy between 1975 and 1985. This period began with much of the country destroyed, with enormous human and economic losses, after the Vietnam War (1955-1975). After the war, Vietnam had a foreign policy of maintaining its traditional friendship with the Soviet Union and its allies. Strained relations with China and the US intensified Vietnam's heavy reliance on economic, technical and military aid from the Soviet Union and Eastern Europe.

With its victory in the war, the Communist Party of Vietnam (CPV) wielded enormous political power to dictate policies to transform North and South Vietnam into a unified socialist economy, but faced significant challenges in solving post-war problems and reviving the domestic economy. Following the Soviet Union's model, the CPV adopted state-led developmental strategies under a strong authoritarian leadership, structurally transforming from an agriculture-bound economy to a centrally-planned economic system in which industry would assume increasing importance. The CPV launched and led two Five-Year Economic Development Plans consecutively between 1976-1980 and 1981-1985, with an emphasis on agricultural development and increasing investment in heavy industry. The goal of reunifying North and South Vietnam provided a political and social foundation for the authoritarianism of the CPV and often served as an instrument of social control. During this period, under the firm control of the CPV, Vietnam entered an era of big government, characteristic of an authoritarian developmental state.

This chapter explores the leading role played by the CPV in setting out and achieving a vision for building socialism in Vietnam. First considered are the environmental factors affecting post-war Vietnam's socialist transformation, with the focus on economic aspects. Then the CPV's adoption of economic policies and their economic and social outcomes delineated.

International Environment

Heavy Reliance on the Soviet Union during the Cold War

The Cold War period was one of sustained political conflict, military tension and economic competition between the Soviet Union and the US. Their conflictual relationship was particularly evident in military coalitions, wars in third countries not allied to each side, a nuclear arms race, and technological competition. The US and some Western European countries made policies designed to prevent the spread of communism and established the military alliance, the NATO to oppose the Soviet Union and its allies. In response, the Soviet Union created the Eastern Bloc with its seven satellite states in Central and Eastern Europe, which united under a collective defense treaty, the Warsaw Pact (1955–1991). In 1955 in Vietnam's region, the US led the formation of the South East Asia Treaty Organization (SEATO), an international organization for collective defense in Southeast Asia. Elsewhere in Latin America and Southeast Asia, the Soviet Union supported communist revolutions, in actions strongly opposed by many Western countries.

The OEEC was initially established in 1948 to run the US-initiated Marshall Plan for the reconstruction of western European countries destroyed by the Second World War. It subsequently developed into the OECD (founded in 1961). Meanwhile, in 1949, as a response to the OEEC, the Soviet Union formed an economic organization that comprised the countries of the Eastern Bloc, named the Council of Mutual Economic Assistance (CMEA).

As a result of involvement in Cold War ideology and political alignment with the Soviet Union, Vietnam's foreign policy resulted in many negative effects for domestic socio-economic development. Owing to strained relations with the US and China, Vietnam relied heavily on economic and military aid from the Soviet Union during the Cold War. As the Soviet Union's Southeast Asian ally, Vietnam joined CMEA in 1978. During the period of 1945-1985, CMEA was the only international organization that Vietnam joined.

US Embargo on Vietnam

After the communists unified Vietnam in 1975, the relations between Vietnam and the US became extremely strained. President Ford extended President Nixon's 1964 trade embargo on Vietnam. The Ford administration also prevented Vietnam from joining the United Nations (UN) by using its veto power three times. As a result, Vietnam's trade with the West was greatly restricted. Diplomatic tensions between the two countries, however, were eased during the presidency of Carter (1977-1981). Although the Carter government did not recognize the Socialist Republic of Vietnam, it did not recognize any Vietnam government-in-exile nor oppose Vietnam's joining any international organizations (Manyin 2005). On July 20, 1977, without a formal vote, Vietnam was admitted to the UN following a UN Security Council recommendation. However, diplomatic relations between the US and Vietnam turned sour again, when Vietnam aligned with the Soviet Union during disputes with China over political, territorial and refugee issues (Manyin 2005). US feared that improving relations with

Vietnam might damage US-China relations (Tran 2010). The formal normalization of diplomatic relations between Vietnam and the US was postponed for nearly 20 years, leaving Vietnam isolated from the international community and even more dependent upon the Soviet Union.

Strained Relations with China

While Vietnam had close ties with the Soviet Union, China-Vietnam relations became strained and tenuous after the Vietnam War. China regarded Vietnam as a small hegemonic country in the south which threatened the existence of China, the big hegemonic country in the north. Vietnam's invasion and occupation of Cambodia between 1977 and 1991 and oppression of ethnic Chinese in Vietnam provoked a prolonged border war between China and Vietnam from 1979 to 1990. Although a small-scale war, it was initiated by Chinese leader Deng Xiaoping to ingratiate China with the US and serve as a warning to Vietnam. It had strong adverse effects on Vietnam's economy. By 1978, China completely stopped all of its aid to Vietnam as soon as a treaty of friendship with the Soviet Union expired. Such tensions with China compelled Vietnam to depend increasingly on the Soviet Union for economic and military assistance. The Soviet Union provided military aid of US$ 1.7 billion annually in the 1982-85 period, remaining as the largest donor of aid and the biggest trade partner to Vietnam during this period (Cima 2002: 117). This pressured Vietnam to join the CMEA group from 1978 and to follow strictly all the regulations imposed by this organization. The relationship limited Vietnam's foreign relations, and significantly affected the way that the Vietnamese government ran the economy, pushing it to take steps toward self-reliance and to assume an initiating role in economic development.

DOMESTIC ENVIRONMENT

The Legacy of Colonial Rule

Vietnam was under Chinese rule for almost 10 centuries (111BC-939AD) before it was occupied by the French colonial power for nearly a century (1858-1954). With growing nationalism, independence movement continued to grow in Vietnam during the World War II. It was the determined Communist leadership under Ho Chi Minh and his organization the "Viet Minh" which came to the forefront in the increasingly bitter struggle for Vietnam's independence. When the French were defeated by Germany during the Second World War (1939-1945), Vietnam was invaded and occupied by Japan until Japan's surrender in 1945.

During the French (1858-1954) and then Japanese occupation (1940-1945), Vietnam was an economically exploited colony. Natural resources were exploited for the benefit of the colonizers and millions of Vietnamese had to work in these industries. The colonial period had a lasting legacy in generating economic differences between the North and South. The French had introduced plantation agriculture (with products such as coffee, tea, cotton and tobacco) and extractive industries (such as the mining of coal and manufacturing) in the North while concentrating on rice cultivation in the South (Gaiduk 2003: 59; International Business Publications 2007: 28).

During the Second World War, Japan's exploitation of Vietnamese resources intensified, creating great suffering, deprivation and starvation amongst the Vietnamese. To make matters worse, bad weather and pests caused a rapid decrease in harvests in North Vietnam. With many roads, warehouses and transportation facilities destroyed during World War II, transportation of rice from the South to the North became extremely difficult. The prices of essential goods — especially foodstuffs — skyrocketed. All these factors led to a deep famine that struck North Vietnam between 1944 and 1945 (Tran M-V 1999). It was estimated that around 1 million people died of starvation out of a population of 10 million in the affected area during this period (Senauth 2012: 17).

After the surrender of Imperial Japan at the end of World War II, Ho Chi Minh declared independence from France and proclaimed the Democratic Republic of Vietnam on 2 September 1945. This was known as the August Revolution of 1945. Ho Chi Minh's Viet Minh forces later defeated the French in the battle of Dien Bien Phu in 1954. The 1954 Geneva Conference, held to secure peace in Vietnam, temporarily divided Vietnam into two, with Ho Chi Minh's communist government ruling the North from Hanoi and Ngo Dinh Diem's anti-communist government ruling the South from Saigon.

Before the reunification in 1975, the North and South had different economic ideologies, communist and capitalist respectively. The communist government in North Vietnam signed agreements with the Soviet Union to underwrite its first Five-Year Plan (1961-1965). The Plan's core characteristics were linked to the classic socialist system, with priority given to heavy industry (although the focus later shifted to agriculture and light industry). With interruptions in electric power, the disruption of transportation routes and labor shortages, however, the North's economy underwent serious strain, leading to a slowdown in industrial and agricultural activity. Meanwhile, the economy in the South became increasingly dependent on foreign aid between 1954 and 1975. The US was the foremost donor that financed the development of Vietnam's military power and the construction of the main infrastructure (such as roads, bridges and ports), and supported the domestic currency and the balance-of-payments (International Business Publications 2007: 28). From the time of the separation of the country, both North and South prepared movements to reunify and rebuild the country; this led to the outbreak of the Vietnam War in 1955.

The Legacy of the Vietnam War (1955-1975)

The armed conflict between the North and South began in 1955 and, with the involvement of the US military, lasted for 20 years. In what is known as the Vietnam War (1955-1975), among the countries that fought for South Vietnam, over 58,000 U.S. soldiers were killed or missing, while

Korea had more than 4,400 killed in action, Australia more than 460, Thailand about 350, and New Zealand 50 (US National Archives and Records Administration 2013; Rohn 2012). In addition, tens of thousands more were wounded or disabled. As the US decided to withdraw from Vietnam in 1973 owing to growing costs and casualties, South Vietnam fell to North Vietnamese forces on April 30, 1975. Finally, Viet Cong communist forces in South Vietnam, and the People's Army of Vietnam (PAVN) forces from the North unified Vietnam under communist rule.

As with the Korean War (1950-1953), the Vietnam War was a conflict intensified by the ongoing Cold War between the US and the Soviet Union, causing widespread damage and destruction. The consequences of the Vietnam War were devastating for Vietnam. The country suffered enormous human and economic losses. It was estimated that nearly 2 million Vietnamese civilians, 1.1 million North Vietnamese soldiers and 200,000 South Vietnamese soldiers were killed during the war. Natural resources and the environment were destroyed, agriculture, infrastructure and industry were in disrepair, and health problems were widespread and persisted for decades. When the war ended, 70 percent of Vietnam's people lived below the official poverty line (Davies 2015).

After the reunification of the country, the CPV faced a number of pressing challenges. First was the task of social and economic integration between North and South, which provided a motivation for authoritarian rule. The damaging experience of war, in conjunction with a long history of colonial rule, influenced Vietnam and the Vietnamese people's general attitude toward foreign powers (especially the US), which remained unfavourable for a long time. The US also changed its policy toward Southeast Asia and assigned a higher priority to its own national interests. While supporting dictatorships friendly to US interests in the region, the US government facilitated the regional economies' reliance on the US.

ECONOMIC POLICIES

The Five-Year Economic Development Plans

After the war, the CPV initiated a centrally planned economy, in which all economic transactions were regulated by the government. The CPV leaders believed that growth of the private economy sector would easily lead to chaos and unfairness, and that only the intervention (by plans and orders) of the government could promote the desired rapid economic development in an orderly manner. Following the example of the first Five-Year Economic Development Plan (1961-1965) conducted in the North, the CPV developed the second Five-Year Economic Development Plan for the period from 1976 to 1980 with a goal to unify the national economy under communism. It was perceived that only the government had sufficient information and strengths to establish order and direction for the economy, and that large-scale operations would bring about greater efficiency.

The second Five-Year Economic Development Plan set extraordinarily high goals for average annual growth rates for industry (16 to 18 percent), agriculture (8 to 10 percent), and national income (13 to 14 percent). It also gave priority to reconstruction and new construction while attempting to develop agricultural resources, to integrate the North and the South socially and economically, and to proceed with communization (International Business Publications 2007).

The plan aimed to lay the foundations of the socialist system through revolutions in the three areas of production, technology and science, and culture. Revolution in production meant the replacement of private ownership with collective ownership in order to achieve the goal of socialist mass production. Cooperatives, family farms and SOEs became the dominant organizational forms in the agricultural and non-agricultural sectors. Revolution in technology and science was also emphasized for the achievement of mass production, while the cultural revolution was to support the socialist ideology at an individual level (Palmujoki 2016).

Continued economic difficulties in the late 1970s prompted changes in attitudes toward individual rights and interests among the national leadership. Understanding that the second plan was too ambitious and was beyond the country's current competencies, the CPV re-established economic goals and constituted the third Five-Year Economic Development Plan (1981–85). The CPV leadership proceeded cautiously with the third plan, presenting the plan one year at a time (International Business Publications 2007: 37). The third plan was more realistic in its objectives, and was based on the adoption of modest measures of gradual reform (Alpert and Sanders 2005). Facing famine and hunger that seriously affected many areas in Vietnam, the highest priority of the plan was to develop agriculture and the production of consumer goods. For this, the CPV decided to integrate the strengths of both collective and individual sectors and improve science and technology capacities in Vietnam. To increase production, economic incentives and price liberalization measures were reintroduced (Alpert and Sanders 2005). Most notably, the concept of the 'family economy' was introduced to allow the peasants' personal use of some economic resources including land. In 1981, the government promulgated the national application of a household contract system under Directive 100, in which individual households were allowed to manage plots of land on their own and could keep or sell surpluses. In addition, government reform of the entire pricing system was conducted twice, in 1981 and 1985. Policies were also adopted involving the decentralization of decision-making to enterprise level, with accompanying programs to improve the managerial skills of government officials. As a result, industrial SOEs were given partial autonomy in management, and were to be held accountable for the outcome of their decisions.

KEY ISSUES

Unified Socialist Economy

After the war, North and South Vietnam were officially reunified on 2 July 1976 under the control of North Vietnam's communist government. The new country was renamed as the Socialist Republic of Vietnam (SRV) with Hanoi, the capital of North Vietnam, as its new capital. The CPV became the only legal political party in Vietnam and was led by Lê Duẩn as General Secretary, a term and position used by Soviet Communists. The government issued a new currency, the Vietnam Dong (VND) in 1978, and unified the financial markets of the North and the South.

Mapping strategies for economic development, the Five-Year Economic Development Plans intensified socialist reform (or revolution). First, the private sector (including private commerce and trade) was eradicated and replaced by state institutions. The government nationalized all manufacturing as well as many services, including French-owned coal mines and other foreign corporations in Vietnam. Second, a rigid centrally planned economy with state ownership became the core of the economy. Third, land was reformed through the abolition of private ownership. Priority within the plan was given to the collectivization of agriculture and the development of heavy industry. The ideology of socialist mass production influenced the development not only of industry but also of agriculture. Large SOEs and big projects were established in the non-agricultural sectors while large-scale cooperatives were formed in the agricultural sector. The collectivization movement had already been under way in the North for a long time after independence. Therefore, the collectivization movement after 1975 focused mainly on the South.

The CPV led by Lê Duẩn gradually carried out the socialist revolution, implementing national strategies for economic development and launching the necessary reforms. The CPV, as they did in the North, abolished the free market economy and forbade private enterprise and private property ownership in the South. They emphasized development of heavy industry and collectivization of agriculture and established many SOEs. Carrying all political characteristics of classical socialism, with the absolute leading role of the Communist Party, Vietnam entered the era of a developmental state, one that was directed in all aspects by big government.

SOE-Initiated Development

SOEs emerged as the dominant form of organization in the non-agricultural sectors. They were seen as the operational arms of the central planning system and the main driver of economic development and industrialization (Wolff 1999). To boost production and provide jobs, SOEs received capital from the state budget, and were oriented to accomplishing the objectives and targets of state planning (Vuong 2010: iii-iv).

As part of the collectivization movement, business establishments in the South, both private and public, were forced to transform into northern-style SOEs. By early 1978, 1500 large and small-scale private enterprises in the South, which employed 130,000 workers or 70 percent of the workforce in the private sector, were nationalized and converted into 650 SOEs (Vu 2002). As a result, the total number of SOEs in non-agricultural sectors rose from about 7,000 to 12,000 from 1976 and 1989, although only a quarter were industrial enterprises (Wolff 1999: 61). Most of the SOEs were small and medium sized. Large SOEs were mostly centrally managed, while smaller firms in light industry were controlled by the provincial and local authorities (Wolff 1999: 61).

But economic difficulties continued so further reforms were undertaken in state-owned industry, foreign trade, agriculture, and the price system in order to improve the viability and production of the planned sector of the economy (Beresford and Phong 2000: 39). With the launch of the third Five-Year Economic Development Plan (1981–85), industrial SOEs were given more autonomy in their production and allowed to dispose of their outputs in free markets. Material incentives were also permitted to improve workers' productivity (Phan 2008).

ECONOMIC OUTCOMES

Growth Outcomes

The post-war government in Vietnam faced many challenges in addressing the adverse consequences of war and generating the recovery of the domestic economy. In addition, following military and financial aid during the war, the Soviet Union played a complex role in CPV affairs after it. Vietnam's two Soviet-supported post-war Economic Development Plans between 1976 and 1985 fell far short of expectations. None of the goals set in the second Five-Year Economic Development Plan (1976-1980) was achieved. During this period, the annual growth rate of national income was only 1.7 percent, much lower than the targeted 13 to 14 percent per year and the average annual growth rate of production in industrial SOEs was only 1.5 percent (Vu 2002: 4). The average GDP growth rate between 1976 and 1980 was a very low 0.9 percent (Phan 2008: 210). In 1979, the Politburo of Vietnam publicly acknowledged that their economic plans had failed, and then initiated a process of planning for moderate reform (Beresford and Phong 2000). The government was still incapable of addressing a myriad of post-war economic challenges and lacked the capacity or favorable circumstances to undertake an ambitious development plan. With resources allocated and utilized according to the plan instead of market demand, the state production operated very inefficiently. In addition, the early years were marked by only modest financial support from the communist countries as western countries came late to assist in the country's socio-economic development. Vietnam thus lacked the required resources to successfully complete its post-war economic plans.

In this context, the focus on heavy industry and a collective economy — not on economic recovery after war — during this period was an expensive burden on Vietnam's economy. With little focus on low labor productivity, unemployment, and insufficient food and consumer goods, Vietnam's economy remained poor, stagnant and dependent on subsidies. For this reason, the economic plan of this period has been characterized as "the most subjective voluntarism" among all economic plans of Vietnam during this period (Dang 2009).

Allowing incentives and the private sale of surpluses, the reforms of the early 1980s had some positive effects on output. GDP gradually increased between 1981 and 1985 with an average growth rate of 6.7 percent (Phan 2008: 210). With an aim of eliminating the gap between state-fixed prices and market-determined prices, the government also implemented price reform for the first time in May 1981. This reform, however, resulted in a rapid increase in market price levels, causing high inflation in 1982. Although the government once again adjusted prices and revalued the Dong in 1985, inflation was exacerbated by a shortage of goods. Average inflation in Vietnam reached 164.9 percent between 1980-1984 with the peak rate of 774 percent at some point in 1986 (Thanh 2008; Vuong and Tran 2009). The reforms eventually pushed the Vietnam's economy deeper into crisis (Tran 2000). The informal private sector began to play an important role in areas such as retail trade, handicrafts and artisanship. With reduced aid from the Soviet Union during the 1980s, the economy in Vietnam kept barely afloat. Vietnam failed to meet its repayments to the IMF in 1985 and became ineligible for further loans.

Collectivization and the SOE-Initiated Socialist Economy

The collectivization movement that extended to the South caused a great imbalance in food production and consumption, as well as pushing up inflation to alarming levels. While the rice cultivated area increased at an annual rate of 1 percent, total rice production in Vietnam continuously decreased at an annual rate of 0.46 percent during the period 1976-80 (Young, Wailes, Cramer and Nguyen 2002: 8). With no rice available for export between 1976 and 1984 (except in 1980), Vietnam became an importer of rice and food grain (Young et al. 2002). However, following the 1981 nationwide application of the household contract system, Vietnam gained remarkable achievements in agricultural production. Between 1981 and 1985, total staples output increased by 21.3 percent while the population grew by 9 percent (Vo 1990: 137).

As part of collectivization, in 1983, a number of import-export firms were integrated into a single enterprise regulated by the state. The import and export activities of Vietnam between 1975 and 1985 were limited to commercial relations with CMEA countries under a state monopoly of foreign trade. The common transaction style was the direct exchange of goods for other goods. The net exports of Vietnam during this period remained negative as imports were always greater than exports (Figure 5-1).

Source: General Statistics Office (GSO) of Vietnam, various years.

Figure 5-1. Exports and Imports in 1980 – 1987 period (million US$).

The imposition of the socialist centrally planned system led to a lack of incentives for productivity and to inefficiency in industrial SOEs. In this context, reform measures in the early 1980s had a positive impact on production efficiency. With the newly acquired autonomy of SOEs, short-term resource utilization was sharply improved and outputs were increased without significant additional inputs, especially in areas sensitive to market demand and easy-to-source inputs (Vu 2002: 5). The SOE reform measures, however, also had adverse effects. With increased autonomy to decide what, how and for whom to produce, management of SOEs tended to scale down industrial production to increase profits (Vu 2002: 6). Lower economic activity led directly to a reduction in state budget revenue and a corresponding increase in the state budget deficit. With limited foreign aid, the deficit was primarily financed by printing money. In 1984, the amount of money in circulation increased by 70 percent compared with 1981. The consequence was high inflation from 1981 (Vu 2002: 6).

SOCIAL AND POLITICAL OUTCOMES

Authoritarianism and the Social and Economic Integration of North and South Vietnam

After reunification, the CPV became the sole source of leadership for the government and society in Vietnam, with the party leader holding dictatorial powers. Political, cultural and religious opposition groups were suppressed through arrests, harassment, surveillance and intimidation. The communist government, the Viet Minh, initially won the support of peasants due to its independence movement during the French colonial period. Its first land reform in the North in the early 1950s also addressed people's expectations as it broke up the colonial landlordism and returned land to peasants. However, the second land reform after reunification involving the transition to collective farming for the whole country caused growing discontent and opposition in rural areas.

The CPV faced challenges in bringing about the social and economic integration between North and South Vietnam. Its quest for a new socialist order in the South was carried out in the form of thought reform, population resettlement, internal exile, surveillance and mass mobilization, which often functioned as instruments of social control. Through the "New Economic Zones" program between 1975 and 1980, all private property in the South was collectivized and millions of people were relocated to uninhabited mountainous forested areas. In this task, CPV policy makers were confronted with the South's resistance to communist transformation, as well as traditional animosities arising from cultural and historical differences between North and South (International Business Publications 2007). Thousands of South Vietnamese "traitors" and "capitalists" including government and military members, intellectuals and academics, Buddhists, Catholics, anti-communist and pro-democracy citizens were sent to re-education camps or New Economic Zones and forced to surrender their property. They were believed to be contaminated by western culture and were forced to endure rigid communist indoctrination. The US Library of Congress recorded that there were about 120,000 Vietnamese in these camps in 1982, facing hard labor, torture or execution (Shinn 1987: 110).

Rationing and Hunger

Introduced in North Vietnam after the defeat of the French colonialists in 1954, the rationing system was extended to the South after the Vietnam War ended in 1975. This extension initiated the period of the subsidy economy called "Thời bảo-cấp" (Rationized Period, 1975-1986), when everything from food to goods became rationed and only available for purchase using government ration cards. Transportation of food and goods between provinces was also controlled by the government.

Under the collective economy, Vietnam faced many difficulties such as a poor and backward agricultural economy, with a fledgling government only having war experience and lacking economic management skills. In this situation, the majority of rice produced was siphoned to the military and communist party members, or exported to the Soviet Union as repayment for wartime assistance to the North. Vietnam soon suffered high inflation, as well as a severe shortage of food and basic necessities. People had to wait in long queues to collect water and buy food. Barley was used instead of rice and condensed milk instead of fresh milk. To avoid starvation and persecution, millions of Vietnamese fled the country, the majority of whom were from South Vietnam. The foreign aid that the country received was inadequate to finance the economic recovery after the war. Thus, Vietnam remained poor and politically isolated until its economic and political reforms in 1986.

Growing Corruption in SOEs and "Fence-Breaking" Activities: The Need for Reform

With their dominance in the economy and good access to funds and influence, SOEs tended to be inefficient and often deeply corrupt. Inefficient SOEs and banks, however, remained heavily subsidized, only to benefit the CPV by keeping its members and adherents wealthy and faithful (Frank 2013). State control of the SOEs, the lack of independent oversight and the artificial protection of SOEs from market forces later led to massive corruption (Frank 2013).

Corruption and abuse of power had been widespread at local government level since pre-colonial times. While Vietnam had a long history of centralized administrative systems, it also had well-established village communities. Traditionally officers at local government were elected by a Council of Notables. They were given a high degree of autonomy from the central government, but were also in good positions to abuse power (Shultz II and Le 1993). Citizens were often abused, detained, beaten and even killed by police with no legitimate cause. Corrupt and abusive officials and police often became causes of public discontent, and demonstrations took place in various parts of the country. Public displays of discontent were integrated into community movements, such as the independence movement during the colonial period and grassroots democracy movements later in 1990s (Kerkvliet 2012).

With increasing difficulties facing the economy from the end of 1979, many local officials began to practice "phá rào (fence breaking)" to instigate local economic growth. Fence-breaking included activities like lobbying officials, using personal connections, operating flexibly, exploiting gaps in laws or even breaking laws. These initiatives were taken to ease or avoid certain legal restrictions and reduce people's struggles and economic hardships. A series of fence-breaking activities took place in different shapes and forms across Vietnam and corruption intensified, becoming an integrated and essential aspect of the economic, social and political systems. Some representative activities included: fence breaking in industry and transport involving contracts at a Fishing Factory in Con Dao, Vung Tau (1979) and contracts at a Bus Company in Ho Chi Minh city (1978); agricultural contracts in Do Son district (1980); breaking the rice price fence in An Giang (1978); and the establishment of a market pricing system in Long An Province (1980). Growing fence-breaking activities, although contributing to economic dynamism, made the existing system unworkable and presented a pressing need for reform (Masina 2006: 70).

This chapter has examined Vietnam's experiences of socialist economic transformation after the war, by looking at the CPV's adoption of the state-led centrally-planned economic system and its failure to achieve post-war recovery.

CONCLUSION

Following the Soviet model, the CPV implemented a centrally planned economy with the aim to unify the national economy under communism. With two consecutive Five-Year Economic Development Plans launched between 1975 and 1985, the CPV began the process of post-war reconstruction while attempting to build the foundations of the socialist system through revolutions in production, technology and science, and culture. However, the CPV was more committed to the socialist transformation of the whole country than to economic recovery. The whole country was forced into massive socialist reforms, eliminating private ownership and transforming it into socialist collective ownership. The CPV nationalized all manufacturing as well as many services, transforming them into SOEs. Poor economic performance led to a rationing system for most products in the North and was extended to the South, initiating the period of the subsidy economy. Everything from food to manufactured goods became rationed and only available for purchase using government ration cards.

Given limited resources, skills and experiences, the CPV was rigid and incapable of undertaking its ambitious five-year development plans. The volumes of economic aid from communist countries were inadequate to give impetus to, Vietnam's domestic economy. Thus, the country had to withstand a period of low and unstable growth, resulting in serious economic crisis accompanied by rampant inflation. Vietnam soon suffered severe shortages of food and basic necessities, and endured high inflation. The fledgling government was authoritarian in its quest for the integration of North and South. With ideological conflicts and cultural and historical differences continuing to exist between north and south, hundreds and thousands of South Vietnamese citizens were sent to re-education camps or New Economic Zones and forced to surrender their property while many others fled the country. In this context, corruption and misconduct were widespread throughout the government and SOEs, further constraining the country's post-war recovery and growth. With the failure of the central planned model, economic reform emerged as a pressing need in Vietnam.

Chapter 5

The Socialist Developmental State and the Transition to a Socialist-Oriented Market Economy (1986 – 2005)

This chapter outlines how, between 1986 and 2005, the CPV transformed the Vietnamese economy from that of an authoritarian socialist state with a closed economy to a socialist developmental state with a socialist-oriented market economic system between 1986 and 2005. As indicated in Chapter 5, the CPV's failure to manage the rigid socialist economic system of the period from 1954 to 1985 had led to massive hunger, poverty and chaos, prompting increasing pressure for economic reform. Whilst the change in direction began in 1986, it was the collapse of the Soviet Union and the communist bloc in Eastern Europe in the early 1990s that consolidated the government's commitment to economic reform.

In 1986, the CPV launched a suite of comprehensive economic and social reform programs known as "*Doi Moi,*" a Vietnamese term meaning "renovation." *Doi Moi* offered a turning point for Vietnam as it initiated the new phase of development, leading to a transition to what can best be described as a socialist developmental state with a market economy. In the more open social atmosphere created by *Doi Moi*, the CPV was able to actively initiate and foster the country's economic liberalization and development.

The first steps in economic reform involved the abolition of the centrally planned economic system in favor of a gradual transformation into a market-oriented economy, allowing competition between SOEs and the private sector. Under *Doi Moi*, the CPV also chose to adopt an open-door policy toward foreign investment. With its continued leading role in the economy, the CPV launched the fourth Five-Year Socio-Economic Development Plan (SEDP) for 1986-1990, followed by two 10-Year Socio-Economic Development Strategies (SEDS) for 1991-2000 and 2001-2010. As a means of addressing and overcoming hunger, poverty and chaos, the key object of the fourth Five-Year SEDP (1986-1990) was to increase production of food, consumer goods and export goods. The first 10-Year SEDS (1991-2000) prioritized labor-intensive manufacturing sectors as a means of enhancing domestic demand and exports, while the second SEDS (2001-2010) focused on the rapid development of high technology production.

The end of the Cold War provided Vietnam with the momentum to take its first steps into the world economy. Vietnam normalized its relations with China in 1991 and the US in 1995, and joined ASEAN in 1995. This opened up opportunities for Vietnam to work with the world's developed economies and international organizations, including multi-lateral donors. It also facilitated Vietnam's integration into the global economy.

Looking at the environmental factors, economic policies and key issues, and outcomes faced by Vietnam's transition economy between 1986 and 2005, this chapter explores how the role of the government can be remain central in steering economic development in the context of a transition to a market economy, particularly with respect to its role in creating the legal and institutional framework for this new form of economy.

INTERNATIONAL ENVIRONMENT

The Collapse of the Soviet Union and Its Impact on Vietnam

The collapse of socialism and the emergence of transitional economies in the Soviet Union and Eastern Europe had significant impacts on Vietnam. On one hand, this meant the loss of its former political and economic fulcrum, placing Vietnam in something of a vacuum of development. On the other hand, the changed international environment provided an opportunity for the Vietnamese government to reconsider its development model as well as its role and management methods in order to adapt to the new situation. Vietnam could no longer rely on the Soviet aid program, and had to approach Western economies and international aid agencies for technical and financial assistance (Wiemann et al. 2006).

The result was a sharp change in the direction of Vietnam's foreign policy. The government recognized the importance of building cohesion with other countries in the region and developing economic ties with powerful countries. It became important to normalize estranged relations with China and the US and to join Asia-Pacific economic communities such as ASEAN and the Asia-Pacific Economic Cooperation (APEC) during the 1990s. Since the late 1980s, Communist Party leaders in Vietnam adopted a more internationally engaged foreign policy with the goal of making "more friends and fewer enemies" and developing cooperation for mutual profit.

Making the First Step into the World Economy

Before 1991, Vietnam's only formal international economic links were those created after 1978, when it joined the CMEA (the Council for Mutual Economic Assistance or Comecon). This organization ran from 1949–1991 under the leadership of the Soviet Union and comprised the countries of the Eastern Bloc along with a number of socialist states elsewhere in the world.

As the Vietnamese economy collapsed as a result of the prosecution of war with Cambodia, Vietnam's party leaders decided to withdraw the country's military forces from Cambodia in 1989. This offered Vietnam an opportunity for normalizing relations with China. Chinese and Vietnamese leaders had an unannounced summit meeting in Chengdu on 3-4 Sep 1990, which provided a turning point in Vietnam-China relations. Delegates of Vietnam included: Nguyen Van Linh, General Secretary of the CPV (1986-991); Do Muoi, President of Council of Ministers; and Pham Van Dong, Advisor to the Party Central Committee. Chinese delegates included General Secretary Jiang Zemin, and Prime Minister Li Peng. At this secret summit, the two countries agreed upon a set of principles for the political settlement of the Cambodia issue and the resumption of relations. On 5 Nov 1991, Do Muoi, General Secretary of the CPV and Vo Van Kiet, President of Council of Ministers, paid a visit to China (Hiep 2013). On 7 Nov 1991, the two countries signed a China-Vietnam trade agreement and a temporary border agreement in Beijing. This normalization of relations later had a significant impact on the way in which the government of Vietnam formed guidelines and policies for socio-economic development.

After more than two decades of an estranged relationship since the Vietnam War, Vietnam and the US also re-established their economic relationship during the 1990s. The end of the bipolar world order of the Cold War in 1991 provided an opportunity for Vietnam to improve its relationship with the US, which emerged as the only superpower. In July 1995, Vietnam-US relations were officially normalized as US President Clinton lifted the then 20-year trade embargo against Vietnam. The signing of the US-Vietnam Bilateral Trade Agreement in December 2001 was a milestone event, which accelerated the development of economic relations between the two countries and also facilitated Vietnam's integration into global markets. Coupled with the normalization of relations with China, the re-establishment of trade linked with the US opened up opportunities to work with the world's developed economies and other international organizations, including multilateral donor agencies such as the World Bank and Asian Development Bank (ADB) (Vuong 2014).

Meanwhile, regional integration also proceeded. Already, by 28 July 1995, Vietnam had been accepted as the seventh member state of ASEAN, which at the time included Malaysia, Singapore, Indonesia, the Philippines, Thailand and Brunei. ASEAN agreed that Vietnam could comply with the requirements of the ASEAN Free Trade Area (AFTA) at a slower pace than the other members. Vietnam's efforts to join ASEAN received strong support from within the country and abroad, although concerns also existed in relation to differences in political and economic systems between Vietnam and ASEAN countries. The regional standoff between Vietnam and ASEAN over Cambodia also remained as an obstacle on the way to Vietnam's gaining ASEAN membership. With the help of Singapore, Canada, Japan, Malaysia and Australia, as well as international organizations such as the United Nations Development Program (UNDP), the Swedish International Development Agency (SIDA), and the British Council. Vietnam signed the Paris Agreements on Cambodia in 1991 and ended two decades of the Cambodian-Vietnamese border war (1977-1991). During the first decade of the current century, Vietnam was to deepen its influence within ASEAN, holding a rotating presidency at the end of 2000s (and hosting the 17th ASEAN Summit in 2010) (Ninh 2010).

In November 1998, Vietnam also joined APEC as part of an effort to accelerate regional economic integration and secure balanced, inclusive, sustainable, innovative and secure growth in the Asia-Pacific region. ASEAN and APEC membership denoted Vietnam's remarkable progress in integrating into the world economy, reflecting important changes in the government's perception of the nation's international position and foreign affairs policy — especially its commitment to regional cooperation. The new integration efforts with both ASEAN and APEC, along with normalization of diplomatic relations, laid the foundation for Vietnam to join the WTO in 2006.

Vietnam's increased openness to international trade also had a negative economic effect. For example, when the 1997 Asian financial crisis substantially destroyed many Asian economies, Vietnam was also adversely affected, although less significantly than others thanks to its belated entry into the world economy. Because many of Vietnam's largest investors (including Thailand and Korea) experienced the currency crisis due to the 1997 Asian financial crisis, Vietnam experienced a decline of over 80 percent in licensed investments between 1995-96 and 1999 (Dapice 2000). Additionally, Vietnam's attractiveness as a trade or investment partner was hampered by overseas perceptions. The Vietnamese bureaucracy had a reputation for inefficiency owing to changing rules that creating delays. The resulting reluctance to invest in Vietnam had a negative impact on Vietnam's economic growth.

DOMESTIC ENVIRONMENT

Doi Moi, Reform for National Development

Facing decades of hunger, economic stagnation and high inflation under the state-controlled economy, as well as significant changes in domestic and international environments, the Vietnamese government was confronted with an urgent need to introduce major changes in its economic policies. The death of Lê Duẩn in 1986, the general secretary of the CPV from 1960 to 1986, who had been strongly committed to a Soviet-type centrally planned economy, provided strong impetus for change. At the 6th National Party Congress in late 1986, Nguyễn Văn Linh was elected new General Secretary and soon assumed leadership of the *Doi Moi* reforms. Aiming to adapt socialism on a new model, Nguyễn Văn Linh urged a liberalization of the Vietnamese economy while maintaining the socialist orientation, winning widespread public approval ("Nguyen Van Linh's 100th birth" 2017).

As the first steps in the economic reform, the centrally planned economic system based on state subsidies was abolished; the economy was transformed into a multi-sector, market-oriented economy with a stronger private sector. Integration into regional and world economies was promoted to improve economic growth. Resources were to be directed to the development of agriculture, the expansion of consumer goods production and the expansion of trade and foreign investment relations (Arkadie and Mallon 2004: 68). In parallel with economic reforms, *Doi Moi* committed to promoting socialist democracy in Vietnam. Although maintaining its one-party regime and refusing to accept the multiple party system, *Doi Moi* had aims of making positive social changes, ensuring the means to strengthen national defense and security in order to stabilize the economy and boost socialist industrialization (*Viet Nam News* 2016b). Political renovation included: innovation in the leadership role of the Party; innovation in international cooperation in an open way; calling for foreign investment and cooperation; and maintaining socialist orientation, channeling economic growth in a socialist direction.

The introduction of the *Doi Moi* policy was a turning point for Vietnam as it proposed a major shift in the role and method of government in managing the national economy. Since 1986, the Vietnamese government gradually increased its control and influence in guiding economic development, providing a legal framework for all socio-economic activities, supplying public goods, maintaining stable macroscopic economy and ensuring social fairness. The old-fashioned agricultural collectives were dismantled, and private enterprise and market prices were introduced. After Nguyễn Văn Linh retired in 1991, Đỗ Mười, the General Secretary of CPV from 1991 to 1996, and Võ Văn Kiệt Prime Minister from 1992 to 1997 continued to advocate extensive reforms.

Vietnam's Demographic Transition

While Vietnam experienced sustained periods of hunger during the immediate Vietnam War period described in Chapter 5, its population rapidly grew since the country's reunification. With over one million people added every year, Vietnam's population growth rate recorded 22.7 percent between 1979 and 1989; by 1999, Vietnam had become the 13th most populous country in the world (Haub and Huong 2003). Population density also became a concern in Vietnam. People living in densely inhabited big cities and major agricultural areas were pressured to leave for more sparsely populated regions. With higher birth rates, rural areas in Vietnam faced higher rates of unemployment and higher levels of poverty (Committee for

Population, Family and Children of Vietnam 2002). The large population size and rapid population growth hindered sustainable development and socio-economic growth in Vietnam, hampering the advance of income per capita (Committee for Population, Family and Children of Vietnam 2002).

In response to these alarming population growth rates, the CPV implemented a series of population policies that garnered positive results. Vietnam's population policy had originally been initiated in North Vietnam in early 1960s and extended nationwide after the country's reunification in 1975. With the launch of *Doi Moi* in 1986, it further developed and matured as an integral part of national socio-economic development plans. The core element of the population policy during this was to promote the social norm of small family size by a vigorous population program, supported by the introduction of birth control measures (Pham, Hill, Hall and Rao 2013). The government's first Decree on birth control was officially issued in 1988 to stipulate a limit on family size to two children. The Resolution 4 on Population and Family Planning issued in 1993 advocated one-to-two children (Pham et al. 2013). As a result, the fertility rate rapidly declined from 3.8 per woman in 1989 to 2.3 per woman in 1999 (Pham et al. 2013). Vietnam experienced a sharp decline in its population growth rate during the 1990s, marking an 18.5 percent increase from 1989 to 1999 (Haub and Huong 2003). Significant progress in slowing population growth contributed to considerable socio-economic growth, especially in rural areas, in the 1990s (Pham et al. 2013). The low fertility rate led to a reduced child dependency ratio, defined as the ratio of the youth population (0 to 19 years) to the working-age population (20 to 64 years). With a better educated workforce making up a larger share of the overall population, Vietnam was able to hasten the process of industrialization. This demographic shift became central to the success of Vietnam's economic transition (Bodewig, Badiani-Magnusson, Macdonald, Newhouse, and Rutkowski 2014).

Economic Policies

Socio-Economic Development Strategies and Plans

Despite its focus on transition to a market economy, the *Doi Moi* policy did not abolish the idea of state regulation. The CPV officially identified the main aim of the *Doi Mo*i policy was to build up "a multi-sectoral commodity economy, regulated by market mechanisms with the state regulation" (*Vietnamnet* 2017b). When renewing the Five-Year Economic Development Plan, the government continued to emphasize the state's leading role in order to broaden the collective economy and to restrict negative aspects of private sectors. With continued commitment to reforms, the CPV, in 1991, launched a new 10-Year SEDS, with main tasks and targets set out in the Five-Year Socio-Economic Development Plans (SEDPs). *Doi Moi* between 1986 and 2005 was based on the fourth Five-Year SEDP (1986-1990) and two 10-Year SEDS (1991-2000 and 2001-2010).

The Fourth Five-Year Socio-Economic Development Plan (1986-1990)

The fourth Five-Year SEDP (1986-1990) began with the major economic objective of increase production of food, consumer goods and export goods. During the first stage of the fourth plan, the biggest difficulties were the poor economy and poverty. Therefore, food production, as in the previous plan, continued to be of primary importance. The aim was to meet domestic demand for food and then to have food reserves. Food and Foodstuff Program strived to reach annual production about 22-23 million tons of grain and 19-20 million tons of rice by 1990, and to bring subsidiary food crops (corns, sweet potatoes, white potatoes and manioc) in the people's diet (International Business Publications 2007: 38). These achievements were possible through the exploitation of the strengths of each locality, taking advantage of labor resources and natural resources, improving import and export, expanding industrial tree plantations (especially fast-growing trees), coupled with the construction of the food processing industry and the decline in population growth rate.

While the food program targeted "enough food," the consumer goods program aimed to meet other basic needs of the people. For example, textile production was promoted to ensure 'enough clothing' for the people. The program also included essential goods such as paper, medicine, sugar, soap, bicycles, watches, sewing machines, radios, etc. The goal was to increase production of consumer goods by an annual average rate of up 13-15 percent until 1990, compared with the 11.3 percent average annual increase recorded during the third Five-Year plan (International Business Publications 2007: 39).

While food and consumer goods programs made important contributions in helping to stabilize the economy as well as the lives of people, the export program proved critical to the development of consumer goods, which were a major component of international trade and economic relations. Priority was given to imports of raw materials in order to protect domestic production of consumer goods. The expected goal of the export program was to achieve an increase of 70 percent in exports compared with the previous Five-Year plan (International Business Publications 2007: 39). The main export goods were agricultural commodities, processed agricultural products, handicrafts, and light industrial and aquatic products.

The export program was based on long-term planning and a specific plan for each period to produce goods for export. It included: streamlining and managing import and export activities; creating favorable conditions to develop foreign exchange generating activities such as tourism, remittances, supply vessels and air service; and sending laborers and professionals to work in other countries.

The program also aimed to promote engagement in international affairs and cooperation with countries or private institutions from other developing and capitalist countries, through the modification of mechanisms and policies in response to changing international environments. Scientific knowledge and development of technology were also promoted as they were regarded as necessary for socio-economic development and the successful achievement of the three production programs (food, consumer goods, and export goods).

The First 10-Year Socio-Economic Development Strategy (1991-2000)

The 7th National Congress of the CPV in 1991 confirmed the government's stronger commitment to the country's industrialization and modernization. The congress adopted a new 10-Year SEDS for the period of 1991-2000 under the principle that economic growth should be attached to social progress and equality, cultural development and protection of the environment. The 10-Year SEDS was the government's main strategy for development that provided a framework and directions for different ministries and sectors to develop their own long-term plans of actions, as well as to deal with any difficulties in their different spheres of operation (Nguyen C M 2011). The action plans by which the 10-Year SEDS was to be implemented were outlined in two consecutive Five-Year SEDPs for 1991-1995 and 1996-2000.

During the 1991-1995 Plan, the government carried out reforms for the task of realizing its conceptualization of a socialist market economy, making the relations of production appropriate to the nature and level of productive forces. According to the 1992 amendment to the constitution, business entities in Vietnam were categorized into three basic forms of ownership: "entire-people" ownership; "collective" ownership; and private ownership.

With national economic development as the main goal, the individual household economy was encouraged as well as the collective economy while private ownership was allowed in certain areas. Linkages between economic sectors were encouraged. Furthermore, the government promoted reforms on economic management mechanisms with a clear determination to remove the system of bureaucratic centralism and subsidization, and build up socialist accounting and business methods. Additionally, the government undertook the rational distribution of labor in each region as well as throughout the country, in order to boost employment opportunities, firstly in urban areas and for young people. The first labor code was created in 1994 to regulate the employment relationship, and to assist and facilitate any activity that would create jobs and promote employment.

While the development of heavy industry (cement and steel) and natural resource-based industries (oil exploitation and mining) remained as a key object of the plan, the priority of the plan was also given to labor-intensive manufacturing sectors for domestic demand (food stuff industries) and export of manufactured products (Nguyen, Luu and Trinh 2016). In the context of high inflation, account deficits, and low labor costs in Vietnam, it was necessary and advantageous to expand the manufacturing industry to support sustainable export development.

Following the initial achievements during the 1991-1995 plan, the 1996-2000 plan set overall goals as follows: overcoming poverty and economic crisis; stabilizing the macro economy; improving people's lives; strengthening defense and security; and enabling the country to grow faster at the advent of the 21st century. The plan continued to emphasize the priorities of the previous Five-Year plan, with greater emphasis on the development of light export-oriented industries (textiles and garments, footwear, paper production) (Nguyen et al. 2016). Specific development targets were set as follows: annual GDP growth rate of 9-10 percent; GDP per capita of 2000 to be doubled of that of 1990; increase in industrial production by 14-15 percent annually; and the annual average growth increase in agricultural production and services sector to be 4.5-5 percent and 12-13 percent respectively (Vietnam Ministry of Planning and Investment 2001).

The Second 10-Year Socio-Economic Development Strategy (2001-2010)

The second SEDS for the period of 2001-2010 was proposed by the Ninth Congress of the CPV after the evaluation of the first 10-Year strategy. The new strategy stated that Vietnam's development vision was to develop the country from an agriculture-based economy to an industrialized economy by 2020. The vision was to achieve rapid development of high technological production, which should reach 45 percent of GDP by 2020. The GDP growth rate target was set at 6.5-7 percent per year, with the decline in the share of agriculture GDP from 25 percent to 16-17 percent. Increased attention was to be given to protecting the environment and natural resources, to climate change measures and to improving human capacity and social welfare (UNIDO 2012:13).

To achieve the strategic goals of the 2001-2010 SEDS, two Five-Year SEDPs (2001-2005 and 2006-2010) were implemented. With a focus on rapid growth, job creation, poverty reduction and social equity as well as continued focus on economic structural changes towards industrialization and modernization, the 2001-2005 plan set out its economic targets as follows: a doubling of GDP by 2010 to be attained through 7.5 percent between 2001-2005; investment to be increased to 30 percent of GDP; exports to grow at more than twice the rate of GDP growth; the share of agriculture GDP to decline from 25 percent to 16-17 percent; industry to increase from 35 percent to 40-41 percent; services to increase from 40 percent to 42-43 percent; the share of agriculture employment to decline from two-thirds to half; and the share of the urban population to increase from a quarter to a third (International Business Publications 2007: 56).

Although the 2001-2005 plan generally continued the previous policies, industrial policies were revised with greater support for the development of SMEs. Through various promotion policies, the government also encouraged the service sector, the establishment of private businesses and employment in industry (Nguyen et al. 2016). By 2001, as many as 11 industries were identified as emerging priority industries to be supported, although this resulted in the dispersion of investment resources and low efficiency (Nguyen et al. 2016).

The 2006-2010 plan also had general goals to achieve as follows: boosting the economic growth rate; achieving rapid and sustainable development; bringing the country out of the low development state. Economic targets of the plan included: GDP in 2010 to be 2.1 times higher than that in 2000; annual average growth rate per capita between 2006 - 2010 to be 7.5 – 8 percent, aiming at over 8 percent; GDP per capita to be about

USD 1,050 - 1,100 at current price (Vietnam Ministry of Planning and Investment 2006).

KEY ISSUES

The State-Led Transition to a Socialist-Oriented Market Economy

With the advent of *Doi Moi*, efforts were made to shift the Vietnamese economy from the centrally planned economy to a market-oriented and globally integrated model. Using macro management tools associated with investment programs based on concentrated capital, the government guided and promoted the restructuring process in order to build and develop the Vietnamese "socialist-oriented market economy." Vietnam's socialist market mechanism promoted the concept of a multi-sectoral economy, as well as open-door policies towards international trade and investment, and recognized private property rights (Vuong 2014). Accordingly, a judicious change was made to shift from a unitary public ownership to a multi-ownership economy through SOE "equitization," the government's term for privatization. The multi-ownership economy enabled non-state and state ownership and collective ownership to legally co-exist. The liberalization of the economy encouraged the establishment of new businesses. SOEs were allowed to operate freely for both social and commercial objectives as independent business entities. They were favored and protected as the main driver of the economic development and industrialization in Vietnam (Wolff 1999).

In addition, the government opened some sectors to foreign investors in 1987 and began to set out legal documents. This change helped the governments extend international relationships as well as maintain and strengthen cooperation with traditional partners. Given the lack of capital and domestic economic structure for economic development, the government had to make various efforts to attract FDI during the early state of *Doi Moi* in the late 1980s.

Following the first few years of adjustments under *Doi Moi*, the government took a further step forward in the transition to a market economy by adopting a macroeconomic stabilization program in 1989. This program aimed to stabilize the economy and facilitate market development, stressing less government intervention and more free market incentives. The key components of the program included monetary and fiscal stabilization and domestic and international trade liberalization. Monetary policies involved the devaluation of market exchange rates and rise in nominal interest rates, while fiscal policies focused on reducing subsidies to SOEs and curbing public sector and state budget expenditures (Le 2008). The government implemented a tight monetary policy to prevent high inflation, narrow the saving-investment gap and reduce dependency on resource exports. Cash management was strengthened; the business and service units were not allowed to keep cash exceeding the regulated amount to meet the business's requirements. To keep price stability, retail prices of consumer goods were maintained near prices of trading business. At the same time, the government regulated supply and demand to prevent commercial products, especially essential goods, from dominating the market. With the cost of living rapidly increasing since *Doi Moi*, in 1987, the government also adjusted the wages with different increases for different groups (Nguyen et al. 2016). Under the Labor Code 1994, minimum wages were officially introduced, although varying across location and the type of firm ownership as determined by the government (Nguyen et al. 2016). Through these state-led regulatory and policy tools, the government hoped to improve the balance of payments and control public and national debt to ensure the security of national finance. The government also made comprehensive development policies in fields such as employment, culture, education, science, health care, natural resources and the environment, emphasizing the role of the state in improving management efficiency and strengthening the rule of law.

Opening up for Door Foreign Investment and Export-Oriented Industrialization

Before *Doi Moi*, international relations of Vietnam were limited to the socialist community, including the Soviet Union, CMEA, the two neighboring countries, Laos and Cambodia. Export and import activities were concentrated within the CMEA bloc. Under *Doi Moi*, the Vietnamese government chose to adopt an open and multilateral approach of economic relations by engaging with diverse nations and organizations. By doing so, the government aimed to actively integrate into the region and the world, extending its diplomatic and economic ties to other nations whilst maintaining and strengthening cooperation with traditional partners. The implementation of an open-door policy was necessary for Vietnam to increase exports of processed goods and reduce the proportion of crude products so that Vietnam could increase profits and advantages of scale, thus ensuring financial stability through a relatively stable market.

With the first foreign investment law approved in 1987, Vietnam was opened to foreign investments in 1988. Given the limited degree of industrialization at the outset of its transition, there was a great need for foreign technology and capital in Vietnam. Vietnam introduced a significant change in government's foreign trade policy, switching from an import-substitution to export-orientation strategy (Nguyen et al. 2016). The Vietnamese government substantially reduced and/or gradually eliminated both tariff and non-tariff barriers (International Trade Centre 2001). The average import tax rate was only around 14 percent in 1997 (International Trade Centre 2001). Quotas on rice exports and fertilizer imports were also abolished in 2001 (Nguyen et al. 2016). To encourage exports and export-oriented investment, the government also introduced and implemented various export-promoting measures and policies including tax incentives, easier access to credit, foreign exchange and land-use rights, easier and quicker business registration and licensing, export awards, and support in trade promotion (International Trade Centre 2001). The government also implemented various foreign investment policies to create a favorable environment for attracting and efficiently using foreign investment capital, and facilitating the process of regional and global economic integration. In addition, export processing zones (EPZs) and Industrial Zones (IZs) were set up to attract foreign investment nationwide. Since then, FDI inflows to Vietnam increased considerably. During the 1990s, most of FDI was concentrated on oil related production, heavy industry or real estate (Harvie 2001: 12). The heavy industry mostly depended on SOEs requiring a high production costs, leading to the loss of international competitiveness.

Between 2001 and 2005, the development of the labor-intensive, light industrial sector was promoted to support sustainable export-led development (Nguyen et al. 2016). The quality of manufactured goods in Vietnam, however, was lower than Chinese products whereas its production cost was higher. With efforts to apply technology in production process, the government put an increasing share of FDI into the light industry. During this period, the government began to forcibly apply tax policies and rates to encourage exports strongly. It showcased innovations in thinking of policymakers at that time. Export targets of five years from 1991 to 1995 was set out more than 2 to 2.5 times higher than the previous five years, until 2000 will accelerate the speed increased by 5 times compared to 1990. In this phase, import policy tended to support the development of production and technological innovation in order to create competitive advantages of the goods, especially goods for export, not just focusing primarily on essential goods such as the previous period.

Together with some reform policies, the introduction of Enterprise Law in 1999 contributed to creating a favorable business environment for private sector development. This law simplified previous detailed documents about the process of establishing enterprises and limited some legal privileges of SOEs. The government also made efforts towards regional integration and trade liberalization by joining the ASEAN (1995) and the WTO (January 2007) and re-establishing diplomatic relations with China and the US.

FDI and Industrial Zone-Led Development

With the key objective of the 2001-2010 SEDS to move Vietnam to an industrial country by 2020, there was demand to develop high-level production capacity with modern technologies as well as production organization systems. As a means of facilitating industrial investment, attracting higher levels of FDI, promoting technology transfers and improving human resource quality of the country, Vietnam introduced a system of Industrial Zones, with the pilot model of EPZs implemented in 1991. After a three-year pilot, the key regulations on developing and managing IZs, EPZs and hi-tech zones were first promulgated in 1997. The 2005 Law on investment paved the way for further development of IPs and their investors. The law introduced the definition of "industrial park" under the economic integration period was also intended to spearhead the decentralization of investment. According to the Law, IPs, hi-tech zones, EPZs and economic zones were classified as areas benefiting from investment incentives. This policy shows strong support of the government for businesses investing in IPs, among other zones. Enjoying benefits from reduced tax and other investment incentives, a number of Industrial Parks (IPs) were established within the IZs under this policy reform and continued to grow as foreign investment poured in.

IZs with their basic infrastructure not only attracted FDI but also promoted technology transfers and improved human resource quality of Vietnam. The spillover effects of technology transfers among enterprises in production chains, especially those in the same or nearby IZs, motivated the establishment of more IZs in Vietnam. This was also expected to help to develop local industries in the provinces having the zones. IZs could also provide a high-quality labor force trained within the zones or from other zones. The economic linkages among businesses in IZs together with higher quality workers led to greater potential for increasing labor productivity of businesses in the IZs as well as those in their value chains (Nguyen, Lee and Nguyet 2017).

However, policy consistency was not always ensured due to weaknesses in the IZ master development plans nation-wide. In some provinces, IZs were formed without considering necessary conditions such as appropriate locations, basic infrastructure, regional economic development trends and labor supply capacity. As a result, a number of IZs failed to attract investors, both domestic and foreign, in building infrastructures. Some IZ licenses were withdrawn, resulting in the waste of social resources such as land left uncultivated for a long time or incomplete compensation procedures for affected citizens. These situations caused unstable social and economic conditions for the government to address (Nguyen et al. 2017).

Towards an Institutionalized Market Economy

The transition to a market economy led the Vietnamese government to initiate the correlative reforms in laws. The process of joining international organizations such as ASEAN, APEC and WTO also pressured Vietnam to build a more transparent legal framework in line with international standards. After applying for WTO membership in 1995, in particular, the government embarked on bold reforms to economic laws in order to provide an equal business environment for both local and foreign enterprises operating in Vietnam (Nguyen 2009: 8). A series of necessary legal frameworks for building up the market economy was also formulated during this period. The introduction of these law reforms marked a significant progression in the development of political and legal systems in Vietnam, in that it unified and standardized economic laws. The law enactment was made in the following three main areas: (i) laws on private economic activities; (ii) laws on finance and tax; and (iii) laws on foreign investment.

Laws on Private Economic Activities

Company law in Vietnam, although originally based on the French commercial law system, was largely influenced by the economic policies of the ruling communist party since the country's independence in 1945. In 1992, the Constitution was promulgated and a number of legal documents related to private land use, investment, enterprises, business competition and others were successively issued.

The Land Law was first enacted in 1987 to regulate the complex changes in land management during the transition economy period. Although reaffirming that the state had total management powers over land, this land law also stipulated the recognition and protection of private land use rights (Le 2015: 155). Central Committee Resolution 10 was also adopted, which formalized the farm household as the main unit of agricultural production and provided for the allocation of land use rights to households. Farm households were allowed to use land over the long term, and sell their products on the free market with no obligation to participate in cooperatives. Still in the early stage to absorb ideas relating to *Doi Moi,* the first land law was not effective, and later was replaced by a new law in 1993. Through the creation of quasi-ownership of land, the new law facilitated the liberalization of farmers' rights in relation to the land they farmed and its produce. The legal framework for land management was further revised through amendments and supplementary provisions in 1998 and in 2001, until the Land Law was finally ratified by the National Assembly in 2003. Under the new law, land acquisition was allowed for both local and foreign investors. Foreign investors were allowed to lease the land directly from the government and paid rent, while local investors could acquire the land via land allocation, paying a land use fee or lease the land paying rent on a yearly basis.

The transition to the globally integrated economy also required Vietnam to implement competition policies and establish an independent competition agency. After years of effort, a number of existing provisions regulating anticompetitive acts or monopolies in some specific areas were integrated into one Competition Law in 2004. This Competition Law aimed to promote a fair-competition environment and govern practices in restraint of competition, unfair competitive practices, the order and procedures for resolution of competition cases, and measures for dealing with breaches of the laws on competition. While implementing the Competition Law aiming to enhance a fair competitive market, Vietnam was also pursuing a conservative industrial policy involving government support such as tax reduction, land and credit accessibility, and other incentives. This contributed to problems in law enforcement. In addition, there were many government and business entities that were excluded from the competition legislation of general application, including government agencies, SOEs and Small and Medium Enterprises (SMEs) (Thanh 2015). In addition to the Land Law and Competition Law, the Commercial Law (1997), the Ordinance on Protection of Consumer Rights (1999) and the Law on Accounting and Auditing (2005) were formulated in order to protect private economic activities.

Laws on Finance and Tax

The commercial banking system of Vietnam used to operate on one level before developing as a central bank in 1976. The banking system was then reformed with two ordinances on banks passed in 1990 that allowed non-state-owned enterprises (NSEs) to operate banking businesses. New banks were created, including the Industrial and Commercial Bank of Vietnam and the Vietnam Bank of Agriculture, both in 1988. As a result, a new banking system was established to replace the old single-level banking system, with a two-level one that separated the functions of management carried out by the state bank from the business activities of commercial banks. After applying for WTO membership, the National Assembly passed the Law on the State Bank of Vietnam and the Law on Credit Institutions in 1997, in order to strengthen monetary policy and enhance the efficiency of credit institutions. Monetary policy aimed to achieve several goals: stabilize the value of currency; curb inflation; promote socio-economic development; consolidate national defense; and foster better living (Nguyen 2009: 16). Under the new Law, interest rates were liberalized and exchange rates were adjusted according to changes in supply and demand. The forms of credit institutions were diversified while the efficiency of banking business was enhanced, for example, through the adoption of an internal audit system and a supervisory board. Insurance institutions were also established while the development of joint-stock enterprises, expansion of types of stocks and bonds and creation of securities market were encouraged. The government also adopted measures to clean up the capital market and currency by preventing usury, fraud and speculation.

In addition, a unified taxation law system was created in 1990 to govern both state-owned and non-state-owned economic sectors. With a need to modernize the taxation system and align with international standards, new laws were also promulgated including the Corporate Income Taxation Law (1997), the Value-Added Taxation Law (1997) and the Excise Taxation Law (1998). Furthermore, a series of revision was carried out on the High-Income Earners Tax, Import and Export Duties and Tax on the Transfer of Land Use Rights.

Other necessary legal frameworks for building up market economy were also formulated: Law on Credit Institutions (1997); Law on Insurance Business (2001); Law on Value Added Tax (1997); Law on Corporate Income Tax (1997); and Law on Customs (2001).

Laws on Foreign Investment

Vietnam introduced the Law on Foreign Investment 1987 and the Law on Private Enterprises and Companies 1990 to offer the first legal corporate framework that could bolster and assist investors' interests and business activities in Vietnam.

The Foreign Investment Law was introduced to expand economic co-operation with foreign countries and to encourage and create favorable conditions for investment in Vietnam by foreign organizations and individuals. It underwent several amendments in 1990, 1992, 1996 and 2000 to offer a more liberal and equal environment for foreign investors. In addition, the Law on Promotion of Domestic Investment was promulgated in 1994 and later amended in 1998. Incorporating the Law on Foreign Investment and the Law on Promotion of Domestic Investment, the government announced the Law on Investment in 2005. The new Investment Law granted greater autonomy to investors, allowing choices for foreign investors to select the sectors to invest in, the form of investment, capital-raising methods, the location and scale of investment, investment partners and the duration of investment (Nguyen 2009: 21). This Law guaranteed investors equal access and eliminated all discrimination.

Similarly, to enhance business freedom and create a congenial business environment for the private sector, the Companies Law and the Private Enterprises Law were enacted by the National Assembly in December 1990 and later replaced by the Enterprise Law in 1999. The adoption of the Enterprise Law, however, led different enterprises to operate under different legislations. Privately-owned enterprises, SOEs and foreign-invested enterprises in Vietnam were governed by the Enterprises Law of 1999, the Law on State-owned Enterprises of 1995 (amended in 2003) and the Foreign Investment Law of 1987, respectively. This called for the adoption of a unified law to govern enterprises operating in different economic sectors in Vietnam (Nguyen 2009). As a result, in 2005, the National Assembly passed new laws, the State-owned Enterprises Law and the Foreign Investment Law. This established a legal basis for the establishment of limited liability and shareholding companies and the regulation of corporate groups.

ECONOMIC OUTCOMES

Growth Outcomes

During the first few years of *Doi Moi* (1986-1990), the chaos caused by the evolving economic structure and the collapse of socialist countries made economic growth in Vietnam low and unstable. From 1986 to 1989, inflation was extremely high. The inflation rate recorded 487 percent, 301 percent, and 394 percent in 1986, 1987 and 1988 respectively. The source of macroeconomic imbalance was deficits of the public sector which were financed by borrowing from the central bank and, until 1990, from the Soviet Union. The rapid expansion of credit resulted in sharp increases in prices. As the rate of inflation increased, more people shifted from dong, the local currency, into US dollars and gold. This triggered further instability of the economy. The inflation also undermined international competitiveness, with the Dong significantly overvalued in real terms. By 1989, three years after the beginning of the reform under *Doi Moi*, the economy was facing a severe crisis (Riedel 1995). Vietnam remained one of the slowest growing countries in the region with average per capita GDP growth of about 1.9 percent until 1991 (Tran 2002). According to a survey with 500 SOEs conducted in May 1989, only 33.7 percent of enterprises could maintain production levels. Severe weather and frequent natural calamities were also serious impediments to poverty reduction and socio-economic development in Vietnam (Glewwe, Gragnolatti and Zaman 2000).

However, compared with other communist countries adopting a capitalist economy in Eastern Europe and the Soviet Union, the economic growth of Vietnam was still regarded as a success. As set out in the 1986-1990 Economic Development Plan, food production increased and the rate of inflation was reduced (Kien and Heo 2008). Total rice production increased 5.19 percent yearly in the period 1988-95 (Young et al. 2002: 8). Vietnam became the world's third largest rice exporter by 1989, following China and the US as well as a major coffee exporter (Vuong 2014: 5). The economic growth during the 1990s was even more impressive. The stabilization program of 1989 and the following law reforms contributed to the increase in fiscal revenue and macroeconomic stabilization. With a relatively stable market, Vietnam's economy constantly developed at a higher rate, with average per capita GDP growth jumping to 6.6 percent between 1991-1995 (Tran 2002). The relation between market economy and currency started to take effect as a result of government promotion. Exports in dollars rose from $2 billion in 1991 to over $9 billion in 1997, and GDP reached US$ 360 per capita (Dapice 2000). Extreme poverty was also greatly reduced. The number of people below the poverty line declined from 75 percent of the population in 1988, to 58 percent in 1993 and 37 percent in 1998 and further down to 29 percent in 2002 (Wang and Balasubramanyam 2011: 722).

The growth of the Vietnamese economy, however, slowed down in the late 1990s due to the influence of external shocks. The Asian financial crisis in 1997 reduced FDI and exports, having an adverse impact on the growth rate. Vietnam's GDP growth rate declined to 4.77 percent in 1998 and committed FDI fell by half compared to 1996 (Vuong 2014: 7). Export growth rate also declined from 26.6 percent in 1997 to 1.9 percent in 1998 (Tran 1999). The Vietnamese government embarked on a small number of adjustment programs to cope with the situation, although most of them were poorly carried out. Fortunately, however, the effects of the 1997 Asian financial crisis on Vietnam's economy were not as strong as in other Asian countries as it was still only partially open to the global economy and largely controlled by the government rather than market forces.

From mid-1999, Vietnam's economy was again on the rise, with a new economic stimulus proposal of the government. In 2000, the export rate of Vietnam increased owing to support from FDI, mostly in the field of manufacturing industry. From 2001 to 2005, an average GDP growth reached 7.5 percent, fulfilling the target growth rate set in the Five-Year plan. The year 2005 saw the highest rate of growth since 1997, attaining 8.4 percent (International Business Publications 2007: 39). In addition, from the early 1990s to 2005, poverty declined from about 50 percent to 29 percent of the population. The outstanding achievement of constant economic growth was that average income increased from US$114 in 1991 to US$1,061 in 2010 (Duong 2012).

The rapid economic growth during this period was greatly attributed to stable economic conditions, both domestic and international (Tran 2002). Through the introduction of the stabilization program in 1989, Vietnam successfully lowered inflation and stabilized commodity prices and the exchange rate, which were all essential for economic development and growth (Le 2008). Besides, foreign aid (e.g., ODA programs) and FDI increased rapidly during this period, which facilitated government's plan for infrastructure development, stimulated export activities, introduced technology know-how and generated job opportunities (Varamini and Vu 2007). Manufacturing companies and other prominent businesses from industrialized countries in the Asian region including Korea (such as Samsung, LG, Lotte and SK) began to move their production plants to Vietnam for cheaper labor and invest a significant amount of capital in Vietnam. While growing investments in the manufacturing sector boosted exports, however, this also led to a surge in imports. On the one hand, this may have indicated strength in domestic demand but on the other, it also revealed a lack of industrial depth and complexity, as local Vietnamese firms did not produce any of the components necessary for the production of exported products.

Structural Changes for Industrialization and Modernization

Changes derived from the state-led *Doi Moi* reform programs in Vietnam were genuinely impressive. The most obvious change was a shift in the system of national accounts in 1988, from Material Product System (MPS) using prices set by the state, to System of National Accounts (SNA) using "market" prices. Economic activities were more controlled by the market than the previous period. Although administrative orders and directions remained in some important fields, basic market principles such as demand-supply and price signal upheld more and more significant roles. In addition, the structure of the economy changed, with an increase of the share for industry and construction and a declining share for agriculture. The shift from agriculture to manufacturing helped to raise labor productivity at an average annual rate of 4.8 percent between 1996 and 2008 (UNIDO 2012: 13).

With increasing importance given to the non-state sector and the introduction of the Enterprise Law in 2000, the private sector in Vietnam developed rapidly during the 2000s. For example, more than 10,000 new private firms registered during the first nine months of 2000 (Harvie 2001). Not only did their number increase, private firms (although largely small or medium scale) also contributed to a larger share in employment and labor-intensive exports (Harvie 2001). With an open-door policy under *Doi Moi*, the number of foreign invested enterprises also rapidly increased in Vietnam.

Facing more competition from private companies as well as an increase in their numbers, SOEs needed further reform. Although still dominating the industrial sector, the inefficiency and inertia remaining in the state sector was a barrier to economic growth. SOEs became a burden for the state budget and the focus of economic reforms in Vietnam since the early 1980s.

The loss of the Soviet commodity aid program in 1989-90 also precipitated cutbacks of administrative resource allocation to SOEs in Vietnam (Fforde 2004). As a component of economic restructuring, the government started the equitization of SOEs with a pilot program in 1992, which involved converting SOEs into a joint-stock or shareholding companies (that is public limited companies or corporations with a portion of the shares being sold at public auction or to strategic investors). The reform program successfully reduced the number of SOEs, from some 12,000 to about 6,000 by April 1995, through closing down and merging insolvent SOEs (Webster and Amin 1998). However, changes in the management and planning mechanism were only moderate (Webster and Amin 1998). The Law on State Enterprises enacted in 1996 provided the first legal framework for the operation of SOEs, which allowed SOEs autonomy and responsibility for their actions. In addition, under the 2005 Investment Law, foreign-invested enterprises (FIEs) were allowed to have joint ventures with SOEs due to their available capacity and political neutrality. However, although equity became available for private purchase, the state retained a majority share and made all management decisions in most equitized firms. In addition, equitization of this period created confusion in economic policy for the SOE sector, as it on one hand suppressed the expansion of SOEs by reducing their number, and on the other facilitated it by providing subsidies to insolvent SOEs. As a result, the progress on equitization was slow and SOEs continued to dominate the economy of Vietnam (Sjöholm 2006).

An FDI and Aid-Dependent Economy

After *Doi Moi*'s open-door policy, FDI inflows to Vietnam increased dramatically, with an annual growth rate of 28 percent (Varamini and Vu 2007). Following the normalization of relations with the US in 1995, over US$10 billion of FDI entered Vietnam in 1996 together with billions of dollars of ODA coming from the World Bank and Asian Development Bank (Muchie, Nguyen, Baskaran and Nguyen 2011). The high rate of foreign direct private capital inflows – as much as US$2 billion a year – created a high level of investment and industrial growth. This inflow alone was 5-10 percent of GDP each year. Aid grew to reach US$1 billion of disbursements in 1997 (Dapice 2000).

The government encouraged foreign investments to enter labor-intensive light industries such as the footwear or garment sectors, regions of socio-economic difficulties and IZs although Ho Chi Minh City attracted most FDI (24 percent of the total capital between 1988 and 2005). The foreign investment law passed in the early 1990s encouraged the establishment of FIEs, which rapidly grew in mining (oil and gas extraction) and manufacturing (IMF 2006: 36). Between 1995-2005, FDI inflows into the industrial sector increased dramatically from only an estimated US$ 1118 million in 1995 to about US$ 2614 million in 2005, although committed FDI declined by half in 1997-1998 due to the 1997 Asian financial crisis (Vuong 2014). During this period, automotive and electronic industries were the major FDI recipients. The four NICs, including Singapore, Taiwan, Japan, Korea, and Hong Kong, were the largest investor countries in Vietnam between 2000 and 2005, together accounting for more than 40 percent of overall FDI inflows into Vietnam (Nguyen 2006). The social and political stability during this period positively contributed to the investment environment in Vietnam (Nguyen et al. 2017).

FDI inflows were important for socio-economic development and created the initial foundation for national industrialization and modernization. They played a very important role, not only in providing capital for development investment but also facilitating technology transfer, export expansion and human resource development as well as job creation and better living conditions. This contributed to favorable conditions for Vietnam to enhance its competitiveness and hasten its integration into the world economy (Anwar and Nguyen 2010).

Despite rapid economic growth resulting from FDI inflows, however, the government of Vietnam lacked the capacity to predict future trends and adjust policies and decisions accordingly in order to sustain constant economic development. Structural changes were still lacking, compared to some other countries whose economic growth was bolstered by the development of science, technology and information. The growth of the

Vietnam economy from 1986 to 2005 was mainly driven by capital (FDI) while the contribution of total factor productivity (TFP) — a measure of how technologically advanced production is — was insignificant, even negative between 2000-2007 (Park 2010). For the same period, contribution of TFP to economic growth of Thailand, the Philippines and Indonesia was 61.7 percent, 48.8 percent and 57.9 percent, respectively (Park 2010). High dependence on capital, although common in most developing countries, could lead to some macroeconomic instability because the marginal productivity of all forces would finally decline.

SOCIAL AND POLITICAL OUTCOMES

Political Corruption

During this period, economic reforms were not followed by political changes in Vietnam. The CPV remained the sole political party and the leading force in Vietnam. Bureaucratic corruption and abuse were rampant and widespread, affecting different sectors of the society. Regulations were frequently changed and enforced in a non-transparent manner so that businesses increasingly relied on patronage and personal relationships with members of the government and the party (Martini 2012). A number of high-ranking officials and party members were found to be connected to serious corruption cases. Doing business in Vietnam commonly involved bribery, bureaucratic interference and facilitation payments. In a 2005 survey, nearly a third of government employees in Vietnam said they would take a bribe if offered (An 2015).

With the realization that corruption was a threat to the legitimacy of the CPV and the socio-economic development of Vietnam, the Vietnamese government began to adopt a number of anti-corruption measures in 2005, including the Anti-Corruption law (Martini 2012). Various government agencies were established to deal with corruption, including the Central Steering Committee for Anti-Corruption (led by the Prime Minister), the

Government Inspectorate, the People's Procuracy and the State Audit of Vietnam, and line ministries and agencies.

Citizens began to complain openly about political corruption, inefficient government policies and unclear bureaucratic procedures. A number of people spoke out and made legal appeals against corruption. But there was a large gap between laws and how they applied. The CPV tightly suppressed any criticism of the state; its leaders and its policies and controlled the media. After openly calling for more democracy and freedom of expression, a high-ranking party member, Tran Do, was expelled from the party in 1999. The need for political reform emerged as a recurrent agenda item in Vietnam.

Emergence of Grassroots Democracy

Economic reform after *Doi Moi* created not only firm foundations for the country's economic development, but also an open and democratic social atmosphere ("Nguyen Van Linh's 100th birth" 2017). The CPV began to allow a greater degree of personal freedom than in the past. With government's poor performance to deal with widespread corruption and inadequate public administration, however, political reform lagged significantly behind market reform during the *Doi Moi* era (Loc 2016). In a market-driven economy after *Doi Moi*, labor relations were severely regulated with the introduction of new laws and policies, starting from the Labor Code 1994.

Increased economic freedom after *Doi Moi* resulted in higher living standards and greater access to education and information, and inevitably drove public demands for increased political rights. The first effort of the CPV to appease such a revolt was the Grassroots Democracy Decree (GDD) issued in 1998. Under the slogan that "the people know, the people discuss, the people do and the people monitor," the GDD provided the first legal framework for direct citizen participation in local government in Vietnam (UNDP 2006). The extensive process of fiscal decentralization and increased sub-national autonomy under *Doi Moi* enabled the agricultural sector and rural areas to play an important role for economic development in the first years of *Doi Moi.* This set the stage for the establishment of a new political actor in the existing governance system of Vietnam, represented by civil organizations and NGOs. An increasing number of anti-colonial organizations such as the Women's Union founded in 1930 were transformed into civil organizations during the *Doi Moi* period to focus on collective action for the promotion of grassroots equality (Larsen 2011). On top of increasing social and economic inequality and economic uncertainty, citizen dissatisfaction with corruption at local government level produced widespread demonstrations and violence demanding grassroots democracy and policy efficiency during the 1990s.

Then the most serious protests erupted in the Central Highlands region in the early 2000s, when religious and ethnic minority groups demonstrated against government's repressive attitudes and policies toward religion and land rights. Due to violent government crackdowns against protestors, thousands of people were arrested and injured. Concerns were raised about government crackdowns during the 9th National Congress of the CPV 2001, which initiated the introduction of the Human Rights Act in 2005. With increasing financial and practical support to promote civil society from international organizations such as the UNDP and the World Bank, the number of civil society organizations skyrocketed in Vietnam. In July 2005, it was estimated that there were 140,000 community-based organizations, in addition to 3,000 cooperatives in industry and services, 1000 locally registered NGOs and 200 charities in Vietnam (Thayer 2009: 5).

Conclusion

This chapter has examined how the CPV initiated and led Vietnam's transition from a centrally-planned economy to a socialist developmental state with a market economy. In the context of high inflation, current account deficits, and drastic effects from the regional and global market during the early years of this period, *Doi Moi* represented a critical turning point in Vietnam's policy direction, marking a radical shift to a free market economy. Although the CPV was still a single political party in the country, its governance progressed towards a less rigid form of government, being more responsive to public demands (Nguyen 2016). Environmental forces, both international and domestic, strengthened government's commitment to reforms.

Despite its decision to transform to the market economy, however, the CPV continued to play a leading role in planning and implementing economic development strategies and plans. During this period, the CPV led the transition to a market economy, the implementation of the open-door policy, industrial zone-led development, and institutionalization of the market economy. The CPV changed the focus of industrial development from heavy industry to labor-intensive light industry and export in order to support sustainable growth and export development. Responding to growing demands of a transition economy under *Doi Moi*, it also conducted a number of corporate law reforms which led to the improvement of the Vietnamese corporate governance system. Applying for WTO membership in 1995 facilitated the establishment of basic institutions of market economy through the gradual improvement of the legal system. With the first foreign investment law approved in 1987, Vietnam began to open its doors to foreign investment in 1988, which allowed massive FDI inflows and the development of industrial zones in Vietnam.

After the first few difficult years since *Doi Moi*, the Vietnamese economy started to thrive from late 1989. With support from FDI, exports greatly increased in the manufacturing industry since the early 2000s, and Vietnam enjoyed rapid economic growth with an average GDP growth of 7.5 percent between 2000 and 2005. Despite these remarkable achievements in economic reforms, bureaucratic corruption and abuse continued to be widespread, especially in SOEs, impeding the country's socio-economic development. The transition economy in Vietnam revealed limitations of CPV's collective leadership system, which hampered flexible responses to changing environments and reforms in politics. However, it is noticeable that, during this period, many civil organizations were established to empower the people at the grassroots, which led to the initiation of the grassroots movements demanding greater voice for citizens and improvements in government policy performance in the 2000s.

Chapter 6

The Adaptive Socialist Developmental State and Challenges from Integration into the Global Economy (2006 – 2016)

This chapter examines Vietnam's economic development since its accession to the WTO in 2006 until 2016, which represented a critical period of its integration into the world economy.

After accession to the WTO, Vietnam signed bilateral trade agreements (BTAs) with many WTO members and achieved social and political stability. These changes made Vietnam an attractive destination for FDI which facilitated economic development during this period. With a strong commitment to reform, the CPV also adopted a new SEDP for 2006-2010, with the continued aim to accelerate the country's industrialization and modernization and enhance its position in regional and international arenas. The plan aimed in particular to shift Vietnam from a low-income country to lower-middle-income economy, and to achieve GDP growth rates of over 8 percent a year.

Vietnam's accession to the WTO, however, not only opened the door for international integration and cooperation but also posed challenges of intense competition between domestic and international enterprises. Being integrated into the world economy, Vietnam was confronted with the spillover effect of the 2008 global financial crisis. With a sharp decrease in foreign investment and aid after the crisis, Vietnam again entered a period of macroeconomic instability accompanied by high inflation, budget deficits, declining foreign exchange reserves, mismanaged fiscal and monetary policies, high unemployment and sluggish commercial activities until the end of 2010 (Vuong 2014).

This economic instability required the CPV to become more responsive and capable. The CPV government first released several urgent measures in an effort to prevent a sharp economic downturn and ensure social stability. In this context, the 11th National Congress of the CPV held in January 2011 was a milestone event that presented a new direction for development. The incoming leadership of the CPV adopted a SEDS for 2011-2020 which, for the first time, attached importance to flexibility and changed its development orientation from rapid growth towards the quality of growth. The strategy identified three key breakthrough areas to achieve Vietnam's development goals: human resource development, economic integration and environmental sustainability. In pursuit of this, a Five-Year Plan was drawn up for 2011–2015, and the CPV was to take a leading role in changing and upgrading the economic structure to adjust to new economic realities. Structural reforms were concentrated in the country's SOEs, financial sector and public investment, with increasing pressure on SOEs to improve their market competitiveness. To better respond to an increasingly interdependent global economy and speed up domestic reforms, the CPV also committed to pursue further integration into the world economy.

This chapter examines how the CPV in Vietnam coped with the development of the socialist market economy from 2006-2016 and the process of international economic integration in Vietnam.

INTERNATIONAL ENVIRONMENT

Growing Globalization and Its Impacts on International Trade

After the global financial-economic crisis, the world economy entered a new era. US power and influence was eroded while the role of emerging and developing markets including Korea and Vietnam became more important in dealing with global-scale problems. There was an expectation that rapid economic growth in the emerging markets would be the main driver behind the significant reduction in global poverty as well as a new foundation for growth in the world economy as a whole (Lagarde 2016). Against expectations, however, many emerging and developing markets entered a period of slower growth and became new sources of global instability. The main factor in the weakening of emerging markets was the slowdown in China's economy. This had a significant impact on the economies of South East Asia as well as Brazil and Australia, the world's major suppliers of raw materials (Kundu 2015). In an era of rising inequality, protectionism, and populism, partnerships between emerging and advanced economies became extremely important for growth and development (Lagarde 2016).

As Vietnam's economic development progressed, the business environment changed to one with an increasingly costly structure of production while productivity was at a standstill. While other Asian countries like China and Indonesia sought to improve their productivity, Vietnam gradually lost its competitiveness. Vietnam's biggest trade deficit was with China from where Vietnam imported many manufactured products. However, Korean companies (especially Samsung) increasingly invested in Vietnam. From 1988 to 2016, South Korean businesses invested US$50 billion in Vietnam, an amount that accounted for 30.8 percent of total FDI (Son 2017). At least 71 percent of the capital went into the manufacturing sector. Despite the FDI, concerns were expressed that increasing imports of Korean products, of better quality than Chinese or Vietnamese products, could be a hurdle to the development of Vietnamese businesses (*Vietnamnet* 2017b).

2007-2008 Global Financial Crisis

The overheated development of economies after the Cold War period, together with low-interest rates of major central banks, created a real estate bubble and huge surplus cash flows around the world. Most of the central banks failed to effectively carry out tight monetary policy to control the real estate market. In August 2007, the US sub-prime mortgage market collapsed and shook the bank system leading it to experience a liquidity crisis. The housing boom was reversed with the decline in housing values not only in the US but also in other industrialized economies. For the first time, the world's major central banks cooperated to adjust interest rates to historic lows. Many major economies experienced significant economic recessions, including the UK, the US, mainland European countries and Japan. During the fourth quarter of 2008, economic growth marked -1.7 percent for Europe; -2.2 percent for the UK; -8.2 percent for the US; and -2.1 percent for Japan (Trading Economics 2017).

By September 2008, many stock markets and large financial institutions across the world had collapsed, forcing governments in even the wealthiest nations to establish rescue packages to bail out large private sector financial organizations. International investors also had to withdraw funds from banks used for trading and commodities in order to shore up their domestic economies. The crisis ended in March 2009 with huge stimulus packages launched simultaneously by different countries in order to make up for the decrease in consumer spending and international investment and commerce.

By exposing the fragility of global markets, the 2008 crisis also had a positive effect as it led governments to pay more attention to discipline in the financial-monetary field, especially banking. Financial reforms were implemented, for example, through the Dodd-Frank Wall Street Reform and Consumer Protection Act 2010 in the US and the 2011 Basel III regulatory requirements for banks globally to limit risks and improve the standards for Capital Adequacy Ratio within the commercial bank system.

As with the 1997 Asian financial crisis, Vietnam was less affected by the global financial crisis than many other countries owing to its comparatively lesser exposure to international financial markets. However, being already in a period of macroeconomic instability, Vietnam's economy could not be free from the ripple effects of surging Inflation and changes in the broader economic environment associated with the crisis. The global financial crisis had negative impacts on trade, FDI and financial capital movement, which consequently affected employment and overall economic growth in Vietnam. Vietnam's economic growth in 2008 slowed down to 6.2 percent, the lowest rate in almost a decade (Le 2009). This experience of external shock provided the government with an opportunity to address vulnerability and structural weaknesses in the economy. It provided the country with an opportunity to proactively change and upgrade the existing structures to respond to effectively to the new economic situation.

DOMESTIC ENVIRONMENT

Increasing Income Inequality: A Source of Social Conflicts

Despite their positive impact on economic growth, the privatization and liberalization aspects of *Doi Moi* resulted in significant increases in social inequality (Tran and To 2003). With rapid economic growth, the country's net household income consistently increased but inequality in income distribution also grew. The gap between the richest 20 percent of the population and the rest widened after 2004, with a rising number of ultra-wealthy individuals. Between 1992 and 2012, the Palma ratio (the ratio between the income share of the top 10 percent to the bottom 40 percent) increased by 17 percent, from 1.48 to 1.74. This trend was mostly driven by a decline in the income share of the bottom 40 percent of the population, from 19.33 percent to 17.28 percent (Oxfam 2017: 14). Greater privatization and user charges in basic social services such as education and health also produced a growing inequality in service use between people who could afford and those who could not (Bloom 1998). The gap between the rich and poor increased from 8 to 20 times especially between 1986 and 2004 (Pham 2008: 3).

Regional inequality in economic development was particularly evident, with higher income and wealth concentrated in urban areas. The abolition of the collective system increased the economic vulnerability of the rural poor, who were already disadvantaged due to geographical remoteness, seasonality, periodic health crises and natural disasters. Poverty was still a social problem, but mainly in rural areas, where some 80 percent of the population lived (Tran and To 2003).

Poverty and hunger were much higher and widespread among ethnic minorities. While representing 15 percent of the population, ethnic minority groups accounted for half of the country's poor and 70 percent of the extreme poor (Dang 2010; Demombynes 2013). Despite efforts made by the government, 61 percent of ethnic minority people were still poor in 2004 (Swinkels and Turk 2006). They were more likely than ethnic majority groups to experience social exclusion, cultural and language barriers, limited access to quality land and markets, and low levels of education, and were hence often in disadvantageous socio-economic positions. In addition, living in remote, lightly populated mountain regions in northern, central and western Vietnam, most of them were highly vulnerable to shocks from climate change, natural disasters, as well as economic and health shocks (World Bank 2017c). Reductions in poverty were spread unevenly across ethnic groups in Vietnam (Dang 2010).

Worsening Corruption and SOEs

Corruption was widespread across many levels of government and agencies. One of the biggest government corruption scandals became public in January 2006, when Dao Dinh Binh, head of Vietnam's ministry of transportation, was arrested for allegedly using millions of dollars from government infrastructure projects for gambling on soccer matches and buying luxury vehicles. Investigators found a total of 17 affiliated institutions and 40 individuals involved in this case. The transport minister resigned and several in his ministry were arrested. The government had to reconsider and adjust its procedures for capital management. Another large government corruption scandal broke out in April 2006 when 17 communist party members were sentenced for their connections with Vietnam's most notorious underworld boss, Nam Cam. Some of them held important positions like former Deputy Minister of Public Security, former Deputy Head of the People's Supreme Procuracy, and former director of the Voice of Vietnam radio station. Given this rampant corruption, Vietnam was ranked 111 out of 163 countries in Transparency International's Corruption Perceptions Index (CPI) in 2006 and did not improve its position over the next decade, coming 113 out of 176 countries surveyed in 2016 (Transparency International 2017).

Widespread and persistent bureaucratism, corruption and wastefulness were key impediments to the economic development of Vietnam (Martini 2012). Corrupt behavior although illegal was tolerated in different forms, including facilitation payments, extortion, abuse of office, fraud, embezzlement, money laundering, and active and passive bribery as common practices for doing business in Vietnam. In a 2014 survey, 66 percent of participating 9,859 Vietnamese firms said they usually paid extra informal charges to facilitate business activities; during the previous year, 41 percent of the survey respondents said they did so (*Saigoneer* 2015). Foreign investors expressed concerns about the level of corruption in Vietnam and warned that it would deter future investment from overseas companies (AmCham 2014).

SOEs, although the main driver of Vietnam's economy, were also greatly affected by corruption as they were often controlled by politically well-connected individuals or industrial groups and allowed to run up massive debts. In 2010, a massive embezzlement scandal occurred at the shipbuilding conglomerate called Vinalines, embroiling the party leaders. Going through the global economic slowdown, Vinalines was struggling under some US$3 billion of debt when six of its executives were arrested for embezzling millions of dollars. Two top executives including chairman Duong Chi Dung were sentenced to death in December 2013. The collapse of major SOEs, such as Vinalines, had a devastating impact on the Vietnam economy and generated a sense of urgency about SOE reforms in Vietnam (Hiep 2017).

ECONOMIC POLICIES

Socio-Economic Development Strategies and Plans

The CPV continued to show its commitment to reforms during this period (2006–2016). After reviewing and evaluating the implementation of the SEDP for the period of 2001-2005, the 10th National Congress of the CPV adopted the new 2006-2010 SEDP with the continuing aim of accelerating the country's industrialization and modernization and enhancing its position in regional and international arenas. The 2006-2010 plan had the major target of shifting Vietnam from a low-income country to lower-middle-income economy. The GDP growth rate was projected at 7.5-8 percent a year, with a goal to achieve over 8 percent a year (Socialist Republic of Vietnam 2017a).

In the context of the global financial crisis, on 11 December 2008, the Vietnamese government additionally released several urgent measures to prevent an economic downturn and ensure social stability. The government also launched a stimulus package of US$ 6 million in 2009, with the main objective being to help enterprises and the economy escape from negative impacts of the global financial crisis with tax cuts, interest rate assistance, as well as increased spending on infrastructure, housing, schools and hospitals. This stimulus package included the implementation of a range of policies such as: credit guarantee for SMEs, deferment and exemption for enterprise taxes, and a 4 percent subsidy for medium and short-term interest rates. (Nguyen and Pham 2011: 6).

Amid the worsening global financial turmoil and economic slowdown, the 11th National Congress of the CPV held in January 2011 was a landmark event, which presented a new direction for development. After reviewing and evaluating the implementation of the SEDS for the period of 2001-2010, the congress proposed the 2011-2020 SEDS and mapped out orientations and tasks for its achievement. Facing economic instability, the new leadership of the CPV attached importance to flexibility and changed its development orientation from rapid growth towards sustainable and effective growth. With this shift in strategy, the new priorities in the growth model were those of quality, productivity, effectiveness and competitiveness. In addition, three "strategic breakthroughs" were defined as follows: (i) improve socialist-oriented market economy regulations with the core objective to create an equal and competitive environment, and to make administrative reform (ii) quickly develop human resources, especially high quality human resources (iii) build an infrastructure system that synchronizes with some modern projects, and focus on improving the traffic system and big urban infrastructure (Government of Vietnam n.d.). For the development of a sustainable socialist economy, various shortcomings and weaknesses were targeted as priorities, including: low quality, low effectiveness and low competitiveness of the economy, the growing gap between rich and poor, and political and social instability (Socialist Republic of Vietnam 2017b).

Preparing the action plan for the 2011-2020 SEDS, the CPV also adopted the Five-Year SEDP for the period of 2011-2015. In consideration of the new context and real situation, the 2011-2015 plan set 2015 targets of a GDP growth by 6.5-7 percent; social investment accounting set at 33.5-35 percent of GDP; a trade deficit of less than 10 percent of export value; a budget deficit below 4.5 percent of GDP; and a public debt reduction to less than 65 percent of GDP. The plan also set the targets of creating jobs for 8 million people, reducing the urban unemployment rate to less than 4 percent, and an annual poverty reduction rate of 2 percent (Socialist Republic of Vietnam 2017b).

The plan identified three key breakthrough areas to achieve Vietnam's development goals: human resource development, economic integration and environmental sustainability. Among these, human resource development was defined as a strategic national priority. Education and training were emphasized for high-profile officials. Competent junior officers were to be given managerial tasks at regional stations, sent overseas to pursue postgraduate degrees or doctorates or offered training courses.

The 2011–2015 plan also highlighted the need for structural reforms within the Vietnamese economy. Radical transformation was required in three areas: SOEs, the banking system and public investment. The aim was to undertake economic restructuring in line with the changes in the growth model and thus increase the competitiveness of the economy (Tran 2014). The government stepped up efforts to reduce public investment by encouraging more investment from the non-state and foreign-investment sectors and improving the efficiency of public investment projects. In addition, the government announced a plan for bank restructuring known as Decision 254 with the focus on restructuring commercial banks and financial organizations. The restructuring program that attracted most interest of the public was restructuring of SOEs.

KEY ISSUES

Speeding up Globalization and Trade Liberalization

Experiencing a sharp decrease in foreign aid during the 1997 Asian financial crisis, the CPV moved to remedy the situation by accelerating the process of international integration. CPV leaders accepted that Vietnam needed to ensure access to leading markets in the region and world. WTO membership was vital to the government's international efforts to improve Vietnam's market access. After 11 years of negotiation, Vietnam officially became a member of WTO in 2006, marking the completion of the long process of integration of Vietnam into the global economy. Despite increased risks and challenges of competing in the domestic and international markets, membership in WTO was expected to generate significant benefits for Vietnam including: access to commodity and service markets in all member countries with deducted import tax and without any discrimination; improvement of the domestic business environment; promotion of synchronous and effective domestic reforms; and effective performance of foreign policy.

As an effective approach to integrating Vietnam into the global economy and speeding up domestic reforms, the government began to develop economic ties and sign bilateral and multilateral FTAs with many countries and groups of countries including the Eurasian Economic Union (EEU), the EU and the Trans-Pacific Partnership (TPP). Vietnam was the first ASEAN country to sign an FTA with the EEU (2015). In the same year, Korean President Lee Myung Bak and Vietnamese President Nguyen Minh Triet also signed a bilateral agreement to upgrade their countries' relationship to a strategic cooperative partnership. This agreement involved establishing a dialogue between their defense and foreign ministries to forge cooperative security and political ties. Other agreements included efforts to double bilateral trade to US$20 billion by 2015 and a joint study on the feasibility of a bilateral free trade agreement (*The Saigon Times* 2009). Vietnam also took part in the establishment of the ASEAN Economic Community (AEC) in 2015, which is expected to expand its opportunities for integration with regional and global economies. As of May 2017, Vietnam was engaged in 16 bilateral and multilateral agreements within or outside the region, which have boosted its international economic integration.

Offering many opportunities for international trade and investment, these bilateral and multilateral agreements were undertaken to create competitive advantage for Vietnam's export-oriented manufacturing industries. FTAs could remove export regulations by lowering trade barriers. FTAs also had positive impacts on FDI flows into Vietnam by enhancing the country's attractiveness to investors (Nguyen and Cao 2016).

To create an even more favorable environment for foreign investors, in November 2014, the National Assembly of Vietnam passed amended versions of the Law on Investment and the Law on Enterprises, replacing the 2005 versions of each law. The new laws eliminated obstacles to foreign investment including strict licensing requirements and other restrictions, and authorized foreign ownership of Vietnamese firms up to 100 percent.

Economic Growth and the Expansion of Industrial Zones (IZs)

With an understanding of the risk of population ageing and the increased threat of automation to low-skill manufacturing jobs, the CPV, in its SEDS, set a new growth model based on labor productivity, competitiveness and quality. The government set a target of boosting labor productivity growth by more than 50 percent to maintain the country's rapid rate of GDP growth. For this, the government planned to increase investment in education and training, and shift employment from agriculture to manufacturing. The role of the private sector was emphasized while the role of the state was to be reduced. The government set a target to increase the share of the domestic private sector in GDP to 48-49 percent by 2020.

With a focus on quality growth, the government also set itself a target that TFP should contribute 30-35 percent of GDP growth by 2020. The goal was to move toward more value-added, more high-tech and innovative manufacturing with lower impacts on the natural environment. To achieve all these objectives, it was important to secure the benefits of global economic integration, which remained as the core of the government's economic agenda, as indicated by ever more FTAs.

The Vietnamese government also implemented a policy to benefit foreign investors in order to strengthen Industrial Zone-led development. With global manufacturing companies setting up production centers in IZs, Vietnam emerged as a hub for manufacturing. Vietnam's exports greatly increased, especially in textiles, garments and footwear exports to the US. The ready availability of cheap labor and openness to FDI were significant contributing factors.

SOE Reform and Privatization

The weakness of the large SOE sector was regarded as the reason behind the inefficiency of the whole economy. Despite their monopoly power, SOEs accounted for only 19 percent of GDP growth and 8 percent of growth in the industrial sector (Pincus, Vu, Pham, Wilkinson and Nguyen 2012).

This inefficiency was influenced by their lack of engagement in exports and failure to develop technological capabilities in new industries (Pincus et al. 2012). Bad debt owned by SOEs posed a challenge to the banking system. Although there are no official statistics, estimates show that 70 percent of bad debt of Vietnam's commercial banks in 2012 was SOE debt (Vietnam Economic Portal 2014). Public attitudes toward SOEs were also negative in Vietnam. In a World Bank survey (2011), an overwhelming majority (69 percent) preferred private ownership as the dominant ownership structure for the enterprise sector, while only 13 percent preferred SOEs, and the rest (19 percent) were indifferent.

The Vietnam government was determined to restructure the SOE sector not only due to state budget deficit pressure but also due to an increasing demand for economic liberalization and transparency as conditions of WTO membership. SOE reform emerged as an inevitable task for the government and one that entailed a long process. The equitization that commenced in the early 1990s was the first and the most important driver of government's SOE reform. Reducing number of SOEs and institutional reform of the remaining SOEs were necessary to increase the efficiency of the SOEs and improving their business operations.

More recently, in 2016, Prime Minister Phuc approved a plan on restructuring SOEs in the 2016-2020 period and issued a list of SOEs to be privatized during that time. Under this plan the government will equitize 137 SOEs and continue to hold a 100 percent stake in 103 SOEs, excluding defense and military enterprises, the State Capital Investment Corporation and the Vietnam Asset Management Company. The plan aims to promote divestment from non-core businesses and increase the SOEs' financial as well as management capacity. It also includes ways to deal with the ineffective operations of SOEs and loss-making projects, particularly 12 projects managed by the Ministry of Industry and Trade (*Vietnamnet* 2017c).

ECONOMIC OUTCOMES

Growth Outcomes

With its WTO accession in 2006 that boosted the confidence of investors, Vietnam experienced a rapid inflow of foreign investment in the following year. The economy grew rapidly reaching a GDP growth rate of 8.48 percent in the fourth quarter of 2007 and the per capita income increased more than six-fold (from 180 US$ in early 1990s to nearly 1,200 US$ in 2010) (Communist Party of Vietnam 2011; Trading Economics 2017). However, the economy soon became overheated and inflation rates soared, averaging 12.63 percent in 2007 (Nguyen and Pham 2011). Too much capital, particularly from foreign investment, collided with bottlenecks in Vietnamese infrastructure and capacity. The education system was not yet producing enough skilled and semi-skilled workers. Many business corporations revealed lack of efficiency and caused losses for the economy.

The 2007-2008 global financial crisis had a significant impact on Vietnam's economic growth and exports. The economic growth rate fell from 8.6 percent in 2007 to 6.2 percent in 2008 while the trade gap continued to widen (Nguyen and Pham 2011). Driven in part by rapid price rises in food, transportation, housing and construction materials, the inflation rate escalated to 28.3 percent in August 2008 (Nguyen and Pham 2011). The fiscal stimulus policy in 2008 failed to maintain macroeconomic stability (Pham V 2011). In addition, the shift in Vietnam's status to a middle-income country in 2008 resulted in a decline in the amount of foreign aid. People also lost confidence in the government to manage the economy. Rumors of price rises led to panic spending on fuel and rice and widespread discontent among workers. Finding it difficult to sustain their urban lifestyle under a factory wage, many manufacturing workers joined a growing wave of strikes and protests across Vietnam and/or returned to their homes in the countryside.

Although quicker than other Asian countries, Vietnam's recovery from the global economic crisis generated uneven results. Many of the targets of the 2006–2010 plan were successfully achieved. The goal set in the 2006-2010 SEDP to achieve lower-middle-income economy was achieved earlier than planned in 2008, which increased Vietnam's access to commercial finance. Industrial production reached an all-time high of 28.40 percent of GDP in January 2010 even though its growth slumped to 7.6 percent in 2009 (Trading Economics 2017; World Bank 2010). The rural economy and farmers' lives also improved. The shift towards greater productivity, through investment in rural infrastructure and the construction of industrial complexes and trading villages, positively affected production and employment levels, hunger eradication and poverty reduction. In addition, significant improvements were made in education, science and technology and cultural spheres, and the protection of natural resources and the environment (IMF 2006).

However, some of the key targets of the 2006–2010 plan were not successfully achieved, thus restraining Vietnam's long-term growth (Phan 2014). The average GDP growth rate (6.3 percent) was lower than the target (7.5 percent) while the average inflation rate (>20 percent) was higher than the expected level (<10 percent) (Phan 2014). With the structure of Vietnam's exports based on raw and simply-processed products, foreign trade — both exports and imports — severely declined, leading to a serious contraction of economic growth. Worsened by a weak currency, debt problems with SOEs, and rising budget deficits and trade deficits, the economic situation worsened in 2010-2011 (Stratfor 2011). The low quality of labor and productivity levels relative to the potential opportunities and development requirements of the country substantially restricted sustainable economic development. Economic development in Vietnam did not seem sustainable. Owing to these constraints, Vietnam's economy faced the onset of severe macroeconomic instability by the end of 2010 (Nguyen D 2011; OECD 2013).

The introduction of austerity measures in 2011 instigated a sharp slowdown in credit and investment growth, which allowed a clampdown on macro imbalances (Peltier 2013). With the achievement of disinflation, current account surpluses, slowly rising foreign reserves and exchange rate stability, the economy stabilized and continued to strengthen in the 2010s. (Peltier 2013). With a robust recovery in economic growth following a painful adjustment period, Vietnam posted a GDP growth rate of 6.68 percent in 2015, the highest rate since 2010 (*Tuoi Tre News* 2016). There was a dramatic reduction in poverty, and social outcomes improved significantly. The proportion of the population living below the national poverty line reached 13.5 percent in 2014, down from 21 percent in 2010 and 60 percent in 1993 (World Bank 2017c). Children were receiving a better education and the population were enjoying higher life expectancy. Access to basic infrastructure such as electricity and clean water had also improved substantially (World Bank 2017c).

Rapid Expansion of Trade

The shift in the government's attitude towards integration into the world economy, manifested in its WTO accession, facilitated openness towards nations other than traditional partners and boosted trade (Figure 7-1).

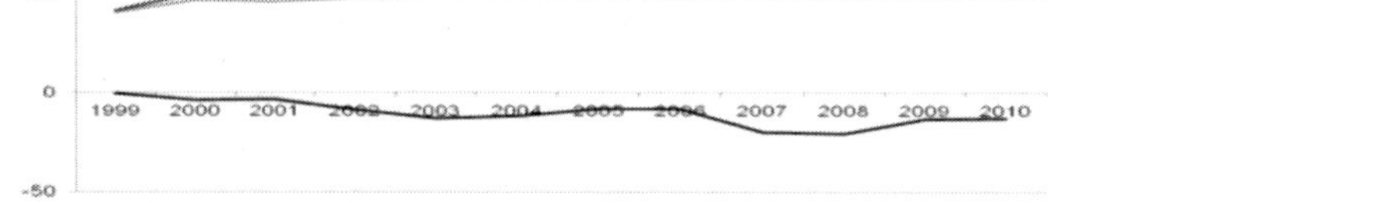

Source: Nguyen, Dinh, Pham & Pham 2012.

Figure 7-1. Vietnam: Openness and Net Export (1999-2010).

But, global integration also posed many difficulties and challenges for Vietnam. For example, lowered import tariffs (from the pre-accession average rate of 17.4 percent to a final upper rate of 13.4 percent) and the dismantling of non-tariff barriers to trade meant greater competition from foreign firms (Cheong, Pham and Nguyen 2011). The lack of decisiveness and timeliness in reforming the domestic structure of the economy and the fact that SOEs were under no pressure to change, led to the result that Vietnam faced considerable difficulties in improving its position in international commerce, making good use of FDI as well as joining the global manufacturing chain. The weakness of supportive industries made export in Vietnam only concentrate on simply processed or low- and average-tech goods. As can be clearly seen by analyzing revealed comparative advantage (RCA), while many competing countries were transforming production to higher value-added goods and establishing footholds in global manufacturing chains, Vietnam was still focused on exporting goods with high labor intensity and low added value. Analyses of the effects of integration and RCA all pointed to the necessity of moving up to higher levels in the global value chain giving greater value added to products and improved labor efficiency. According to the WTO, there was no improvement in the export structure of Vietnam in terms of its products after joining the WTO. Meanwhile, Indonesia and Malaysia were now competing against Vietnam in some commodity groups that Vietnam previously held an advantage. Singapore, Philippines and Thailand kept their competitive advantages in manufacturing.

The 2008 global financial crisis adversely affected the market for Vietnam's exports and led the economy to experience a drastic decline in export turnover. Due to Vietnam's dependency on processing-based exports, imports correspondingly decreased, particularly at the beginning of 2008. The fall in imports was also caused by a fall of domestic demand for consumption and industrial goods. With fiscal policy tightened after the global financial crisis, many companies found it difficult to borrow from banks and to increase or maintain their production. Recovery of exports depended heavily on the recovery of the world economy, particularly recovery in major trading partners in the region such as China and Korea, who were also negatively impacted by the global financial crisis (Nguyen and Pham 2011).

FDI-Led Growth and Industrial Zones

Thanks to increasing FDI flows into Vietnam, the number of IZs in Vietnam continued to rise. By July 2015, 299 IZs were established across the country, with 212 zones in operation as of 2017 (Chau 2016). The northern province of Bac Ninh, although the smallest province in Vietnam with a total area of only 822.7 km^2, has been one of the leading provinces in attracting FDI. In the 2011-15 period, Bac Ninh attracted more than US$12.1 billion in investment, of which FDI accounted for $10.7 billion (*Viet Nam News* 2016b). In 2015, Bac Ninh led the nation in investment attraction with global economic giants including PepsiCo, Samsung, Canon, ABB and Microsoft among those contributing to the US$ 3.7 billion FDI in the province ("Bac Ninh attracts foreign investors" 2016). Since establishing a new handset factory in 2009 in Yen Phony Industrial Park in Bac Ninh province, Samsung (Korea) increased its investment in Bac Ninh province at a very rapid rate. In 2010, Samsung and other Korean companies jointly invested in 32 industrial projects at a total registered capital of US$916.3 million, ranking first in investment capital and in the number of FDI projects in Bac Ninh province. Korean companies had more than 400 projects, accounting for about 50 percent of total FDI capital for Bac Ninh province. They included large companies such as Samsung, Orion, Daewoo, Flexcom, Intops, Nano Tech (Ngoc 2016). Samsung in particular set up a major production base in Vietnam and became Vietnam's largest exporter accounting for about 20 percent of the nation's total export turnover (Nguyen D 2017).

The establishment of IZs in Vietnam contributed to making both new urban areas and new rural opportunities in the provinces. This helped to create good infrastructure, employment, and shifts of economic and labor structures from agriculture to industry and services. The IZs made important and practical contributions to socio-economic development in their specific local areas as well as in the country as a whole. However, critics argue that the performance of the IZs has still not reached full potential due to: lack of cohesion between enterprises in the IZs in manufacturing and processing industries; the failure to form production clusters offering scale economies and close linkages; and too few production and processing bases in the IZs. Therefore, it is necessary to develop IZs into key processing and manufacturing areas with strong linkages in production among secondary enterprises in the IZs, and to improve operational efficiency (Nguyen et al. 2017).

FDI flows into Vietnam have continued to grow, confirming the country's position as the third most attractive country in terms of FDI in Asia, just behind China and India. According to the World Bank, this growth will continue (Santander Trade Portal 2017). In 2016, Vietnam granted new licenses to 2,556 FDI projects worth US$ 15.182 billion up 9 percent in value and 27 percent in volume from the previous year (*The Business Times* 2016). The quality of FDI in Vietnam is also improving. Vietnam has attracted large-scale technology, industrial and human resources projects. The largest investors have been Korea, Malaysia and the United Kingdom, and the manufacturing sector has attracted the most FDI. Korean investors pledged the most funds in 2016, including US$ 1.5 billion for LG Display's OLED screens plant and Innotek's US$ 550 million camera plant ("Vietnam's 2016 FDI inflow" 2016).

This influx of foreign investment has led the economy of Vietnam to be heavily dependent on FDI; it accounted for 71 percent of total export turnover and 59 percent of total import turnover in 2015 (Gunnion 2016). But domestic firms often lack linkages and know-how and have faced increased market pressure for their products. Export industries also import large amounts of products for assembly. Critics argued that foreign industrial enterprises (FIEs) in Vietnam have contributed a great deal to trade deficit as compared to those in China that generated a trade surplus because they focused on exporting high value-added products (Pham S 2011). There were also pressures in Vietnam to consolidate the legal framework for the economy to ensure they comply with international standards.

Vietnam also became one of the favored destinations for mergers and acquisitions (M&A) for foreign investors, particularly from Japan, Korea and Singapore. The number of reported M&A deals in 2015 was 40 percent higher than in 2014 with total value of US$ 4.3 billion, and higher than 2012 when the value reached a record high of US$ 4.2 billion (*Vietnamnet* 2017d).

Analysts commented that foreign companies were attracted by the predicted GDP growth rate of 6.7 percent in 2016, a nine-year high, and by the country's large market with 60 percent of the population aged under 35 years ("Vietnam may see record number" 2017). Key sectors of interest have included real estate, food and beverage, retail, and to a lesser extent, manufacturing. However, the Vietnamese government has not yet consolidated the laws governing M&A to streamline capital flow from foreign countries while counterbalancing the protection of local business, as it planned. Vietnam's local enterprises have not yet developed a win-win mentality when approaching M&A. As a consequence, many M&A negotiations took too long and closing deals could be difficult to achieve (Le 2014).

Slow Progress in SOE Reform as a Key Burden for Economic Development

Despite the transition to a market economy, SOEs continued to play a leading role in the Vietnamese economy (Figure 7-2). Although the share of SOEs declined to 24 percent of GDP after WTO accession in 2006, SOEs still controlled 70 percent of fixed assets and 45 percent of new investments (Lakatos 2015). In 2007, Vietnam adopted a strategy to exploit economies of scale in production and technology by transforming large SOEs into 19 State Economic Groups (SEGs), taking large conglomerates — particularly Korean chaebols — as role models (Pincus et al. 2012). SEGs were given monopoly status in many heavy industries thus protecting them from foreign competition. Whilst some SEGs (e.g., VNPT, EVN, Petro Vietnam) played an important role in achieving economies of scale, many contributed to economic instability, especially after the 1997 Asian financial crisis.

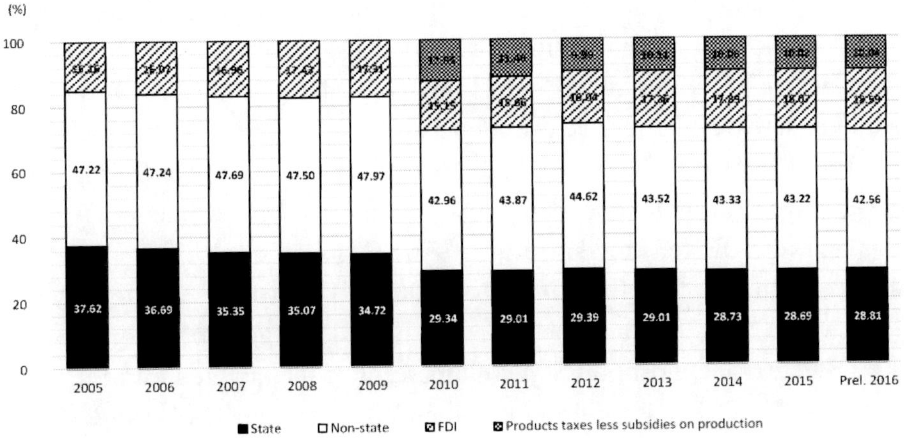

Figure 7-2. Share in GDP at current prices by types of ownership (2005-2016).

Prompted by the government's desire to boost the economy after the global economic crisis, state-owned banks readily handed out loans to SEGs. Being encouraged by the government to expand their business areas, many SEGs invested the money in unrelated sectors including banking and real estate. Investment activities of SEGs in the financial and real estate sector aggravated asset price bubbles in the late 2000s, with some even speculating against the Vietnam Dong in late 2009 and early 2010. Many SEGs were unable to repay their loans and required rescuing. For example, the Vietnam national shipbuilding conglomerate known as Vinashin, following its executives' poor investment decisions, collapsed in 2010 under more than US$4 billion in debts — Vietnam's biggest state-owned company failure (*Reuters* 2012). Incurring major losses, SOEs share of national employment dropped by 22 percent between 2006 and 2010 (Pincus et al. 2012).

The weakness of the SOE system contributed to decreased efficiency of the whole economy on top of the instability from the beginning of the 2000s. Economic growth in Vietnam changed the economic structure. Agriculture's share in GDP decreased from 16 percent (1995) to 17 percent (2008), industry's share increased from 30 percent (1995) to 42 percent (2008) while services' share decreased from 40 percent (1995) to only 38 percent (2008) (Pham 2010). Labor and capital productivity were lower in the service sector than in the industry sector. One possible reason was that SOEs still accounted for a considerable amount of activity in the service sector (Pham 2010). Thus, the problem facing the Vietnamese government involved how to re-design the roles of different types of enterprise to achieve a more modern, active and effective economic structure.

In an effort to democratize economic life and encourage the development of non-state economic sectors, the government has been engaged in SOE reforms since the 1990s (Nguyen et al. 2012). Through these reform attempts, the number of SOEs fell from 12,000 enterprises in 1990 to 6,000 in 2006 and then to 3,199 by 2013 (Nguyen 2016). Between 2011 and 2015, almost 600 SOEs, 96 percent of the targeted number, were equitized (Do 2017). In addition, due to increasing numbers of joint ventures between FIEs and SOEs since the 2005 Investment Law, the FDI sector surpassed the state-owned sector within a decade, contributing the most to Vietnam's industrial growth (Vu 2015). The SOE sector was a different story. Aside from wastefulness and corruption in public investment, there was ineffective and inefficient investment undertaken by business groups and corporations in the state-owned sector. As of 2014, SOEs contributed less than a third to Vietnam's GDP, but accounted for nearly half of public investment and 60 percent of bank lending (Nguyen 2015).

Vietnam's SOE reform effort has had a number of limitations. First, restructuring SOEs was not put in the context of the overall economic reform program. Therefore, resources were not redistributed to the private sector. Second, there was not yet a controlling organization that had enough political power to maintain the restructuring process. Third, in the new Law on Enterprises passed in 2014, SOEs included enterprises in which the state holds 100 percent of the equity but it excluded numerous other enterprises partially owned by the state thus obscuring the true number of SOEs in Vietnam (Bureau of Economic and Business Affairs 2016).

To reduce the role of SOEs and expand the private sector, the new leadership in the CPV announced their plan to accelerate the equitization and divestment of SOEs through a series of liberalization reforms, including the lifting of restrictions on foreign investment and the negotiation of FTAs ("South Korea becomes" 2017). With the ascendancy of a more conservative party leadership, however, progress in the planned privatization of SOEs is anticipated to remain slow (Wagner 2016).

Social and Political Outcomes

Growing Demand for More Equitable Economic Growth

With labor relations strictly regulated since *Doi Moi,* restructuring of the unions lagged behind the development of the market economy (Beresford and Nyland 1998). Rising inflation and social hardships, however, led to a spate of strikes for higher pay and better working conditions in the garment, footwear, toy and electronic industries. In 2008, for instance, nearly 7,000 workers at a Taiwanese-owned shoe company in northern Vietnam declared a strike, demanding an increase to their monthly wage of US$50 and a reduction of long working hours. Most were required to work 13-hour shifts. The firm made shoes for Nike and exported them to countries in Europe and Asia (Divjak 2008). The number of strikes started to rise sharply between 2005 and 2006 and reached a record 857 in 2011, with a total of 4,142 strikes over the period from 1995 to 2011 (Nguyen T 2017).

The alarming number of labor conflicts and economic difficulties tested the management ability of the CPV government and raised a question about the model of "big government" of the party. In the context of continued integration into the world economy, the direct intervention of the government was likely to have an attenuated effect due to asymmetric information (or information failure). While Vietnam has made progress in improving macroeconomic fundamentals, more time is needed to complete the agenda of economic modernization and structural transformation in the future. Freedom of expression, freedom of religion freedom, and civil society activism are still highly restricted and the use of social media and the internet by citizens to transmit uncensored information and organize dissenting voices is increasingly repressed (Freedom House 2017).

The Rise of Pro-Democracy Movement

During this period (2006-2016), pro-democracy activists and groups at the grassroots level began to form numerous explicitly political organizations (self-described as political parties) dedicated to the promotion of democracy, human rights and religious freedom. In 2006, three out of four (74 percent) people were involved in at least one such organization in Vietnam (Larsen 2011).

In 2006, a group of activists representing diverse professionals formed a nationwide political network, later known as Bloc 8406. They began to issue political statements (e.g., a Manifesto on Freedom and Democracy for Vietnam) and distribute them widely throughout the country via the Internet. As Hanoi was set to be the focus of global attention due to the 2006 APEC summit, the Vietnamese police began to act against Bloc 8406 to nip any planned political rallies in the bud. This effectively stopped Bloc 8406's activities during the summit, but later provoked continuous public protests and led to the expansion of political organizations in number and size. There were also overseas activists who formed a political network to promote democracy in Vietnam, including the Vietnam Reform Party (also known as Viet Tan). In the same year, Block 8406 released A Manifesto on Freedom and Democracy for Vietnam calling for democratic reforms, signed by 118 dissidents who advocated for a multi-party state. The support later expanded to include thousands of citizens even though signing such documents triggered a police investigation, detention and often imprisonment (Freedom House 2010). Peaceful dissidents and government critics were subjected to censorship, arrest, and detention.

In 2013, a petition signed by 72 intellectuals and politicians under the leadership of former Justice Minister Nguyễn Đình Lộc gained international attention. One of the central demands of this so-called "Petition 72" was the revision of Article 4 of the constitution, which stipulates the guarantee of the leadership of the CPV. They demanded a multi-party system, calling for the provision of human rights in accordance with the United Nations' Universal Declaration of Human Rights.

In response to these political movements, the CPV adopted a dual approach to preserve its ability and right to govern. While repressing prominent pro-democracy activists, the party also appeared more tolerant of moderate criticisms, and undertook limited political reforms to calm critics and to address problems that the party itself considered detrimental to its legitimacy. Experimental political reforms, however, were limited to local levels. In 2010, for example, the local party congress in Danang, Vietnam's third-biggest city, directly elected the municipal party chief for the first time, possibly paving the way for more accountability among the leadership. Critics, however, argued that such change was only cosmetic and did not mean the party intended to give up its monopoly on power, as enshrined in the constitution (Ruwitch 2010). In Vietnam, the Communist party has been in power since 1975 and most people still have no direct say in how their leaders are elected. Party leaders believe that one-party rule is best for Vietnam (Associated Press in Hanoi 2016). However, there is growing belief that, to continue its fast growth and economic development, Vietnam is required to build a political system that is suitable for the market economy (Vietnam Investor Network 2015).

Taking Steps towards Transparent Government

Vietnam's Anti-Corruption Law introduced in 2005 was not extensive in its scope nor sufficiently enforced to deal with complex issues and widespread incidence of corruption. There was still no law regarding access to information or the acceptance of gifts, hospitality and other benefits by government and public officials. The Anti-Corruption Law was revised in 2007, criminalizing several types of corruption in the public sector and setting out rules on asset disclosure for politicians and civil servants. It also offered protection for whistleblowers and stipulated the development of rules and regulations specific to each ministry, sector and locality. The aim was to encourage public participation in anti-corruption activities. The Law on Procurement and several other directives were also amended. However, the new legislation was too complex and incoherent for both public officials and businesses to understand and implement. In addition, most of the decrees and decisions either were not translated into English or were translated by different bodies, creating confusion for foreign investors and businesses (Martini 2012).

In order to increase the effectiveness of the law, in May 2009, the government adopted the National Strategy on Anti-Corruption toward 2020 and its accompanying Action Plan. This represented a major step forward, as it explicitly recognized the role of openness and transparency in reducing corruption. More importantly, the government established compulsory corruption training at all educational levels in order to raise corruption awareness. In the same year, Vietnam ratified the UN Convention Against Corruption, confirming its commitment to international cooperation in the prevention and combatting of corruption. Under the National Strategy on Anti-Corruption, in November 2011, the government approved the Denunciation Law which increased whistleblower protection when exposing wrongdoings. The Central Steering Committee for Anti-Corruption was expanded and reorganized into a new anti-corruption body in 2013 known as the CPV Central Commission of Internal Affairs.

However, Vietnam's anti-corruption efforts are still considered to be localized and not sufficient to address the root causes, which include a lack of transparency, accountability, and media freedom, as well as low pay for government officials and inadequate systems for holding officials accountable for their actions (Bureau of Economic and Business Affairs 2013). In response to both inside and outside concerns, Vietnam's government has strengthened its anti-corruption capacity in recent years by enhancing the anti-corruption legislation and its enforcement. The 10-year implementation of the Anti-Corruption Law was reviewed for a comprehensive revision of the law. With the first draft of Vietnam's revised anti-corruption law published in June 2016, the government collected opinions from ministries and sectors to modify the draft. This revised law is expected to promote transparency and responsibility of heads of anti-corruption agencies. In addition, in May 2017, eight inspection teams were established to inspect and supervise the process of probing, prosecuting, investigating and judging high-profile corruption and economic crime cases related to the standing boards of 20 provincial party committees. They are expected to reduce government inefficiency and waste during the process.

CONCLUSION

This chapter has examined how the CPV in Vietnam has continually developed the socialist-oriented market economy and further integrate it into the international economy since WTO accession in 2006. With successful economic transition and international economic integration, Vietnam made rapid economic growth up until the global economic crisis in 2008, with an average annual GDP growth rate reaching an all-time high of 8.48 percent in late 2007. Given the government's focus on sustainable growth, most sectors and areas of the economy (including agriculture) achieved satisfactory results, leading to Vietnam's attainment of lower middle-income status in 2008. After two decades since the *Doi Moi* reforms, however, the Vietnamese economy started to reveal weaknesses, ranging from the small-scale of many business operations and low efficiency to persistent corruption in SOEs. Rapid economic growth within a short period of time, in addition, resulted in significant increases in income inequality and widening socio-economic gap between citizens. In this context, WTO accession in 2006 accelerated Vietnam's integration into the world economy and facilitated expanding trade and openness, but at the same time brought serious challenges resulting from increasing foreign influence and competition. With spillover effects of the 2007-2008 global financial crisis, Vietnam faced severe macroeconomic instability accompanied by high inflation, a big trade deficit and complicated financial and monetary markets between the late 2000s and the early 2010s.

Facing the worsening global financial turmoil and economic slowdown, the new leadership in the CPV adopted a flexible response. The 2010-2020 SEDS and 2011-2015 SEDP brought a marked change in Vietnam's development orientation, with its focus shifting from rapid growth towards the quality of growth. For this, the CPV committed to (i) the globalization and trade liberalization of the Vietnam economy, (ii) shifting the growth engine toward more value-added, more high-tech and innovative manufacturing, with the focus on the development of IZs, and (iii) SOE reform and privatization. As a result, the CPV expanded economic ties and signed bilateral and multilateral free trade agreements with various countries and groups of countries during the 2000s. Policies to benefit foreign investors were implemented which strengthened the IZ-led development. With rapid expansion of foreign investment and trade, Vietnam made rapid economic growth during this period, with 7 percent annual GDP growth between 2006-2010 and 5.91 percent between 2010 and 2015 (Dao 2016).

Leading the process of building a socialist developmental state, the CPV was actively involved in all aspects of economic reform and took full ownership of Vietnam's economic growth and development, which granted them decades of legitimacy and popularity. The expansion of the market economy and international economic integration, however, called for flexibility and a change in the role of government in the economy. SOEs, the significant economic organizations of the communist system, became a crucial obstacle to Vietnam's economic development for their ineffectiveness, monopoly power, huge debt and corruption. Considering their prolonged negative impact on the economy, SOE reform has been an inevitable and urgent task for the country. The 2011-2015 SEDP proposed structural reforms within SOEs, the banking system and public investment. Government reform efforts concentrated on restructuring of SOEs. Despite the transition to a market economy, SOEs continued to play a leading role in the Vietnamese economy despite the ineffectiveness and poor performance of many. With reform, the number of SOEs was reduced and their efficiency increased, although the restructuring of SOEs took time and was slow-paced.

In contrast to its significant role in the economic reforms, the CPV has not been successful in making necessary political reforms, with civil and political rights remaining strictly controlled. A large number of labor conflicts and the growth of a pro-democracy movement posed challenges for the CPV. Aspiring to its fast growth and economic development, the CPV government is now confronted with myriad political, economic and institutional challenges.

Chapter 7

CONCLUSION

THE ROLE OF GOVERNMENT IN ECONOMIC DEVELOPMENT IN KOREA AND VIETNAM: AN OVERVIEW

This book has mapped the highly successful paths to economic development in Korea and Vietnam over the past several decades and what role the government of each country has played in engineering such positive outcomes. As a representative example of the East Asian model, Korea achieved sustained and rapid economic growth from the 1960s. The journey started under a strong authoritarian government that focused on economic development directed by the state. The orientation was to export-led industrialization and comprehensive short- to medium-term economic development policies. During the export-driven industrialization period under President Park Jung-hee (1962-1979), the Korean government extended state control over limited resources and invested heavily in selected strategic industries. In order to expand the nation's economy, the Park government also began to support selected export businesses which grew into the debt-based and volume-oriented large conglomerates known as *chaebols*.

While this authoritarian development model was highly successful in terms of economic growth it also led to increasing economic and social inequalities and the suppression of civil and political rights and freedoms, and faced widespread public resistance from the late 1980s onwards. The model, while successful, was not sustainable as the country became affected by the trend towards global economic integration and neoliberalism in the 1990s. Since then, Korea has transformed from an authoritarian developmental state to a more inclusive and democratic state. The role of the government in economic development began to manifest itself in more diverse and complex forms, such as the developmental welfare state or the neoliberal state supporting developmentalist policies, the particular ideological mix depending on the strength and ideological commitment of the democratically elected government. The characteristics of policy interventions fluctuated in response to complex and complicated political and economic issues confronting each government, leading to a multiplicity of policies and strategies often co-existing uneasily.

From the end of the Vietnam War in 1975 until 1985, the communist government of re-unified Vietnam was committed to the construction of a socialist state. The economic system was based on the Soviet central planning model. This entailed transforming the capitalist system of South Vietnam into a socialist one. However, the Soviet-style collectivist command economy, combined with the lack of government capacity, led Vietnam to suffer a period of economic crisis, poverty and hunger. Nearing the end of the Cold War in the mid-1980s, the old socialist economic system was no longer able to offer a solution to poverty. Under the banner of a "socialist market economy," the new government formally abandoned central planning and adopted a multi-sectoral economy in which market-oriented private firms co-existed with state-owned companies to facilitate economic growth and development through competition. In the early years of these so-called *Doi Moi* reforms, however, the government lacked the capacity to effectively manage the reforms, causing considerable confusion in Vietnam and often disappointing results. The government then implemented strong developmentalist short- and long-term economic reforms with the focus on export-led economic growth, the control and allocation of foreign investment to support selected strategic industries, and the growth of SOEs as a main driver of economic development. This approach led to rapid growth of the economy during the 1990s. In the late 2000s, Vietnam, with increased involvement in the global economy enjoyed rapid further economic expansion. As labor-intensive industries that had led rapid growth stagnated with decreased competitiveness, the government sought new initiatives to maximize its role in macroeconomic management, and become a capable and developmental state. The government could no longer micro-manage the economy, but laid down the fundamental laws and regulations governing economic activity. Within these broad parameters, it was increasingly required to be flexible in order to cope with the rapidly changing global economic environment.

In this book, Korea's economic development in the past four decades has been divided into three distinct stages as presented in the table below (Table 8-1).

The first stage (1962-1979) of Korea's economic development began with the emergence of the authoritarian developmental state under Park Jung-hee, a military general, who seized power via military coup in 1961 and assumed dictatorial powers for 18 years. Out of the ruins of the Korean War, Park committed himself to developing the national economy. The ultimate goal of economic growth provided legitimacy for Park's dictatorship to exercise full control over Korean citizens and their political rights (Kim and Vogel 2011:380; Moon 2009:26). Based on massive foreign economic assistance, especially from the US, and an educated, cheap workforce, the Park government instituted central economic planning and government intervention in the market through four of the state-led Five-Year Economic Development Plans (FYEDPs). As the command center for economic development, the Park government initiated export-oriented industrialization with the focus on the expansion of the manufacturing sector during the 1960s and the heavy and chemical industries during the 1970s. The authoritarian developmental state during this period was very effective in achieving the goal of economic development, recording average GDP growth rates exceeding 9 percent per year between 1962 and 1979 (Yau 2009:158). This achievement, however, came at the expense of civil rights and democracy. Park's state-led development strategy also produced negative impacts on the economy, including debt-based and volume-oriented expansion of *chaebols* and structural imbalance in the Korean economy, which began to reduce Korea's export competitiveness and increase income inequality. In this context, the major oil crisis in 1979 resulted in the Korean economy suffering greatly. With the sudden death of Park in the late 1979, Korea experienced enormous social and political turmoil as well (KDI 2017).

Table 8-1. A brief history of Korea's economic development

Periods	Characteristics	Governments	Key economic policy issues
Period 1	The authoritarian developmental state and rapid industrialization (1962-1979)	• Park-Jung-hee (1961-1979)	• Five-Year Economic Development Plans (FYEDPs) • Government-led industrialization • Export-oriented industrialization • Big Push into the heavy and chemical industries • Partnership with large private businesses *(chaebols)*
Period 2	The adaptive developmental state and challenges of economic liberalism (1980-1997)	• Choi Kyu-hah (1979-1980) • Chun Doo-hwan (1981-1988) • Roh Tae-woo (1988-1993) • Kim Young-sam (1993-1998)	• Continuation of FYEDPs • Structural reforms for an advanced industrialized economy • Economic stabilization program • Policies of economic liberalization and globalization (WTO accession in 1995)
Period 3	The capable state and globalization of the economy (1998-2016)	• Kim Dae-jung (1998-2003) • Roh Moo-hyun (2003-2008) • Lee Myung-bak (2008-2013) • Park Geun-hye (2013-2017)	• State-led neoliberal restructuring • Search for new growth engines • Expansion of welfare policies • Reinforcing neoliberalism through FTAs

Amid the domestic economic, social, and political turmoil, the second stage of government- of economic development (1980-1997) began with another military coup led by army generals, Chun Doo-whan and Roh-Tae-woo, both of whom became presidents. During their presidencies, pro-democracy protests against prolonged authoritarian military rule erupted throughout the country, resulting in the re-establishment of the general presidential election system in 1987 and then the rise of a less authoritarian developmental state. This stage was further complicated by changes in the international environment, including the end of the Cold War, the emergence of neoliberalism and the international energy crises followed by high levels of inflation. In response to these complicated domestic and international environments, the Korean government during the 1980s emphasized stability as the top priority of their economic policy. Various measures were put in place to control inflation and rectify prolonged structural imbalances in the economy such as the overinvestment in the heavy-chemical industrial sector during the Park government. Despite political instability and an increasingly active labor movement, the Korean economy grew rapidly, owing to the continuation of government-led development plans and the favorable international environment (including the "three lows" economic boom between 1986 and 1988). Achieving an average GDP growth rate over 8.5 percent between 1980 and 1997 (Countryeconomy.com 2016a) and a rapid increase in trade surplus, the Korean government began to feel under pressure, especially from the US, for market liberalization. In addition, many government interventions targeting the promotion of market competition resulted instead in increased industrial concentration, leading to the further expansion of *chaebol* power. In this context, the government of Kim Young-sam, the first elected civilian president since 1962, advocated "globalization" as a new growth strategy and Korea joined the WTO in 1995 and the OECD in 1996. His government opened capital and financial markets and the rice market and loosened the political control over foreign investment which had been restricted to protect domestic businesses since the Park era. With economic structural problems lingering after the failure of structural reforms in the 1980s, however, the Korean economy plunged into the crisis upon the outbreak of the 1997 Asian financial crisis.

The third stage (1998-2016) began in the aftermath of the 1997 Asian financial crisis and involved massive economic and political liberalization and the 2008 global financial crisis, both of which posed great challenges for Korea's developmental state. When a progressive politician, Kim Dae-jung, became President in 1998, the IMF requested a series of restructuring measures for the Korean government and economy as conditions for a rescue package. With active governmental engagement in economic restructuring (including *chaebol* reforms), the Korean economy recovered from the crisis quicker than any other country, but it entered a low-growth period with an average GDP growth rate of around 4 percent between 1998 and 2016 (Countryeconomy.com 2016a), accompanied by rising social inequality and polarization. State-led neoliberal reforms, reluctantly imposed by the progressive governments of Kim Dae-jung and his successor Roh Moo-hyun, were intensified and reinforced by conservative governments under Lee Myung-bak and Park Geun-hye through extended economic liberalization reforms and deregulation. As the foreign business environment became more unfavourable and FDI declined, the Korean government began to enter into bilateral FTAs from the late 1990s onward, removing trade barriers such as tariffs and import quotas with other countries. Amid the neoliberal transition, however, the slowing rate of growth led Korean governments to still search for developmentalist opportunities. With recognition of the value and necessity of interventionist economic policies learned from the success of the previous developmental state, progressive governments supported venture companies in high-technology and knowledge industries, while conservative governments promoted massive construction projects and SMEs in new industries. Unlike those of the previous authoritarian developmental state, developmentalist approaches of this period supported the role of government as provider of welfare and as "senior partner" rather than "commander-in-chief" in the economy (Cherry 2005). With the growth of civil society that led democratic political transitions, more emphasis was given to the efficiency of government and its role in a welfare state. This enabled Korea's developmental state to transform or evolve into a capable state, expected to champion sustainable economic, social and political development.

The history of Vietnam's economic development has also been divided into three different stages as presented in the table below (Table 8-2).

The first stage (1975-1985) covers the first decade of the post-Vietnam War period, after reunification and before the introduction of *Doi Moi* in 1986. It was the era of an authoritarian socialist state. After the war, Vietnam's foreign policy focused on maintaining the traditional friendship with the Soviet Union and its allies. Strained relations with China and the US intensified Vietnam's heavy reliance on economic, technical and military aid from the Soviet Union. With the communist victory in the Vietnam War, the CPV carried out massive socialist reforms of the economy in a reunited Vietnam. Continuing with Soviet-style five-year economic development plans, the CPV government emphasized the development of heavy industry and the collectivization of agriculture. All private and public business establishments were transformed into state-owned industrial enterprises that became the largest employers and the main driver of economic growth. In the early days of building socialism, the CPV faced many challenges. With resources allocated and utilized according to the plan instead of market demand, most state-run enterprises were operated inefficiently and focused on heavy industry. The collective economy was expensive to run and failed to boost productivity by the desired amounts. With an average GDP growth rate of 3.7 percent (although this figure varies among different sources), the overall economic situation hardly changed (Phan, Nguyen and Phan 2003). In addition, the goal of social and economic integration between North and South Vietnam offered a strong motivation for the authoritarianism of the CPV and functioned as instruments of social control over the people. Corruption and abuse of power in government were also rampant at both national and local levels. Vietnam's economy soon collapsed under the weight of food shortage and galloping inflation during this period. To avoid starvation and political persecution, many Vietnamese fled the country.

Table 8-2. A brief history of Vietnam's economic development

Periods	Characteristics	Leaderships of CPV	Key economic policy issues
Period 1	The authoritarian socialist state with a centrally planned economy (1975-1985)	• Lê Duẩn (1960-1986)	• Five-Year Economic Development Plans • Unified socialist economy • Emphasis on the development of heavy industry and collectivization of agriculture • Establishing socialist SOEs
Period 2	The socialist developmental state and the transition to a socialist-oriented market economy (1986-2005)	• Trường Chinh (1986-1986) • Nguyễn Văn Linh (1986-1991) • Đỗ Mười (1991-1997) • Lê Khả Phiêu (1997-2001) • Nông Đức Mạnh (2001-2011)	• Socio-Economic Development Strategies and Plans (SEDSs and SEDPs) • Government-led institutionalization of a socialist-oriented market economy • Macroeconomic stabilization program • Export-oriented industrialization strategy • FDI and industrial zone-led development • Developing SOEs as a main driver of the economy
Period 3	The socialist capable developmental state and challenges from the integration into the global economy (2006-2016)	• Nông Đức Mạnh (2001-2011) • Nguyễn Phú Trọng (2011-Present)	• Continuation of SEDSs and SEDPs • Speeding up the country's integration into global economy (WTO accession in 2006) • Shifting growth engines and expansion of IZs for international competitiveness • Transformation of SOEs into conglomerates and SOE reform

The second stage (1986-2005) covers the first two decades of Vietnam's radical transition to a socialist-oriented market economy that began in 1986. After the complete failure of the socialist economic system, the CPV government was under increasing pressure for economic reform and launched its *Doi Moi* program, followed by radical market reform in 1989. The collapse of the Soviet Union and the communist bloc in Eastern Europe and their transition to market economies in the early 1990s strengthened government's commitment to reforms. The CPV played a leading role in the economic liberalization process and paved the way for the development of the domestic economy. The government launched a series of 10-Year SEDS and Five-Year SEDPs as the strategic guides for development, while establishing legal frameworks and economic policies for private economic activities, finance and foreign investment. The CPV changed the focus of industrial development from heavy industry to labor-intensive light industry oriented to exports, and introduced a system of Industrial Zones in 1991 to support sustainable export-led growth. Adopting an open-door policy, the CPV normalized its relations with China (1991) and the US (1995) and joined ASEAN (1995), all of which encouraged FDI inflows to Vietnam and integration into the global economy. The CPV regarded SOEs as an important tool for the state to ensure the effective implementation of macro-economic policies and achievement of economic growth. With annual GDP growth averaging 6.8 percent, macroeconomic stabilization working well and export expansion during this period, the CPV laid down solid foundations for Vietnam to continue to develop in later years. The CPV's launch of *Doi Moi* also contributed to the country's transition to a "socialist democracy," a less severe version of authoritarian rule. Following the issue of the Grassroots Democracy Decree in 1998, many civil society organizations were established to empower the people at the grassroots. However, the CPV faced challenges in the transition to a market economy. SOEs, while still dominating the industrial sector, continued operating at a loss and were prone to corruption while maintaining monopoly power. They emerged as a barrier to economic growth, thus calling for massive reforms including privatization.

The third stage (2006-2016) of economic development began with Vietnam's accession to the WTO in 2006. This formally placed the country on the path to economic globalization and liberalization. In the context of growing globalization and the emergence of other newly industrializing exporting such as China and Indonesia, Vietnam gradually lost its international competitiveness during this period. In addition, despite its positive impact on economic growth, the privatization and liberalization of *Doi Moi* resulted in significant increases in income inequality in Vietnam. With BTAs signed with WTO members and domestic political stability, the CPV successfully attracted large volumes of FDI during this period. Supported by rapidly increasing FDI flows, the CPV expanded the IZs to facilitate technology transfer, export expansion and human resource development as well as job creation and better living conditions in Vietnam. Leading the country's economic transition and integration into the international economy, the CPV continued to achieve rapid economic growth marking 6.1 percent annual real GDP growth between 2005 and 2016 (Countryeconomy.com 2016b). The global financial crisis and in 2008-2009, however, had serious spillover effects on Vietnam's export-led economy, leading to a period of high inflation, budget deficits, declining foreign exchange reserves, mismanaged fiscal and monetary policies, high unemployment and sluggish commercial activities. To be more responsive to and capable of dealing with the new economic realities, the CPV again took a leading role in changing and upgrading the country's economic structure. Government reform efforts concentrated on improve the market competitiveness of SOEs. With a sluggish reform process, however, SOEs, although reduced in number, remained a crucial obstacle to Vietnam's economic development as many were still inefficient monopolies with huge debt and riddled with corruption. Continuing economic slowdowns and rising political movements began to undermine the legitimacy of the CPV's reform efforts and slowed its progress, revealing limitations of the socialist developmental state of Vietnam. As a way to facilitate the country's integration into the global economy and speed up domestic reforms, the Vietnamese government was increasingly required to become more effective and responsive to its people who were pushing for better economic, social and political conditions.

THE ROLE OF GOVERNMENT IN ECONOMIC DEVELOPMENT IN KOREA AND VIETNAM: CONVERGENCE OR DIVERGENCE?

This book set out to determine whether the East Asian model of economic development, as exemplified by Korea, can be used to explain the economic development of Vietnam. For an answer to this, we asked two research questions: (i) whether there is convergence or divergence of economic development between Korea and Vietnam; and (ii) whether political and other environmental changes in the study countries have led to changes in the roles of their governments in their economies. To find the answers to these questions, we have examined the development trajectories of Korea and Vietnam and compared environments, government roles, economic policies and growth engines of the two countries.

Korea and Vietnam shared an important feature of the developmental state model in that both countries' governments were strongly committed to rapid growth. As in post-war Korea, the experience of hunger, poverty and economic backwardness led the communist government of a reunified Vietnam to give the highest priority to economic development by transiting from a central planning model to a market economy. Despite being geographically located in Southeast Asia and an important member of ASEAN, Vietnam manifests a development trajectory nearer to those of Northeast Asian countries rather than countries in Southeast Asia. Vietnam, unlike other Southeast Asian countries, has a culturally, ethnically and linguistically homogeneous population, with over 85 percent being ethnic Vietnamese. It is noticeable that, while other Southeast Asian countries underwent internal or interstate conflicts, Vietnam achieved political unification following the communist victory in the war. In both countries, the political legitimacy and authority of their regimes were supported by their people's collective commitment to social, political, or economic transformation and sustained by its economic achievements.

In this historical, social and cultural setting, authoritarian regimes, although not an essential feature of the developmental state model, played a leading role in economic take-off in both countries. While happening in different political systems and at different times, Vietnam's state-led industrialization occurred under the absolute leadership of the CPV, similar to Korea's authoritarian developmental state under the military leadership of the Park Jung-hee era. Both governments gave priority to their nations' economic development, which granted them the power and justification to control the political and social lives of their people, and enhance their regimes' political legitimacy.

In both countries, active state intervention was the key to economic growth and development strategies. Governments were responsible for formulating and implementing the medium- to long-term economic development plans, which functioned as the key policy interventions to direct and organize economic change. Economic policies were implemented according to the medium- to long-term economic development plans devised by governments to take the economy to its potential level of growth.

Both Korea and Vietnam selected an export-led growth strategy as a tool to achieve high economic growth. In both countries, the manufacturing industry — especially labor-intensive light manufacturing — assumed great importance as the first "take-off" industry for export expansion. Both states engaged in deliberate policies of export promotion such as the establishment of export-processing zones (Korea) or Industrial Zones (Vietnam). In addition, they both fostered and supported the development of strategic industries selected as growth engines through the government's capacity to control and allocate limited resources and finance. Investment was concentrated into key industries in each stage of economic development.

In both countries, industrial development was oriented toward a few large companies selected and supported by the government to play a leading role in generating rapid economic growth and achieving economies of scale. The Korean government openly supported selected groups of private companies with foreign loans, relaxed regulations and gave tax cuts, while the Vietnamese government, with government investment, favored and protected SOEs as the pillars of the economy although they were not a part of the developmental state model. In Korea, the favored companies grew into the mega-conglomerates known as *chaebols* via debt-based and volume-oriented expansion strategies. In Vietnam, the chosen SOEs were combined by the government into large general corporations following the model of Korean *chaebols*.

The development paths of Korea and Vietnam, although manifesting patterns of convergence, also displayed divergence. The nature of government's role in the economy is fundamentally different between Korea and Vietnam. This is largely attributable to the differences in their political systems as determined by different ideological principles. After the Korea War, an anti-communist authoritarian government was established in Korea and an economy based on the principles of Western capitalism. The devastation from the war provided the reason for the active role of the government in the economy. This involved supporting and stimulating private sector development especially through support for *chaebols*. In contrast, Vietnam emerged from war as a one-party socialist state, While Korea eventually democratized its political system, in Vietnam, the unelected CPV continues to rule and exert strong control over the society. In this political context, SOEs have been the key organizations for government control and direction of the economy.

In Korea, which is already in the post-developmental state era with an advanced economy, the role of government has changed significantly, unlike in Vietnam which is now in the developmental state era. In the aftermath of the 1997 Asian financial crisis, Korea's developmental state was challenged and undermined by the increasing demand for economic globalization and liberalization. As part of the IMF rescue program, the Korean government, in a short period of time, opened its market to international competition and foreign investment while eliminating or reducing financial and tax regulations for businesses. With radical neoliberal restructuring, direct government involvement in the economy (typical for the East Asian model) seemed to lose its role in Korea. However, bouncing back from economic slowdown, the Korean government managed to demonstrate its capacity to act as a developmental state. Governments of different types -developmentalist, neoliberals or welfare champions-, took new policy initiatives to achieve a more sophisticated economy (Hundt 2009). The transition economy in Vietnam was also challenged by neoliberalism (Gainsborough 2010). With the rise of the private sector and FDI inflows for the past two decades, Vietnam's developmental state may be on the verge of change. Although the role of government has not yet significantly changed as in Korea, there is a subtle and embryonic change (Gainsborough 2010).

Political Transition and Changes in the Role of Government in Korea and Vietnam

Despite disparities in political and social systems, Korea and Vietnam showed convergence as well as divergence in terms of political development. Both countries experienced political transitions as they pursued economic development. In Korea, the authoritarian developmental state during the military rule, despite its remarkable results for economic development, generated economic, social and political inequalities, and was resisted by some citizens. In the context of a growing democracy movement, Korea's authoritarian developmental state became no longer effective and underwent a transformation to a more socially responsive and democratic welfare state. In the new environment, the role of government has manifested in conflicting forms — the developmental state, the neo-liberal state and the welfare state — taking place at different times or at the same time.

In Vietnam, the role of the government also changed in response to external influences. Its introduction of a socialist-oriented market economy in the 1980s, achieving major results in terms of economic growth and initiated Vietnam's transformation from a backward agricultural economy into a developmental state (Masina 2012). Vietnam's developmental state at that time planned and implemented policies in all sectors to construct a market economy and economic development. After an initial stage of economic development, a socialist developmental state was increasingly required to change in response to the changing environment. First, as the market-based economy further expanded and was integrated into neoliberal-driven globalization, the ability of the government' autonomy in economic policy-making was greatly reduced. Secondly, with the erosion of Vietnam's competitiveness in labor-intensive industries, the government was increasingly required to search for new growth engines. Thirdly, the government was required to realize a socialist state and at the same time address income inequalities and other social and political demands of the people. This new environment has led the Vietnamese government to become more inclusive, institutionalized and adaptive to deal with the challenges it faces. In other words, it is required to have: more macro control than unilateral and rigid micro control; management of a complex market economy by an appropriate institutional system; more inclusive labor policies and acknowledgment of some political diversity; the development of new industry policy to maintain economic growth; and infrastructure to accommodate and encourage that growth.

Although Vietnam conforms to the East Asian model in terms of economic development policies and changes in the nature of government's role in the economy, a fundamental constraint on the emergence of a fully-fledged East Asian development state model lies in contrasting ideologies and their effects on the political systems. With an ultimate political goal being the realization of a socialist state, Vietnam is run by a single-party. Others are illegal. Although CPV rigidity has been softened to some extent, it maintains a monopoly on power and does not tolerate political challenges to its authority. With this rigid political system, government involvement in the economy seems inevitable and will continue.

Vietnam has not yet achieved political transformation as in Korea. However, if the market-based economy continues to grow and has an impact on more than society's economic relations, Vietnam could move towards a more competitive political system or, at least, one in which citizens have greater voice. A number of factors could facilitate this transition.

The first factor concerns the market-based economic structure and its development. Although, at least in the past, economic development in

Vietnam has been largely led by SOEs, it is increasingly becoming based on the market. This market needs to be more transparent, and governed by a set of rules or institutions — not simply by the directions of the government or CPV. As observed earlier, developmentalist market intervention has been restricted to some extent in Vietnam by neoliberalism and increasing need to fit with globalization.

The second factor is associated with the nature and trend of the global economy. The world economy has increasingly been integrated into a single market based on neoliberalism. This trend will eventually reduce the degree or capacity of developmentalist state intervention by the Vietnamese government. As an export-oriented economic system, Vietnam's integration into the global economy is considerable and growing leading to government being unable to maintain a developmental state.

The third factor is the growth of civil society. The pattern of economic growth in which some groups benefit more than others inevitably causes inequalities. This inequality can be political and can give rise to pressure for political change. As shown in the Korean example, political change has been an important feature of the East Asian development model. For example, in Korea influential democracy movements included the 1987 June Struggle and the 2016 candlelight protests., The 1998 anti-Suharto protests in Indonesia that led to the dictator's overthrow provide another case of popular action causing political change. This phenomenon, although very gradual, is also occurring in Vietnam. It is further facilitated as Vietnam's social system is increasingly opened to and integrated into the international society. Vietnam's relations with foreign countries are not limited to socialist countries, but also extend to developed and developing democratic nations through social, political and cultural exchanges, that can help lay the foundations for greater political diversity in civil society.

REFERENCES

Adelman, I. (1999). *The role of government in economic development. Working Paper* No. 890. University of California at Berkeley, Department of Agricultural and Resource Economics and Policy.

Adesnik, A. D. & Kim, S. (2008). *If at first you don't succeed: The puzzle of south Korea's democratic transition.* Working Paper No. 83. Center on Democracy, Development, and the Rule of Law. Retrieved from https://cddrl.fsi.stanford.edu/sites/default/files/No_83_AdesKimSouth Korea.pdf.

Aghevli, B. B. & Márquez-Ruarte, J. (1985). *A case of successful adjustment: Korea's experience during 1980-84. Occasional Paper* No. 39. Washington DC: International Monetary Fund.

Ahn, K. (1997). Trends in and determinants of income distribution in Korea. *Journal of Economic Development, 22*(2), 27-56.

Alpert, W. T. & Sanders, S. (2005). Recent economic history: A stalled expansion. In W. T. Alpert (Ed.), *The Vietnamese economy and its transformation to an open market system* (pp. 32-43). Armonk: M. E. Sharpe.

AmCham. (2014). *Vietnam falling short in tackling corruption: Party Secretary Nguyen Phu Trong. AmCham Vietnam*, HoChiMinh City Chapter. Retrieved from http://www.amchamvietnam.com/vietnam-falling-short-in-tackling-corruption-party-chief/.

Amsden, A. H. (1986). *Growth and stabilization in Korea 1962-84*. Paper presented at the World Institute for Development Economics Research Conference Project on Stabilization Programs in Developing Countries, Helsinki, August.

Amsden, A. H. (1989). *Asia's next giant*. New York: Oxford University Press.

An, D. (2015). Business as usual: Bribery remains a way of life in Vietnam, *Thanhnien News*, 16 April. Retrieved from http://www.thanhniennews.com/politics/business-as-usual-bribery-remains-a-way-of-life-in-vietnam-42245.html.

Anwar, S. & Nguyen, L. P. (2010). Foreign direct investment and trade: The case of Vietnam. *Research in International Business and Finance, 25*(1), 39-52.

Arkadie, B. V. & Mallon, R. (2004). *Viet Nam: A transition tiger?* Canberra: Asia Pacific Press.

Asia Centre. (2014). *How unique is South Korea's official development assistance (ODA) model?* Asia Centre, Paris. Retrieved from http://www.centreasia.eu/sites/default/files/publications_pdf/note_oda_-_bondaz_-_allard_-_21112014.pdf.

Associated Press in Hanoi (2016). One-party rule best for Vietnam, says leader. *The Guardian*, 28 January. Retrieved from https://www.theguardian.com/world/2016/jan/28/vietnam-nguyen-phu-trong-one-party-rule-leader.

Azulai, M., Bandiera, O., Blum, F., Kleven, H., La Ferrara, E., Padró, G. & Tejada, C. M. (2014). *State effectiveness, growth, and development. Evidence Paper*. International Growth Centre, LSE-University of Oxford. Retrieved from https://www.theigc.org/wp-content/uploads/2014/09/IGCEvidencePaperState.pdf.

Baer, W. (1972). Import substitution and industrialization in Latin America: Experience and interpretations. *Latin American Research Review*, *7*(1), 95-122.

Bank of Korea. (Various years). *Korean Economy Statistics*. Seoul: Bank of Korea.

Beeson, M. (2004). The rise and fall (?) of the developmental state: The vicissitudes and implications of East Asian interventionism. In L. Low (Ed.), *Developmental states: relevancy, redundancy or reconfiguration?* New York: Nova Science Publishers.

Beeson, M. & Pham, H. H. (2012). Developmentalism with Vietnamese characteristics: The persistence of state-led development in East Asia. *Journal of Contemporary Asia, 42*(4), 539-559.

Belassa, B. (1988). The lessons of East Asian development: An overview, *Economic Development and Cultural Change. 36*(3), 273-290.

Beresford, M. & Nyland, C. (1998). The labour movement of Vietnam [online]. *Labour History,* 75, 57-80. Retrieved from http://search.informit.com.au/documentSummary;dn=200004710;res=IELAPA.

Beresford, M. & Phong, D. (2000). *Economic transition in Vietnam: Trade and Aid in the Demise of a Centrally Planned Economy*. Cheltenham: Edward Elgar Publishing.

Berger, P. L. (1988). An East Asian development model? In P. L. Berger & H-H. M. Hsiao (Eds.), *In search of an East Asian development model* (pp. 3-11). New Brunswick: Transaction Books.

Besada, H. & Tok, E. (2014). South Africa in the BRICS: Soft power balancing and instrumentalization. *Journal of International and Global Studies, 5*(2), 76-95.

Bloom, G. (1998). Primary health care meets the market in China and Vietnam. *Health Policy, 44*(3), 233–252.

Bodewig, C., Badiani-Magnusson, R., Macdonald, K., Newhouse, D. & Rutkowski, J. (2014). *Skilling up Vietnam: Preparing the Workforce for a Modern Market Economy*, Washington DC: World Bank. Retrieved from http://documents.worldbank.org/curated/en/283651468321297015/Skilling-up-Vietnam-preparing-the-workforce-for-a-modern-market-economy.

Boltho, A. & Weber, M. (2009). Did China follow the East Asian development model? *The European Journal of Comparative Economics, 6*(2), 267-286.

Booth, A. (1999). Initial conditions and miraculous growth: Why is Southeast Asia different from Taiwan and South Korea? *World Development, 27*(2), 301–321.

Breu, M., Dobbs, R., Remes, J., Skilling, D. & Kim, J. (2012). *Sustaining Vietnam's growth: The productivity challenge*. McKinsey Global Institute. Retrieved from https://www.mckinsey.com/global-themes/asia-pacific/sustaining-growth-in-vietnam.

BRINK Asia (2016). *Asia's $527 billion makes it top foreign investment destination for 2015. BRINK Asia, 14 December*. Retrieved from https://www.brinknews.com/asia/asias-527-billion-makes-it-top-foreign-investment-destination-for-2015/.

Bureau of Economic and Business Affairs. (2013). *2013 investment climate statement: Vietnam.* February. U.S. Department of State, Bureau of Economic and Business Affairs. Retrieved from https://www.state.gov/e/eb/rls/othr/ics/2013/204760.htm.

Bureau of Economic and Business Affairs. (2016). *Investment climate statements for 2016: Vietnam.* U.S. Department of State, Bureau of Economic and Business Affairs. Retrieved from http://www.state.gov/e/eb/rls/othr/ics/investmentclimatestatements/index.htm?year=2016&dlid=254329.

Cameron, F. (2010, September). *The European Union as a model for regional integration.* Working Paper, September, International Institutions and Global Governance Program, Council on Foreign Relations, New York: Retrieved from https://www.cfr.org/sites/default/files/pdf/2010/09/IIGG_Eurozone_WorkingPaper_Cameron.pdf.

Campbell, J. R. (2012). US foreign policy towards Northeast Asia. *PERCEPTIONS, 17*(4), 3-26. Retrieved from http://sam.gov.tr/wp-content/uploads/2013/03/1Joel_Campbell.pdf.

Centeno, M. A. & Cohen, J. N. (2012). The arc of neoliberalism. *The Annual Review of Sociology, 38*(3), 17–40.

Cha, V. D. (1993). Politics and democracy under the Kim Young Sam government: Something old, something new. *Asian Survey, 33*(9), 849-

863. Retrieved from https://www.jstor.org/stable/pdf/2645233.pdf?refreqid=excelsior:d37bdb7a0f95a808940e5aeee752149e.

Chau, N. (2016). *Promoting Industrial Zones and Economic Zones as key areas for processing and manufacturing after 2015. Vietnam Industrial Parks.* Retrieved from http://khucongnghiep.com.vn/en/tabid/125/articletype/ArticleView/articleId/1550/default.aspx.

Cheng, L. C. (2008). *The Korea Brand: the cultural dimension of South Korea's branding project in 2008*. In *SAIS US-Korea Yearbook 2008* (pp. 73-85). Washington DC: The US-Korea Institute at Johns Hopkins SAIS. Retrieved from http://uskoreainstitute.org/wp-content/uploads/2010/02/Cheng.pdf.

Cheong, I. & Cho, J. (2009). *The Impact of Free Trade Agreements (FTAs) on business in the Republic of Korea. ADBI Working Paper Series* No. 156. Retrieved from https://www.adb.org/sites/default/files/publication/156011/adbi-wp156.pdf.

Cheong, K. C., Pham M. D., Nguyen, T. (Eds.). (2011). *From low-income to industrialized: Vietnam in the next decade and beyond.* Hanoi: Thế giới Publishers.

Cherry, J. (2005). 'Big Deal' or big disappointment? The continuing evolution of the South Korean developmental state. *The Pacific Review, 18*(3), 327–354.

Chew, D. H. & Gillan, S. L. (2009). *Global corporate governance*. New York: Columbia University Press.

Cho, D. (2010) Responses of the Korean economy to the global crisis: another currency crisis? Paper presented at the *EWC / KDI Conference on Global Economic Crisis: Impacts, Transmission, and Recovery, 19-20 August.* Retrieved from https://www.ssc.wisc.edu/~mchinn/02Cho-Aug2010.pdf.

Cho, H. Y. (2004). *Democratization movement of Korea*. Seoul: Korea Democracy Foundation. Retrieved from http://en.kdemo.or.kr/about/democratization-movement-of-korea.

Cho, Y. J. (1997). Government intervention, rent distribution and economic development in Korea. In A. Masahiko, O. Masahiro & H. K. Kim

(Eds.), *The role of government in East Asian economic development* (pp. 208–232). Oxford: Clarendon Press.

Choi, S. J. (2016). Park belatedly tries to clean up predecessor's mess. *The Korea Times,* 15 June. Retrieved from http://www.koreatimes.co.kr/www/tech/2017/06/693_207028.html.

Chu, Y. (2009). Eclipse or reconfigured? South Korea's developmental state and challenges of the global knowledge economy. *Economy and Society, 38*(2), 278–303.

Cima, R. J. (2002). Vietnam: Historical background. In V. Largo (Ed.), *Vietnam: Current issues and historical background* (pp. 73-190). New York: Nova Science Publishers.

Clift, B. (2014). *Comparative political economy: States, markets and global capitalism*. London: Palgrave.

Coe, D. T. & Kim, S. J. (2002). Introduction. In D. T. Coe & S. J. Kim (Eds.), *Korean crisis and recovery* (pp. 1-12). Washington DC: International Monetary Fund.

Collins, S. M. & Park, W. A. (1989). External debt and macroeconomic performance in South Korea. In J. D. Sachs (Ed.), *Developing country debt and the world economy* (pp. 121-140). Chicago: University of Chicago Press.

Committee for Population, Family and Children of Vietnam. (2002). Country report. Paper presented at the *Fifth Asia-Pacific Population Conference*. Retrieved from www.unescap.org.

Committee for the Sixty-Year History of the Korean Economy. (2010). *The Korean economy: Six decades of growth and development*. Seoul: Korea Development Institute.

Communist Party of Vietnam. (2011). *Political report of the Communist Party of Vietnam's 10th Central Committee to the 11th National Party Congress*. Hanoi. Retrieved from http://vietnamlawmagazine.vn/political-report-of-the-communist-party-of-vietnams-10th-central-committee-to-the-11th-national-party-congress-5022.html.

Cooper, W. H. (2009). *Russia's economic performance and policies and their implications for the United States*. CRS Report for Congress.

Washington DC: Congressional Research Service. Retrieved from https://fas.org/sgp/crs/row/RL34512.pdf.

Croissant, A. & Trinn, C. (2009). Culture, identity and conflict in Asia and Southeast Asia, *ASIEN*, *110*(S), 13-43. Retrieved from http://citeseerx.ist.psu.edu/viewdoc/download?doi=10.1.1.531.5748&rep=rep1&type=pdf.

Countryeconomy.com (2016a) *South Korea GDP*: Gross Domestic Product. Countryeconomy.com website. Retrieved from: https://countryeconomy.com/gdp/south-korea.

Countryeconomy.com (2016b) *Vietnam GDP: Gross Domestic Product.* Countryeconomy.com website Retrieved from: https://country economy.com/gdp/south-korea.

Cummings, L. (2008). *Gorbachev's Perestroika and the collapse of the Soviet Union.* Retrieved from https://www.lagrange.edu/resources/pdf/citations/2012/08_Cummings_History.pdf.

Customs News (2016). Vietnam emerges top export market of ROK. (2016). *Customs News*, 16 September. Retrieved from https://customsnews.vn/vietnam-emerges-top-export-market-of-rok-1019.html

Dang, H. A. (2010). Vietnam: a widening poverty gap for ethnic minorities. In G. Hall & H. A. Patrinos (Eds.), *Indigenous peoples, poverty and development.* Draft Manuscript. Washingto DC: World Bank. Retrieved from http://siteresources.worldbank.org/EXTINDPEOPLE/Resources/407801-1271860301656/Chapter_8_Vietnam.pdf.

Dang, P. (2009). *Vietnam economics' mindset 1975 – 1989*. Ho Chi Minh City: Tri Thức Publisher.

Dallago, B. & Rosefielde, S. (2016). *Transformation and crisis in Central and Eastern Europe: Challenges and prospects*. Abingdon: Routledge.

Dao, T. (2016). Vietnam eyes annual GDP growth of 6.5-7 percent from 2016-2020. *VN Express,* 22 March. Retrieved from http://e.vnexpress.net/news/news/vietnam-eyes-annual-gdp-growth-of-6-5-7-percent-from-2016-2020-3374114.html.

Dapice, D. O. (2000). *An overview of the Vietnamese economy after the Asian Crisis*. Harvard University, John F. Kennedy School of Government, Center for Business and Government. Retrieved from https://sites.hks.harvard.edu/m-rcbg/research/d.dapice_cbg_overview.vietnam.econ.pdf.

Das, D. K. (1991). *Korean economic dynamism*. London: Macmillan.

Davies, N. (2015). Vietnam 40 years on: how a communist victory gave way to capitalist corruption. *The Guardian*, 22 April. Retrieved from https://www.theguardian.com/news/2015/apr/22/vietnam-40-years-on-how-communist-victory-gave-way-to-capitalist-corruption.

Demombynes, G. (2013, Oct 15). *Why is ethnic minority poverty persistent in Vietnam?* World Bank, East Asia & Pacific on the rise. Retrieved from http://blogs.worldbank.org/eastasiapacific/why-ethnic-minority-poverty-persistent-vietnam.

Deyo, F. (1987). *The Political economy of the new Asian industrialization*. Ithaca, NY: Cornell University Press.

Divjak, C. (2008). *Inflation fuels social unrest in Vietnam*. World Socialist Web Site, 31 July. Retrieved from https://www.wsws.org/en/articles/2008/07/viet-j31.html.

Dixon, C. (2003). Developmental lessons of the Vietnamese transitional economy. *Progress in Development Studies, 3*(4), 287–306.

Do, H. (2017). Privatizing SOEs: implications for foreign investors. *KPMG Vietnam Webinar, 18 May*. Retrieved from https://home.kpmg.com/content/dam/kpmg/vn/pdf/publication/2017/privatizing-soe-implication-for-foreigns-investors.pdf.

Doner, R., Ritchie, B. & Slater D. (2005). Systemic vulnerability and the origins of developmental states: Northeast and Southeast Asia in comparative perspective. *International Organization, 59*(2), 327-361.

Dong-A Ilbo. (2011). Gap between the rich and poor. *Dong-A Ilbo*, 8 December. Retrieved from http://english.donga.com/List/3/all/26/402703/1.

Dong-A Ilbo. (2014). Korea's birth rate remains lowest among OECD countries. *Dong-A Ilbo*, 25 June. Retrieved from http://english.donga.com/List/3/all/26/408564/1.

Duong, M. T. (2012). The role of Vietnamese local government in the establishment of science parks for green economy development. Paper presented at the *16th Asia Science Park Association annual conference, Ho Chi Minh City, October*. Retrieved from http://www.eng.shtp.hochiminhcity.gov.vn/News/news/Lists/Posts/Post.aspx?ID=131.

EIU (Economist Intelligence Unit). (2015). Democracy Index 2015 Democracy in an age of anxiety. *The Economist.* Retrieved from https://www.yabiladi.com/img/content/EIU-Democracy-Index-2015.pdf.

Encyclopedia of Korean Culture. (2015). Cement. *Encyclopedia of Korean Culture*, Retrieved from http://encykorea.aks.ac.kr/Contents/Index?contents_id=E0032353.

ETNEWS. (2017).Vietnam emerges as the main production base for South Korea's component manufacturers. *ETNEWS*, 8 March. Retrieved from http://english.etnews.com/20170308200003.

Fforde, A. (2004). Vietnamese State Owned Enterprises: 'real property', commercial performance and political economy. *Southeast Asia Research Centre Working Papers Series*, No. 69, University of Hong Kong. Retrieved from http://unpan1.un.org/intradoc/groups/public/documents/apcity/unpan024765.pdf.

Fforde, A. & De Vylder, S. (1996). *From plan to market: the economic transition in Vietnam*. Boulder, COL: Westview Press.

Finger, J. M. (1974). Gatt tariff concessions and the exports of developing countries--United States concessions at the Dillon Round. *The Economic Journal, 84*(335), 566-575.

Fox News (2016). South Korea cuts key rate to record low of 1.25 percent. *Fox News*. Retrieved from http://www.foxnews.com/world/2016/06/08/south-korea-cuts-key-rate-to-record-low-125-percent.html.

Frank, S. (2013). *State-Owned enterprises and economic reform in Vietnam.* Newport, RI: Naval War College. Retrieved from http://www.dtic.mil/get-tr-doc/pdf?AD=ADA594023.

Frank, C. R., Kim, K. S. & Westphal, L. E. (1975). Economic growth in South Korea since World War II. In C. R. Frank, K. S. Kim & L. E. Westphal (Eds.), *Foreign trade regimes and economic development: South Korea* (pp. 6-24). New York: NBER Books.

Freedom House. (2010). *Countries at the crossroads 2010: Vietnam*. Retrieved from https://freedomhouse.org/report/countries-crossroads/2010/Vietnam.

Freedom House. (2011). *South Korea: Freedom of the press 2011*. Retrieved from https://freedomhouse.org/report/freedom-press/2011/south-korea.

Freedom House. (2016). South Korea: *Freedom of the press 2016*. Retrieved from https://freedomhouse.org/report/freedom-press/2016/south-korea.

Freedom House. (2017*). Freedom in the world 2017: Vietnam profile*. Retrieved from https://freedomhouse.org/report/freedom-world/2017/vietnam.

Fuller, E. (2016). Vietnam poised to be Asia's next economic tiger. *Forbes*, 7 September.Retrieved from https://www.forbes.com/sites/edfuller/2016/09/07/vietnam-poised-to-be-asias-next-economic-tiger/#fc042ca44cf5.

Gaiduk, I. V. (2003). *Confronting Vietnam: Soviet policy toward the Indochina conflict, 1954-1963*. Stanford: Stanford University Press.

Gainsborough, M. (2010). Present but not powerful: Neoliberalism, the state, and development in Vietnam. *Globalizations*, *7*(4), 475-488.

General statistics office of Vietnam. (Various years). Retrieved from https://www.gso.gov.vn.

Glewwe, P., Gragnolatti, M. & Zaman, H. (2000). Who gained from Vietnam's boom in the 1990s? An analysis of poverty and inequality trends. *Policy Research Working Paper No. 2275, World Bank*. Retrieved from https://openknowledge.worldbank.org/handle/10986/22283 License: CC BY 3.0 IGO.

Gluck, C. (2001). Seoul pays off its IMF debts. *BBC News*, 23 August. Retrieved from http://news.bbc.co.uk/2/hi/business/1505131.stm.

Government of Vietnam. (n.d.). *Vietnam's socio-economic development strategy for the period of 2011-2020*. Hanoi: Government of Vietnam. Retrieved from http://www.economica.vn/Portals/0/Documents/1d3f7ee0400e42152bdcaa439bf62686.pdf.

Graham, E. M. (2003). *Reforming Korea's industrial conglomerates.* Washington DC: Institute for International Economics.

Gregory, G., Harvie, C, & Lee, H. H. (2002). *Korean SMEs in the wake of the financial crisis: strategies, constraints, and performance in a global economy*. Working Paper 02-12, Department of Economics, University of Wollongong. Retrieved from http://ro.uow.edu.au/cgi/view content.cgi?article=1057&context=commwkpapers.

Greig, A., Hulme, D. & Turner, M. (2007). *Challenging global inequality: Development theory and practice in the 21st century*. Basingstoke: Palgrave Macmillan.

Gunnion, L. (2016). Vietnam: In the fast lane: Asia Pacific economic outlook. *Deloitte Insights*, 6 April. Retrieved from https://dupress.deloitte.com/dup-us-en/economy/asia-pacific-economic-outlook/2016/q2-vietnam.html.

Haggard, S. & Moon, C. (1983). Liberal, dependent or mercantile? The South Korean state in the international system. In J. Ruggie (Ed.), *Antinomies of interdependence* (pp. 131-191). New York: Columbia University Press.

Haggard, S. & Moon, C. (1993). The state, politics, and economic development in postwar South Korea. In H. Koo (Ed.), *State and society in contemporary Korea* (pp. 51-94). Ithaca and London: Cornell University Press.

Hahm, C. (2008). South Korea's miraculous democracy. *Journal of Democracy, 19*(3), 128-142. Retrieved from http://www.rand.org/content/dam/rand/pubs/reprints/2008/RAND_RP1370.pdf.

Harvie, C. (2001). *Competition policy and SMEs in Vietnam.* Working Paper 01-10, Department of Economics, University of Wollongong. Retrieved from http://ro.uow.edu.au/cgi/viewcontent.cgi?article=1040&context=commwkpapers.

Haub, C. & Huong, P. T. T. (2003). *An Overview of Population and Development in Vietnam.* Population Reference Bureau, February. Retrieved from http://www.prb.org/Publications/Articles/2003/AnOverviewofPopulationandDevelopmentinVietnam.aspx.

Hayashi, S. (2010). The developmental state in the era of globalization: Beyond the Northeast Asian model of political economy. *The Pacific Review, 23*(1), 45–69.

Hiep, L. H. (2013). Vietnam's hedging strategy against China since normalization. *Contemporary Southeast Asia: A Journal of International and Strategic Affairs*, 35(3), 333-368.

Hiep, L. H. (2017). Vietnam's new wave of SOE equitization: drivers and implication. *Perspective Issue:* 2017 No. 57, ISEAS Yusof Ishak Institute. Retrieved from http://hdl.handle.net/11540/7363.

Hirschman, A. (1968). The political economy of import-substituting industrialization in Latin America. *The Quarterly Journal of Economics, 82*(1), 1-32.

Holmes, F. (2016). How gold came to South Korea's rescue. US Global Investors, *Frank Talk, 27 September.* Retrieved from http://www.usfunds.com/investor-library/frank-talk/how-gold-came-to-south-koreas-rescue/#.WRKn_2ddC70.

Hong, W. (1979). *Trade, distortions and growth in Korea*. Seoul: Korea Development Institute.

Huff, W. G., Dewit, G. & Oughton, C. (2001). Credibility and reputation building in the developmental state: A model with East Asian applications. *World Development, 29*(4), 711-724.

Hundt, D. (2005). A legitimate paradox: Neo-liberal reform and the return of the state in Korea. *Journal of Development Studies, 41*(2), 242–60.

Hundt, D. (2009). *Korea's developmental alliance: State, capital and the politics of rapid development*. London: Routledge.

Hundt, D. (2015). Neoliberalism, the developmental state and civil society in Korea. *Asian Studies Review, 39*(3), 466-482. Retrieved from http://www.tandfonline.com/doi/full/10.1080/10357823.2015.1052339.

Im, H. B. (2014). Globalization, democracy and social polarization. In Y. Kim (Ed.), *Korea's quest for economic democratization: Globalization, polarization and contention* (pp. 21-40). Cham: Palgrave Macmillan.

IMF (International Monetary Fund). (2006). *Vietnam: Poverty Reduction Strategy Paper: annual progress report.* IMF Country Report No. 06/340), September. Retrieved from https://www.imf.org/external/pubs/ft/scr/2006/cr06340.pdf.

IMF (International Monetary Fund). (2011, September). *The world economic outlook: slowing growth, rising risks*. Washington DC: IMF. Retrieved from http://www.imf.org/en/Publications/WEO/Issues/2016/12/31/Slowing-Growth-Rising-Risks.

IndexMundi (2016). *South Korea GDP: real growth rate. (2016).* IndexMundi website. Retrieved from http://www.indexmundi.com/south_korea/gdp_real_growth_rate.html.

inflation.eu (2017). *Historic inflation South Korea: CPI inflation.* inflation.eu website. Retrieved from: http://www.inflation.eu/inflation-rates/south-korea/historic-inflation/cpi-inflation-south-korea.aspx.

International Business Publications. (2007). *Vietnam economic & development strategy handbook.* Washington DC: International Business Publications USA.

International Trade Centre. (2001). *Trade Promotion Network in Viet Nam: Is it Working?* Geneva: International Trade Centre. Retrieved from http://www.intracen.org.

Jin, D. Y. (2017). How to understand the emergence of digital Korea. In Y. Kim (Ed.), *Routledge handbook of Korean culture and society* (pp. 179-192). London: Routledge.

Johnson, C. (1982). *MITI and the Japanese miracle*. Stanford: Stanford University Press.

Jomo, K. (2001). Rethinking the role of government policy in Southeast Asia. In J. Stiglitz & S. Yusuf (Eds.), *Rethinking the East Asian miracle.* Washington DC: World Bank.

Jung, S. (2017). Korean companies' FDI in Vietnam exceeded $50 billion. *Business Korea*, 5 October. Retrieved from http://www.businesskorea.co.kr/english/news/industry/18343-1-investor-vietnam-korean-companies%E2%80%99-fdi-vietnam-exceeded-50-billion.

Jung. Y. (2014). On the universality and specificity of economic development in Korea. Paper presented at the *2014 Joint Conference on Economics, Seoul, February*. Retrieved from www.kdea.re.kr (in Korean).

Jung, Y. H. (2012). How did law matter for Korean economic development? Evidence from 1970s. Paper presented at the *15th KEA International*

Conference Celebrating the KEA's 60th Anniversary, Seoul, June. Retrieved from http://www.kea.ne.kr.

Kalinowski, T., Rhyu, S. & Croissant, A. (2016). *South Korea report: Sustainable governance indicators 2016*. Bertelsmann Stiftung. Retrieved from http://www.sgi-network.org/docs/2016/country/SGI 2016_South_Korea.pdf.

Kanbur, R., Rhee, C. & Zhuang, J. (2014). *Inequality in Asia and the Pacific: Trends, drivers, and policy implications*. Abingdon: Asian Development Bank and Routledge.

Kang, D. C. (2002). *Crony capitalism: Corruption and development in South Korea and the Philippines*. Cambridge: Cambridge University Press.

Kang, N. H. (2012). The vacillation of culture in neoliberal South Korea.*SOAS-AKS Working Papers in Korean Studies*, No. 37). Retrieved from http://www.soas.ac.uk/japankorea/research/soas-aks-papers/.

Kapur, D., Lewis, J. P. & Webb, R. C. (2010). *The World Bank: Its first half century*. Washington DC: Brookings Institution Press.

KDI (Korea Development Institute) (2017). *Development overview: overviews of Korea's development experience*. K-Developedia. Retrieved from https://www.kdevelopedia.org/experience/list/ALL. do#.WbXiNWdlK70.

Kerkvliet, B. J. T. (2012, November 26). Reconsidering Vietnam's political system. *East Asia Forum*, 26 November.Retrieved from http://www.eastasiaforum.org/2012/11/26/reconsidering-vietnams-political-system/.

Khaled, M. (2007, August). Park Chung-hee's industrialization policy and its lessons for developing countries. Paper for the *World Congress for Korean Studies-2007, Busan, August*. Retrieved from http://www.geocities.ws/mortuzakhaled/park.pdf.

Kien, T. N. & Heo, Y. (2008). Doi Moi policy and socio-economic development in Vietnam, 1986-2005. *International Area Review*, *11*(1) 205-232.

Kil, B. (2017). *Security policy dynamics: Effects of contextual determinants to South Korea*. New York: Routledge.

Kim, B. K. & Vogel, E. F. (2011). *The Park Chung Hee era*. Cambridge, MA: Harvard University Press.

Kim, B. P. (1995). *Two Koreas in development: A comparative study of principles and strategies of capitalist and communist Third World development*. New Brunswick: Transaction Publishers.

Kim, D. (2009). *Korean experience of overcoming economic crisis through ICT development*. ESCAP Technical Paper. United Nations Economic and Social Commission for Asia and the Pacific.

Kim, D. & Koh, Y. (2010). Korea's industrial development. In I. SaKong & Y. Koh (Eds.), *The Korean economy: Six decades of growth and development* (pp. 83-122). Seoul: Korean Development Institute.

Kim, D. S. (2017). Korea aging faster than expected. *The Chosunilbo*, 22 February. Retrieved from http://english.chosun.com/site/data/html_dir/2017/02/22/2017022201512.html.

Kim, E. M. (2010). Limits of the authoritarian developmental state of South Korea: Potentials and challenges. In O. Edigheji (Ed.), *Constructing a democratic developmental state in South Africa* (pp. 97-125). Cape Town: HSRC Press.

Kim, H. & Heo, U. (2017). Comparative analysis of economic development in South Korea and Taiwan: Lessons for other developing countries. *Asian Perspective, 41*(1), 17-41.

Kim, H. A. (2004). *Korea's development under Park Chung Hee: Rapid industrialization*, 1961-1979. London: RoutledgeCurzon.

Kim, J., Cho, W., Moon, M., Park, H., Cho, J., Park, J. and Song, J. (2015). *Education for all 2015 national review report: Republic of Korea. UNESCO*. Retrieved from http://unesdoc.unesco.org/images/0022/002297/229721E.pdf.

Kim, J. D. & Hwang, S. I. (2000, January). The role of foreign direct investment in Korea's economic development: Productivity effects and implications for the currency crisis. In T. Ito & A. O. Krueger (Eds.), *The role of foreign direct investment in East Asian economic development* (pp. 267-294). Chicago: University of Chicago Press.

Kim, J. K., Shim, S. D. & Kim, J. I. (1995). The role of the government in promoting industrialization and human capital accumulation in Korea.

In T. Ito & A. O. Krueger (Eds.), *Growth theories in light of the East Asian experience* (pp. 181-200). Chicago: University of Chicago Press. Retrieved from http://www.nber.org/chapters/c8549.pdf.

Kim, K. (2009). Global financial crisis and Korean economy. Paper presented at the *Asia Economic Policy Conference.* Retrieved from https://core.ac.uk/download/pdf/6780817.pdf.

Kim, K. & Park, I. (2004). East Asian financial crisis and the reformation of the Korean state. In L. Low (Ed.), *Developmental States: relevancy, redundancy or reconfiguration?* (pp. 117-132). New York: Nova Publishers.

Kim, K. S. (1991). The Korean miracle (1962-1980) revisited: Myths and realities in strategy and development. *Kellogg Institute Working Paper* No. 166. Retrieved from https://kellogg.nd.edu/sites/default/files/old_files/documents/166_0.pdf.

Kim, L. (1997). *From imitation to innovation.* Boston: Harvard Business School Press.

Kim, P. H. (2015). The political economy of South Korean development cooperation with Vietnam: The impact of economic aid and the Knowledge Sharing Program. Paper presented at *Inequality in the 21st Century, joint conference with the LSE Department of Sociology and the British Journal of Sociology, London, July.*

Kim, S. (2008). Rapid expansion of higher education in South Korea. In D. P. Baker & A. W. Wiseman (Eds.), *The Worldwide transformation of higher education* (pp. 223-268). Bingley: Emerald Group Publishing.

Kim, S., Han, C. & Jang, J. (2008). State-society relations in South Korea after democratization: Is the strong state defunct? *Pacific Focus, 23*(2), 252–270.

Kim, S. H. (2007). Finance and growth of the Korean economy from 1960 to 2004. *Seoul Journal of Economics, 20*(4), 377-418.

Kim, S. Y. (2014). South Korea's policy responses to global economic crisis. Paper presented at *the First Middle East Conference on Global Business, Economics, Finance and Banking, October.* Retrieved from http://globalbizresearch.org/Dubai_Conference/pdf/pdf/D426.pdf.

Kim, T. (2016). *Evaluation of Park Geun-hye government's economic policy and subsequent tasks* [In Korean], Discussion Paper, 30 March. Retrieved from web.yonsei.ac.kr.

Kim, Y. (2015). Exploring economic policy from the Chun Doo Hwan regime to Lee Myung-bak. *Weekly Hyundae*, 11 May. Retrieved from http://m.hyundaenews.com/13231#05G1.

Kim, Y. M. (2017). Korea's debt-to-GDP ratio continues to rise in 2016. *The Korea Herald* 4 April. Retrieved from http://www.koreaherald.com/view.php?ud=20170404000704.

Koh, W. (2007). Reflection on the economic progress since democratic government and a search for new strategy for economic policy [In Korean]. *Democratic Society and Policy Research, 11*(1), 161-190.

Koh, Y. (2010). The growth of the Korean economy and the role of government. In I. Sakong & Y. Koh (Eds.), *The Korean economy: six decades of growth and development* (pp. 7–82). Seoul, Korea Development Institute.

Koo, H. (1984). The political economy of income distribution in South Korea: The impact of the state's industrialization policies. *World Development*, *12*(10), 1029–1037.

Koo, H. (2014). Inequality in South Korea. *East Asia Forum*, 1 July. Retrieved from http://www.eastasiaforum.org/2014/07/01/inequality-in-south-korea/.

Korea Customs Service. (2017). FTA trend in Korea. *FTA Portal, Korea Customs Service*. Retrieved from http://www.customs.go.kr/kcshome/main/content/ContentView.do?contentId=CONTENT_ID_000002320&layoutMenuNo=23225.

Korea Herald (2017). What Moon Jae-in pledged to do as president. *Korea Herald*, 11 May Retrieved from http://www.koreaherald.com/view.php?ud=20170509000521.

Krueger, A. O. (1982). *The developmental role of the foreign sector and aid.* Cambridge, MA: Harvard University Press.

Krugman, P. R. (1994). The myth of Asia's miracle. *Foreign Affairs, 73*(6), 62-78.

Kundu, T. & Bhuyan, R. (2015). How China's slowdown affects the rest of the world. *Livemint*, 18 September. Retrieved from http://www.livemint.com/Politics/Z1XH8glAU56bfeh24olPTP/How-Chinas-slowdown-affects-the-rest-of-the-world.html.

Kwack, T. W. (1985). *Depreciation allowance and capital income taxation* [In Korean], Seoul: Korea Development Institute.

Kwon, H. J. (2007). Transforming the developmental welfare states in East Asia. *DESA Working Paper* No. 40. Retrieved from http://citeseerx.ist.psu.edu/viewdoc/download?doi=10.1.1.643.2660&rep=rep1&type=pdf.

Kwon, S. H. & O'Donnell, M. (2001). *The chaebol and labour in Korea: The development of management strategy in Hyundai*. London: Routledge.

Kwon, S. H. & Suh, C. S. (2003). The chaebol and Korean capitalism: The Hyundai business group. In C. S. Suh & M. J. Tcha (Eds.), *The Korean economy at the crossroads: Triumphs, difficulties and triumphs again* (pp. 127-152). London: RoutledgeCurzon.

Kwong, K. S., Chau, L. C., Lui, F. T. & Qiu, L. D. (2001). *Industrial development in Singapore, Taiwan, and South Korea*. Singapore: World Scientific Publishing.

Lagarde, C. (2016). The role of emerging markets in a new global partnership for growth. *Speech at University of Maryland, 4 February*. Retrieved from https://www.imf.org/en/News/Articles/2015/09/28/04/53/sp020416.

Lakatos, A. (2015, March). Investment in Vietnam and the commitments made in the Asian investment area. *International Economics Strategic Analysis for Growth and Development: International Trade and Economics Series, March*. Retrieved from http://www.tradeeconomics.com/cw/wp-content/uploads/2016/09/Investment-in-Vietnam-and-the-commitments-made-in-the-ASEAN-Investment-Area.pdf.

Larsen, R. K. (2011). Reinventing rural development in Vietnam: Discursive constructions of grassroots democracy during the renovation reform. *Asia Pacific Viewpoint, 52*(3), 316–332.

Le, A. M. (2008). Macroeconomic policy analysis of Vietnam: a macro-econometric model approach. *Forum of International Development Studies*, 36, 193-214.

Le, N. (2014). *Mergers and acquisitions in Vietnam – pitfalls and resolutions*. Financier Worldwide website, November. Retrieved from https://www.financierworldwide.com/mergers-and-acquisitions-in-vietnam-pitfalls-and-resolutions/#.WRVEY2ddC70.

Le, T. (2015). Perspectives on land grabs in Vietnam, In C Carter & A. Harding (Eds.), *Land grabs in Asia: What role for the law?* (pp. 150-166). London: Routledge.

Le, T. T. V. (2009). The global crisis and Vietnam's policy responses. *East Asian Policy* 1(2), 63-74Retrieved from http://www.eai.nus.edu.sg/publications/files/Vol1No2_LeThiThuy.pdf.

Yonhap News. (2017). Leaders of S. Korea, Vietnam agree to boost bilateral trade, cooperation. *Yonhap News*, 8 July. Retrieved from http://english.yonhapnews.co.kr/news/2017/07/08/0200000000AEN20170708000400315.html.

Lee, H. (2014). A lost 10 years? Comparing the results between DJ, Roh and MB [In Korean]. *Money Today*. Retrieved from http://news.mt.co.kr/mtview.php?no=2014052308467641313.

Lee, H. H., Lee, M. & Park, D. (2012, December). *Growth policy and inequality in developing Asia: lessons from Korea. ERIA Discussion Paper* 2012-12. Economic Research Institute for ASEAN and East Asia. Retrieved from http://www.eria.org/publications/discussion_papers/growth-policy-and-inequality-in-developing-asia-lesson-from-korea.html.

Lee, H. K. (2004, June). Re-examination and policy implications of social safety net in Korea. *Proceedings of the Symposium of the Korean Academy of Social Welfare* (pp. 1–22).

Lee, H. Y., Kim, J. & Cin, B. C. (2013). Empirical analysis on the determinants of income inequality in Korea. *International Journal of Advanced Science and Technology*, 53, 95-110.

Lee, J. H. & Yun, S. J. (2011). A comparative study of governance in state management: focusing on the Roh Moo-hyun government and the Lee Myung-bak government. *Development and Society, 40*(2), 289-318.

Lee, J. W. (1995). Government interventions and productivity growth in Korean manufacturing industries. *NBER Working Paper* No. 5060, National Bureau of Economic Research, Cambridge, MA. Retrieved from http://www.nber.org/papers/w5060.

Lee, J. W. (2016). The Republic of Korea's economic growth and catch-up: implications for the People's Republic of China. *ADBI Working Paper* No.571. Tokyo: Asian Development Bank Institute. Retrieved from http://www.adb.org/publications/republic-korea-economic-growth-catch-up-implications-prc/.

Lee, K. (2016). Structural changes in the Korean economy and Korean investment in China and ASEAN. In S. J. La Croix (Ed.), *Emerging patterns of East Asian investment in China: From Korea, Taiwan and Hong Kong* (pp. 217-238). Armonk: M. E. Sharpe.

Lee, M. Y. (2011). *The Park Chung Hee era: The transformation of South Korea.* Cambridge, MA: Harvard University Press.

Lee, N. (2007). *The making of Minjung: democracy and the politics of representation in South Korea*. New York: Cornell University Press.

Lee, Y. H. (1997). *The state, society and big business in South Korea*. London: Routledge.

Lee, J. H. & Yun, S. J. (2011). A comparative study of governance in state management: focusing on the Roh Moo-hyun government and the Lee Myung-bak government. *Development and Society, 40*(2), 289-318.

Lim, D. (2014). *Economic growth and employment in Vietnam.* London: Routledge.

Lim, H. (2009). Democratization and the transformation process in East Asian developmental states: Financial reform in Korea and Taiwan. *Asian Perspective*, *33*(1), 75-110.

Liou, T. (2008). South Korea's FTA Strategy. *Foreign Trade Review, 43*(1), 42-65.

Loc, D. (2016, February 19). Vietnam's stalled reform agenda. *East Asia Forum*, 19 February. Retrieved July 29, 2017, from East Asia Forum website: http://www.eastasiaforum.org/2016/02/19/vietnams-stalled-reform-agenda/.

Malesky, E. & London, J. (2014). The political economy of development in China and Vietnam, *Annual Review of Political Science, 17*, 395-419.

Manyin, M. E. (2005, June). The Vietnam-U.S. normalization process. *CRS Issue Brief for Congress.* Washington DC: Congressional Research Services. Retrieved from https://fas.org/sgp/crs/row/IB98033.pdf.

Martini, M. (2012). *Overview of corruption and anti-corruption in Vietnam. Transparency International, Anti-corruption Resource Centre, U4 Expert Answer.* Retrieved from https://www.transparency.org/files/content/corruptionqas/315_Overview_of_corruption_and_anti-corruption_in_Vietnam.pdf.

Masina, P. (2006). *Vietnam's development strategies.* London: Routledge.

Masina, P. (2012). Vietnam between developmental state and neoliberalism: The case of the industrial sector. In K-S. Chang, B. Fine & L. Weiss (Eds.), *Developmental politics in transition: The neoliberal era and beyond* (pp. 188-210). Basingstoke: Palgrave Macmillan.

Metraux, D. (1997). The economy. In A. M. Savada & W. Shaw (Eds.), *South Korea: A country study* (4th ed.) (pp. 135-196). Collingdale, PA: DIANE Publishing.

Minh, A. (2017). Vietnam's biggest trade deficit is no longer with China but S. Korea. *VnExpress International,* 29 July. Retrieved from https://e.vnexpress.net/news/business/data-speaks/vietnam-s-biggest-trade-deficit-is-no-longer-with-china-but-s-korea-3619855.html.

Ministry of Employment and Labor. (2012). *2012 employment and labor policy in Korea. Seoul: Ministry of Labor.* Retrieved from http://www.moel.go.kr/english/data/130111_2012_Employment%20and%20Labor%20Policy.pdf.

Moon, S. (2009). The cultural politics of remembering Park Chung Hee. *The Asia-Pacific Journal: Japan Focus, 7*(19), 5. Retrieved from http://apjjf.org/-Seungsook-Moon/3140/article.pdf.

Muchie, M., Nguyen, Q. T., Baskaran, A. & Nguyen, N. (2011). The Nature and Growth of Foreign Direct Investment and its Impact in Vietnam: A

National Innovation System Perspective. *Development Research Series* No. 148, Aaalborg Universitet, Institut for Kuktur og Globale Studier.

Mundy, S. (2016, February 24). South Korea household debt pile mounts. *Financial Times*, 24 February. Retrieved from https://www.ft.com/content/f1fa1254-dad1-11e5-9ba8-3abc1e7247e4?mhq5j=e3.

Nam, C. H. (2007). The role of trade and exchange rate policy in Korea's growth. In T. Ito & A. O. Krueger (Eds.), *Growth theories in light of the East Asian experience* (pp. 153-179). Chicago: University of Chicago Press.

Ngoc, C. (2016). Hanwha Techwin to invest $50 million in Bac Ninh. *Vietnam Economic Times,* 26 December. Retrieved from http://vneconomictimes.com/article/business/hanwha-techwin-to-invest-50-million-in-bac-ninh.

Nguyen, C. M. (2011). Overview of Vietnam socio-economic development strategy. Paper presented at the *Korean Association for Public Administration (KAPA) International Conference*, Retrieved from http://www.dbpia.co.kr/Journal/ArticleDetail/NODE06714888.

Nguyen, D. K. L. & Cao, T. H. V. (2016). Do free trade agreements generally and individually raise foreign direct investment into Vietnam? Paper presented at the *Ninth Vietnam Economists Annual Meeting, Da Nang City, 11-12 August.* Retrieved from http://veam.org/wp-content/uploads/2016/08/64.-Cao-Thi-Hong-Vinh.pdf.

Nguyen, D. T. (Ed.). (2011). *Vietnam annual economic report 2011: The economy at a crossroad.* Hanoi: Hanoi National University Press.

Nguyen, D. T., Dinh, T. M., Pham, T. A. & Pham, S. T. (2012). Toward a macroeconomic policy agenda for Vietnam in medium and long-term, *Macroeconomic Policy Dialogue*, 21 March.

Nguyen, D. T. U. (2017). Vietnam's economy takes knock as Samsung production drops. *Bloomberg*, 29 March. Retrieved from https://www.bloomberg.com/news/articles/2017-03-29/vietnam-s-economy-expands-at-slower-pace-in-first-quarter.

Nguyen, M. H., Lee, M. & Nguyet, T. N. (2017). State capacity to implement reform policy for industrial zones in Vietnam: the Case of Yen Phong Industrial Zone. *Proceedings of the KRI-OPDC Reform Policy*

Symposium & Research Workshop (pp. 237-256) April. Sydney: University of New South Wales.

Nguyen, P. L. (2006). *Foreign direct investment and its linkage to economic growth in Vietnam: A provincial level analysis*. University of South Australia Centre for Regulation and Market Analysis. Retrieved from https://editorialexpress.com/cgi-bin/conference/download.cgi?db_name=ESAM07&paper_id=24.

Nguyen, T. A. V. (2009). Economic law reform in Vietnam: Before and after WTO accession. *CALE Discussion Paper* No.1, Nagoya University, Center for Asian Legal Exchange. Retrieved from http://journals.sagepub.com/doi/pdf/10.1177/223386590801100112.

Nguyen, T. H. (2016). Strategic management in Vietnam State-Owned Enterprises (SOE), *International Journal of Business and Management, 11*(2), 197-204.

Nguyen, T. K. (2015). Manufacturing exports and employment generation in Vietnam. *Southeast Asian Journal of Economics, 3*(2), 1-21.

Nguyen, T. P. (2017). Workers' strikes in Vietnam from a regulatory perspective. *Asian Studies Review, 41*(2), 263-280.

Nguyen, T. T. A., Luu, M. D. & Trinh, D. C. (2016). The evolution of Vietnamese industry. In C. Newman, J. Page, J. Rand, A. Shimeles, M. Söderbom & F. Tarp (Eds.), *Manufacturing transformation: Comparative studies of industrial development in Africa and emerging Asia*. Oxford: Oxford University Press.

Nguyen, M. H. & Pham, S. A. (2011). Impacts of the global economic crisis on foreign trade in lower-income economies in the Greater Mekong Sub-region and policy responses: the case of Vietnam and its implications for Lao PDR and Cambodia. *Asia-Pacific Research and Training Network on Trade Working Paper Series* No.102, May. Retrieved from http://www.unescap.org/sites/default/files/AWP%20No.%20102.pdf.

Ninh, K. N. B. (2010). Vietnam hosts final summit as ASEAN chair. In *Asia*, The Asia Foundation. Retrieved from https://asiafoundation.org/2010/10/27/vietnam-hosts-final-summit-as-asean-chair/.

Nixon, R. M. (1971). *Public papers of the Presidents of the United States: Richard M. Nixon, 1970*. Washington DC: United States Government Printing Office.

OEC (Observatory of Economic Complexity). (2017). *Vietnam. OEC website*. Retrieved from http://atlas.media.mit.edu/ko/profile/country/vnm/.

(OECD) Organisation for Economic Co-operation and Development. (1994). *OECD Economic Surveys: Korea 1994*. Paris: OECD. Retrieved from http://www.oecd-ilibrary.org/economics/oecd-economic-surveys-korea_19990707.

(OECD) Organisation for Economic Co-operation and Development. (1996). *OECD economic surveys: Korea 1996*. Paris: OECD. Retrieved from http://www.oecd-ilibrary.org/economics/oecd-economic-surveys-korea_19990707.

(OECD) Organisation for Economic Co-operation and Development. (2012). How does Korea compare? *OECD Employment Outlook 2012*. Retrieved from https://www.oecd.org/korea/Korea_final_EN.pdf.

(OECD) Organisation for Economic Co-operation and Development. (2013). Southeast Asian economic outlook 2013: *With perspectives on china and India: Structural policy country notes Viet Nam. Paris: OECD*. Retrieved from http://www.oecd.org/dev/asia-pacific/saeo2013.htm.

(OECD) Organisation for Economic Co-operation and Development. (2014). *OECD economic surveys: Korea 2014*. Paris: OECD. Retrieved from http://www.oecd-ilibrary.org/economics/oecd-economic-surveys-korea_19990707.

Oh, J. H. & Mah, J. S. (2017). The patterns of Korea's foreign direct investment in Vietnam. *Open Journal of Business and Management, 5*(2), 253-271.

Ohno, K. (2003). The role of government in promoting industrialization under globalization: The East Asian experience. Paper presented at *National Graduate Institute for Policy Studies (GRIPS), Tokyo, 28 November*. Retrieved from http://www.grips.ac.jp/vietnam/KOarchives/doc/EP15_Role.pdf.

Oxfam. (2017, January). *Even it up: How to tackle inequality in Vietnam.* Oxfam Briefing Paper. Hanoi: Oxfam in Vietnam, January, Retrieved from https://www.oxfam.org/sites/www.oxfam.org/files/file_attachments/bp-vietnam-inequality-120117-en.pdf.

Palmujoki, E. (2016). *Vietnam and the world: Marxist-Leninist doctrine and the changes in international relations, 1975–93.* Basingstoke: Palgrave Macmillan.

Pang, E. S. (2000). The financial crisis of 1997–98 and the end of the Asian development state. *Contemporary Southeast Asia, 22*(3), 570–593.

Park, J. (2010). Projection of long-term Total Factor Productivity growth for 12 Asian economies. *ADB Economics Working Paper Series* No. 227. Retrieved from https://www.adb.org/sites/default/files/publication/28428/economics-wp227.pdf.

Park, K. (2008). *Who controls the Korean policy making?* Morrisville, NC: Lulu Press.

Park, S. Y. (2011). Restoring or killing rivers? The political economy of sapjil and citizens movements in Lee Myung-bak's South Korea. *The Asia Pacific Journal: Japan focus, 9*(48), 2.

Park, Y. C. (2013). Financial development and liberalization in Korea. In Y. C. Park & H. Patrick (Eds.), *How finance is shaping the economies of China, Japan, and Korea* (pp. 225-301). New York: Columbia University Press.

Peltier, C. (2013). Vietnam, painful adjustment. *BNP Paribas*, July. Retrieved from http://economic-research.bnpparibas.com/Views/DisplayPublication.aspx?type=document&IdPdf=22527.

Peng, I. & Wong, J. (2004). *Growing out of the developmental state: East Asian welfare reform in the 1990s*. Paper available on Institut d'études internationals de Montréal (IEIM-UQUAM) website. Retrieved from http://www.ieim.uqam.ca/IMG/pdf/Ombres_Wong-Peng.pdf.

Pham, B. N., Hill, P. S., Hall, W. & Rao, W. (2013). The evolution of population policy in Viet Nam, *Asia-Pacific Population Journal*, *27*(2), 61-75.

Pham S. T. (2011). Comparing effectiveness in attracting FDI between China and Vietnam. *Economic Management Journal*, 1 – 2.

Pham, T. N. (2008). The state of democratic governance in Vietnam. Paper presented at *The Asian Barometer Conference on The State of Democratic Governance in Asia, Taipei, 20-21 June*. Retrieved from http://www.asianbarometer.org/publications/the-asian-barometer-conference-on-the-state-of-democratic-governance-in-asia-june-20-21-2008-taipei.

Pham, V. H. (2010). Overview of the Vietnamese economy 2009. In D. T. Nguyen (Ed.), *Vietnam annual economic report 2010: Choices for sustainable growth*. Hanoi: Hanoi National University Press.

Pham, V. H. (2011), Overview of the Vietnamese economy 2010. In D. T. Nguyen (Ed.), *Vietnam annual economic report 2011: The economy at a crossroad*. Hanoi: Hanoi National University Press.

Phan, M. N. (2008). Sources of Vietnam's economic growth. *Progress in Development Studies, 8*(3), 209-229.

Phan, M. N., Nguyen, T. P. A. & Phan, T. N. (2003). Exports and long-run growth in Vietnam, 1975-2001. *ASEAN Economic Bulletin, 20*(3), 211-232.

Phan, S. H. (2014). A qualitative review of Vietnam's 2006–2010 economic plan and the performance of the agriculture sector. *Asian Journal of Agriculture and Development, 11*(1), 39-63.

Pincus, J., Vu, T. T. A., Pham, D. N., Wilkinson, B. & Nguyen, X. T. (2012). Structural reform for growth, equity, and national sovereignty. Policy discussion paper for *the Vietnam Executive Leadership Program, February*. Retrieved from http://www.fetp.edu.vn/cache/VELP%20 Framework%20Paper%202012.01.18-E-2012-09-20-10063958.pdf.

Pike, D. (1994). Vietnam in 1993: Uncertainty closes in. *Asian Survey, 34* (1), 64-71.

Plunk, D. (1985). *South Korea's Kwangju incident revisited. Report No. 35 1985*, The Heritage Foundation. Retrieved from http://www.heritage.org/report/south-koreas-kwangju-incident-revisited.

Rajagopal. (2007). *Dynamics of international trade and economy: An inquiry into emerging markets*. New York: Nova Science Publishers.

Regnier, P. (2011). Developmental states and hybrid regimes in South-east Asia: The socio-economic and political challenges of global crises (1998-2008). *ASIEN,* 120, 10-27.

Ren, S., Collins, N. & Zhu, Y. (2014). Leadership self-development in China and Vietnam. *Asia Pacific Journal of Human Resources, 52* (1), 42–59.

Reuters (2012) Vietnam jails former Vinashin executives after downfall. *Reuters*, 30 March. Retrieved from http://www.reuters.com/article/vietnam-vinashin/vietnam-jails-former-vinashin-executives-after-downfall-idUSL3E8ER36Q20120330.

Riain, S. O. (2000). The flexible developmental state: Globalization, information technology, and the "Celtic Tiger." *Politics & Society, 28*(2), 157-193.

Riedel, J. (1995). The transition to market economy in Vietnam. Reprinted from *HKCER Letters*, Vol. 25, November 1995. Retrieved from http://www.hkcer.hku.hk/Letters/v35/rriedel.htm.

Rohn, A. (2012). Vietnam War casualties. *The Vietnam War website*, 10 December. Retrieved from http://thevietnamwar.info/vietnam-war-casualties/.

Routley, L. (2012). *Developmental states: A review of the literature*. ESID Working Paper No. 03, University of Manchester, Effective States and Inclusive Development. Retrieved from https://assets.publishing.service.gov.uk/media/57a08a9a40f0b6497400069c/esid_wp_03_routley.pdf.

Ruwitch, J. (2010). Vietnam political reform experiments move up a notch. *Reuters,* 29 September. Retrieved from http://www.reuters.com/article/us-vietnam-politics-idUSTRE68S1VH20100929.

Sachs, J. (1996). Reforms in Eastern Europe and the former Soviet Union in light of the East Asian Experiences. *NBER Working Paper* No. 5404, National Bureau of Economic Research, Cambridge, MA, Retrieved from http://www.nber.org/papers/w5404.

Saigoneer (2015) Corruption is getting worse in Vietnam: Report. *Saigoneer*, 20 April. Retrieved from https://saigoneer.com/vietnam-news/4254-corruption-is-getting-worse-in-vietnam-report.

Santander Trade Portal. (2017). Vietnam: foreign investment. *Santander Trade Portal website*. Retrieved from https://en.portal.santandertrade.com/establish-overseas/vietnam/investing.

Sato, Y. (2004). Growth and governance in Asia: Framework of analysis. In Y. Sato (Ed.), *Growth and governance in Asia* (pp. 1-8). Honolulu, HI: Asia-Pacific Center for Security Studies.

Saxer, C. J. (2013). Democratization, globalization and the linkage of domestic and foreign policy in South Korea. *The Pacific Review, 26*(2), 177-198.

Schenk, C. R. (2011). *International economic relations since 1945*. London: Routledge.

Scholte, J. A. (2005, October). The sources of neoliberal globalization, overarching concerns. *Programme Paper* No. 8, Geneva, United Nations Research Institute for Social Development.

Seekins, D. M. (1997). The society and its environment. In A. M. Savada & W. Shaw (Eds.), *South Korea: A country study* (pp. 67-134). Washington DC: Library of Congress.

Senauth, F. (2012). *The making of Vietnam*. Bloomington: AuthorHouse.

Shin, J. S. & Chang, H. J. (2003). Restructuring 'Korea Inc.': *Financial crisis, corporate reform, and institutional transition.* London: Routledge.

Shim, J. S. & Lee, M. (2016). *The Korean economic system: Governments, big business and financial institutions*. Aldershot: Ashgate Publishing,

Shim, T. Y. (2011). Korea Inc.: Building pre-entrepreneurship in Korea. In T. Y. Shim (Ed.), *Korean entrepreneurship: The foundation of the Korean economy* (pp. 17-42). New York: Springer.

Shin, K. & Ciccantell, P. S. (2009). The steel and shipbuilding industries of South Korea: Rising East Asia and globalisation. *American Sociological Association, 15*(2), 167-192.

Shinn, R. S. (1987). The society and its environment. In R. J. Cima (Ed.), *Vietnam: A country study* (pp. 81-140). Washington DC: US Library of Congress.

Shultz II, C. J. & Le, K. (1993). Vietnam's inconsistencies between political structure and socio-economic practice: Implications for the nation's future. *Contemporary Southeast Asia, 15*(2), 179-194.

Sirowy, L. & Inkeles, A. (1990). The effects of democracy on economic growth and inequality: A review. *Studies in Comparative International Development, 25*(1), 126–157.

Sjöholm, F. (2006). State-owned enterprises and equitization in Vietnam. *Scandinavian Working Papers in Economics* No. 228. Retrieved from http://swopec.hhs.se/eijswp/papers/eijswp0228.pdf.

Snyder, S. (2009). Lee Myung-bak's foreign policy: A 250-day assessment. *Korean Journal of Defense Analysis, 21*(1), 85-102.

Socialist Republic of Vietnam. (2017a). Viet Nam's Five-year Socio-economic Development Plan, 2006-2010. *Hanoi, Socialist Republic of Vietnam Government Portal*. Retrieved from http://www.chinhphu.vn/portal/page/portal/English/strategies/strategiesdetails?categoryId=29&articleId=10050684.

Socialist Republic of Vietnam. (2017b). Resolution on the 2011-2015 Socio-Economic Development Plan. *Socialist Republic of Vietnam Government Portal*. Retrieved from http://www.chinhphu.vn/portal/page/portal/English/strategies/strategiesdetails?categoryId=30&articleId=10057591.

Sohn, P. (2015). President Park Geun-hye's 'Creative Economy' budget 21.5 trillion won...close to the 'Four Rivers Project" budget. *The Kyunghyang Shinmun,* 8 September. Retrieved from http://news.khan.co.kr/kh_news/khan_art_view.html?artid=201509081725261#csidx115ca4aa2dc9ed9ac0ed4b67b6f1e9b (in Korean).

Son, J. H. (2017, June 12). Korea's direct investment in Vietnam tops $50b in 2016. *The Korean Herald,* 12 June. Retrieved from http://www.koreaherald.com/view.php?ud=20170612000743.

Song, B. N. (2003). *The rise of the Korean economy* (3rd ed.). New York: Oxford University Press.

Song, H. K. (2003). The birth of a welfare state in Korea: The unfinished symphony of democratization and globalization. *Journal of East Asian Studies 3*(3), 405–432.

Song, S. H. (2014, February 26). Park aims for overhaul of economy with '474 Vision'. *Korea JoongAng Daily*, 26 February. Retrieved from http://koreajoongangdaily.joins.com/news/article/Article.aspx?aid=2985510.

Stallings, B. & Kim, E. M. (2017). *Promoting development: The political economy of East Asian foreign aid*. Singapore: Springer.

Stratfor (2011). The potential for unrest in Vietnam. *Stratfor Worldview*, 9 March. Retrieved from https://worldview.stratfor.com.

Stubbs, R. (2009). Whatever happened to the East Asia developmental state? The unfolding debate. *The Pacific Review 22*(1), 1–22.

Suh, C. S. (1996). Korea in the 1990s: Lttle dragon or new giant in Asia? In D. K. Das (Ed.), *Emerging growth pole: The Asian Pacific economy* (pp. 577–601). Singapore: Prentice Hall.

Suh, C. S. & Kwon, S. H. (2014). Whither the developmental state in South Korea? Balancing welfare and neoliberalism. *Asian Studies Review, 38*(4), 676-692.

Suh, J. J. (2009). *The Lee Myung-bak government's North Korea policy: A study on its historical and theoretical foundation*. Seoul: Korea Institute for National Unification. Retrieved from http://citeseerx.ist.psu.edu/viewdoc/download;jsessionid=E7629E944B5ED32A986F471CC09F136F?doi=10.1.1.233.2160&rep=rep1&type=pdf.

Swinkels, R. & Turk, C. (2006). Explaining ethnic minority poverty in Vietnam: a summary of recent trends and current challenges. Draft background paper for *CEM/ MPI meeting on Ethnic Minority Poverty Hanoi*. Retrieved from http://www.worldbank.org/.

Thanh, B. T. K. (2008). *Inflation in Vietnam over the period 1990-2007*. Unpublished Master's thesis. Institute of Social Studies, The Hague. Retrieved from https://thesis.eur.nl.

Thanh, P. C. (2015). Competition law enforcement of Viet Nam and the necessity of a transparent regional competition policy. *ERIA Discussion Paper Series*, Jakarta, Economic Research Institute for ASEAN and East Asia. Retrieved from http://www.eria.org/ERIA-DP-2015-86.pdf.

Thayer, C. A. (2009). Vietnam and the challenge of political civil society. *Contemporary Southeast Asia*, *31*(1), 1–27.

The Business Times. (2016). Vietnam's 2016 FDI inflow hits record high of US$15.8b: govt. *The Business Times,* 28 December. Retrieved from http://www.businesstimes.com.sg/government-economy/vietnams-2016-fdi-inflow-hits-record-high-of-us158b-govt.

The Saigon Times (2009). Vietnam, S. Korea upgrade ties to strategic partnership. *The Saigon Times*, 22 October. Retrieved from http://english.thesaigontimes.vn/7081/Vietnam-SKorea-upgrade-ties-to-strategic-partnership.html.

Thurbon, E. (2016). Full flowering of financial activism. In E. Thurbon (Ed.), *Developmental mindset: The revival of financial activism in South Korea* (pp. 125-142). Ithaca, NY: Cornell University Press. Retrieved from http://www.jstor.org/stable/10.7591/j.ctt18kr603.13.

Trading Economics. (2017). Economic indicators. *Trading Economics website*. Retrieved from https://tradingeconomics.com.

Tran, D. L. (2014). Public investment restructuring: problems and solutions. *Vietnam Law & Legal forum, 23 October.* Retrieved from http://vietnamlawmagazine.vn/public-investment-restructuring-problems-and-solutions-3528.html.

Tran, M. (2011). South Korea: a model of development? *The Guardian,* 28 November. Retrieved from https://www.theguardian.com/global-development/poverty-matters/2011/nov/28/south-korea-development-model.

Tran, M. V. (1999). Japan through Vietnamese eyes (1905-1945). *Journal of Southeast Asian Studies, 30*(1), 126-146.

Tran, N. T. (2010), *Vietnam-America relations - reality and prospects.* Hanoi: Information and Communications Publishing House.

Tran, T. Q. & To, X. P. (2003). Doi Moi policy and its impact on the poor. *Social Watch website*. Retrieved from http://www.socialwatch.org/node/10854.

Tran, V. T. (Ed.) (2000), *Vietnam economy 1955 – 2000*. Hanoi: Statistical Publishing House.

Tran, V. T. (2002). Economic development in Vietnam during the second half of the 20th century: How to avoid the danger of lagging behind. In

T. N. Binh & D. P. Chi (Eds.), *The Vietnamese economy awakening the dormant dragon* (pp. 15-29). London: RoutledgeCurzon.

Transparency International. (2017). Vietnam. *Transparency International website*. Retrieved from https://www.transparency.org.

Tuoi Tre News (2016). PM urges Vietnam to overachieve on GDP growth. *Tuoi Tre News*, 1 March. Retrieved from http://tuoitrenews.vn/business/33476/pm-urges-vietnam-to-overachieve-on-gdp-growth.

Turner, M., Kwon, S. H. & O'Donnell, M. (2017). Integrity, institutions and ethical leadership with special reference to South Korea. *Proceedings of the KRI-OPDC Reform Policy Symposium & Research Workshop, April (pp. 41-51)*. Sydney: University of New South Wales.

(UNDP) United Nations Development Programme. (2006). *Deepening democracy and increasing popular participation in Viet Nam. UNDP Vietnam Policy Dialogue Paper* 2006/1. Retrieved from http://www.vn.undp.org/content/vietnam/en/home/library/democratic_governance/deepening-democracy-and-increasing-popular-participation-in-viet.html.

United Nations Industrial Development Organization. (2012). *UNIDO activities in the Socialist Republic of Viet Nam.* UNIDO Evaluation Group, Independent Country Evaluation. Retrieved from https://www.unido.org/fileadmin/user_media/About_UNIDO/Evaluation/Country_Reports/VietNam_Ebook.pdf.

U.S. National Archives and Records Administration. (2013). *Statistical information about casualties of the Vietnam War.* Retrieved from https://www.archives.gov/research/military/vietnam-war/casualty-statistics.html.

Varamini, H. & Vu, A. (2007). Foreign direct investment in Vietnam and its impact on economic growth. *International Journal of Business Research, 7*(6).

VBN (2016). RoK to provide US$1.5 bln ODA for VN in 2016-2020. *Vietnam Breaking News (VBN)*, 15 June. Retrieved from https://www.vietnambreakingnews.com/2016/06/rok-to-provide-us1-5-bln-oda-for-vn-in-2016-2020/.

VBN (2017). Nguyen Van Linh's 100th birth anniversary commemorated. *Vietnam Breaking News.Com. (VBN),* 8 March. Retrieved from https://www.vietnambreakingnews.com/2017/03/nguyen-van-linhs-100th-birth-anniversary-commemorated-viet-nam-news/.

Vietnam Economic Portal. (2014). Bad debt settlement - critical issues in bank restructuring in Vietnam. *Vietnam Economic Portal.* Retrieved from http://www.vnep.org.vn/en-US/Moneytary-Policy/Bad-debt-settlement-critical-issues-in-bank-restructuring-in-Vietnam.html.

Vietnam Investor Network. (2015). *Speech by Bui Quang Vinh, Minister of Investment and Planning, at the National Party Congress.* Retrieved from https://www.ahvietnam.com/economy/vietnam-economic-and-political-reform-process/.

Vietnam Ministry of Planning and Investment. (2001). *The 5-year plan for socio-economic development (2001-2005).* Hanoi: Ministry of Planning and Investment. Retrieved from http://siteresources.worldbank.org/INTVIETNAM/Resources/5yr_Soc_Eco.pdf.

Vietnam Ministry of Planning and Investment. (2006). The 5-year plan for socio-economic development (2006-2010). *Hanoi: Ministry of Planning and Investment.* Retrieved from http://siteresources.worldbank.org/INTPRS1/Resources/Vietnam_PRSP(July-2006).pdf.

Vietnamnet. (2017a) Vietnam's top ten 2016 exports. *Vietnamnet,* 3 February. Retrieved from http://english.vietnamnet.vn/fms/business/172030/vietnam-s-top-ten-2016-exports.html.

Vietnamnet. (2017b). Vietnam eases reliance on Chinese products, but imports more from South Korea. *Vietnamnet,* 16 July. Retrieved from http://english.vietnamnet.vn/fms/business/182035/vietnam-eases-reliance-on-chinese-products--but-imports-more-from-south-korea.html.

Vietnamnet. (2017c). Vietnam to equitise 137 more state-owned enterprises by 2020. *Vietnamnet,* 31 May. Retrieved from http://english.vietnamnet.vn/fms/business/179482/vietnam-to-equitise-137-more-state-owned-enterprises-by-2020.html.

Vietnamnet. (2017d) Vietnam may see record number of M&A deals in 2016. *Vietnamnet,* 25 January. Retrieved from http://english.vietnam net.vn/fms/business/150223/vietnam-may-see-record-number-of-m-a-deals-in-2016.html.

Viet Nam News. (2016a) MoF to accelerate SOE equitization. *Viet Nam News*, 13 June. Retrieved from http://vietnamnews.vn/economy/ 298088/mof-to-accelerate-soe-equitisation.html#cq34jYs6pfJjpYp3. 97.

Viet Nam News. (2016b). Report of the Party's XIth-tenure Central Committee. *Viet Nam News*, 29 January. Retrieved from http://vietnamnews.vn/politics-laws/281839/report-of-the-partys-xith-tenure-central-committee.html#tbpsfLjPU22DOP4p.97.

Viet Nam News. (2016c). Bac Ninh attracts foreign investors. *Viet Nam News*, 7 January. Retrieved from http://vietnamnews.vn/economy/280 809/bac-ninh-attracts-foreign-investors.html#qBXdw3dozFxb3fv4.97.

Viet Nam News. (2017). South Korea becomes VN's second largest trade partner. *Viet Nam News*, 28 July. Retrieved from http://vietnamnews. vn/economy/381007/south-korea-becomes-vns-second-largest-trade-partner.html#s2iTeYjmkdDTMF7U.99.

Vo, N. T. (1990). *Vietnam's economic policy since 1975*. Singapore: Institute of Southeast Asian Studies.

Vu, M. K. (2015). Can Vietnam achieve more robust economic growth? Insights from a comparative analysis of economic reforms in Vietnam and China. *Journal of Southeast Asian Economies, 32*(1), 52-84.

Vu, Q. N. (2002). The state-owned enterprise reform in Vietnam: process and achievements. *Visiting Researchers Series* No. 4, Institute of Southeast Asian Studies, Singapore. Retrieved from http://citeseerx.ist.psu.edu/viewdoc/download?doi=10.1.1.201.2122&rep=rep1&type=pdf.

Vuong, Q. H. (2010). *Financial markets in Vietnam's transition economy, facts, insights, implications*. Saarbrücken: VDM Verlag Dr. Müller Aktiengesellschaft & Co.

Vuong, Q. H. (2014). Vietnam's political economy: A discussion on the 1986-2016 period. *CEB Working Paper* No. 14/010, Centre Emile Bernheim, Solvay Brussels School, Economics and Management. Retrieved from https://econpapers.repec.org/paper/solwpaper/2013_2f163371.htm.

Vuong, Q. H. & Tran, T. D. (2009). Financial turbulences in Vietnam's emerging economy: transformation over 1991-2008 period. In Jagadeesha and S. Deene (Eds.), *2009 contemporary issues in finance* (pp. 43-61). New Delhi: Excel Books.

Wagner, J. (2016). Vietnam's political transition: economic implications. *The Diplomat,* 30 April. Retrieved from https://thediplomat.com/2016/04/vietnams-political-transition-economic-implications/.

Wang, C. & Balasubramanyam, V. N. (2011). Aid and foreign direct investment in Vietnam. *Journal of Economic Integration, 26*(4), 721-739.

Webster, L. & Amin, M. R. (1998). *Equitization of state enterprises in Vietnam: Experience to date. Private Sector Discussions* Number 3, Mekong Project Development Facility, Hanoi. Retrieved from http://documents.worldbank.org/curated/en/392021468173655407/pdf/367380State0enterprises0PSDP1No131EN.pdf.

Wiemann, J., Effner, H., Grammling, S., Henke, K., Kommer, C. & Mühlich, L. (2006). *Vietnam – the 150th WTO-member: Implications for industrial policy and export promotion. Bonn*: German Development Institute. Retreived from http://www.fes-globalization.org/geneva/documents/GDI_Study_implications_Vietnams_WTO_accession.pdf.

Wolff, P. (1999*) Vietnam, the incomplete transformation.* London: Psychology Press.

Wong, J. (2004). The adaptive developmental state in East Asia. *Journal of East Asian Studies*, *4*(3), 345–362.

Woo-Cumings, M. (1999). Introduction: Chalmers Johnson and the politics of nationalism and development. In M. Woo-Cumings (Ed.), *The developmental state* (pp. 1-33). Ithaca: Cornell University Press.

Workman, D. (2017). South Korea's top trading partners. *WTEx website, 2 September*. Retrieved from http://www.worldstopexports.com/south-koreas-top-import-partners/.

World Bank. (1997). *World Development Report*. New York: Oxford University Press.

World Bank. (2010). *World Bank East Asia and Pacific economic update 2010, volume 2: robust recovery, rising risks*. Retrieved from https://openknowledge.worldbank.org/handle/10986/14469.

World Bank. (2011, December 6). *Market economy for a middle-income Vietnam*. Retrieved from http://documents.worldbank.org/curated/en/495721468327934602/pdf/659800AR00PUBL0elopment0Report02012.pdf.

World Bank. (2017a). *World Bank national accounts data, and OECD national accounts data files*. Retrieved from http://data.worldbank.org/indicator/NY.GDP.MKTP.KD.ZG.

World Bank. (2017b). *Where we work*. Retrieved from http://www.worldbank.org/en/where-we-work.

World Bank. (2017c). *The World Bank in Vietnam*. Retrieved from http://www.worldbank.org/en/country/vietnam/overview.

(WTO) World Trade Organization. (2017). Korea, Republic of. Retrieved from http://stat.wto.org/CountryProfile/WSDBCountryPFView.aspx?Country=KR&Language=F.

Worsnip, P. (2008, April 16). S. Korea's Lee calls for new strategic bond with U.S. *Reuters,* 16 April. Retrieved from http://www.reuters.com/article/us-usa-korea-lee-idUSN1527979420080416.

Wright, J. & Blomenhofer, M. (2017). *The rise of Korean investment in Vietnam: How Korean companies can continue to thrive in an exciting but challenging jurisdiction*. New York: Kroll. Retrieved from http://www.kroll.com/CMSPages/GetAzureFile.aspx?path=~%5Cmedia%5Cimages%5Cintelligence-center%5Ctht-inv-apac_rise-of-korean-investment-in-vietnam_feb-2017_web.pdf&hash=4dbb223eb291d58bdca8fc648161b3b008523ac3522ee32fb5bcdac7cc7784a2.

Yang, E. (2008). *South Korean government under the former CEO, President Lee Myung-Bak. UNISCI Discussion Papers* No. 18, October, Unidad de Investigación sobre Seguridad y Cooperación, Universidad Complutense de Madrid. Retrieved from https://www.ucm.es/data/cont/media/www/pag-72511/UNISCI%20DP%2018%20-%20YANG.pdf.

Yang, J. J. (2012). The Korean welfare state in economic hard times: democracy, partisanship, and social learning. *Taiwan Journal of Democracy, 8*(1), 51-68.

Yau, K. S. (2009). Imagining others: a study of the "Asia" presented in Japanese cinema, In D. M. Nault (Ed.), *Development in Asia: Interdisciplinary, post-neoliberal, and transnational perspectives* (pp. 135-164), Boca Raton: Universal-Publishers.

Yeung, H. W. (2017). Rethinking the East Asian developmental state in its historical context: finance, geopolitics and bureaucracy. *Area Development and Policy, 2*(1). 1-23.

Yonhap News (2014). S. Korea has fastest aging population among advanced economies. *Yonhap News,* 9 September Retrieved from http://english.yonhapnews.co.kr/full/2014/09/09/34/1200000000AEN20140909001800320F.html.

Yoon J. C. & Hellmann, T. (1993). *The government's role in Japanese and Korean credit markets: a new institutional economics perspective.* Working Paper, Financial Sector Development, World Bank. Retrieved from http://documents.worldbank.org/curated/en/899891468774541126/The-governments-role-in-Japanese-and-Korean-credit-markets-a-new-institutional-economics-perspective.

You, J. S. (2015). The Cheonan Incident and the declining freedom of expression in South Korea. *Asian Perspective, 39*(2), 195–219.

Young, K. B., Wailes, E. J., Cramer, G. L. & Nguyen, T. K. (2002). *Vietnam's rice economy: Developments and prospects. Research Report No. 968*, Arkansas Agricultural Experiment Station. Retrieved from http://arkansasagnews.uark.edu/968.pdf.

Yousefi, M. (1997). Economic development and gender equity in South Korea, In J. M. Rives & M. Yousefi (Eds.), *Economic dimensions of gender inequality: A global perspective* (pp. 57-74). Westport: Greenwood Publishing Group.

Zysman, J. & Doherty, E. (1995). *The evolving role of the state in Asian industrialization. Working Paper* No. 84, The Berkeley Roundtable on International Economy. Retrieved from https://www.kdevelopedia.org/Resources/economy/evolving-role-state-asiindustrialization-05201410290135026.do?fldIds=TP_ECO%7CTP_ECO_EA#.Widx1WdlKUk.

ABOUT THE AUTHOR

Seung-Ho Kwon, PhD
Executive Director
Korea Research Institute (KRI),
University of New South Wales. Australia
Email: s.kwon@unsw.edu.au

Dr. Seung-Ho Kwon received his PhD degree from the School of Industrial Relations and Organisational Behaviour at the University of New South Wales in 1997. In 1998, he began his career as a senior research fellow at the School of International Business, the University of New South Wales. He is a founding member of Korea Research Institute at the University of New South Wales (KRI@UNSW) established in 2000. Currently, he is the Executive Director of the KRI. Through his work at KRI@UNSW, he has made a substantial contribution to the creation of a strong research network for Korean Studies scholars across Australasia, Korea and Southeast Asia and the promotion of Korean Studies in these regions. He has also played an instrumental role in establishing the Korean Studies Association of Southeast Asia (KoSASA) consisting of the leading national universities from eight Southeast Asian countries (Thailand, Malaysia, Indonesia, The Philippines, Vietnam, Laos, Cambodia and Laos). His research interests include cultural and copyright industries, state capacity and public policy, globalisation strategies and Asian multinational corporations and employment relations.

INDEX

A

D

E

F

G

H

I

J

K

L

Q

R

S

T

U

V

W

Russia: Background, Issues and Recent Developments

Author: Ulyana Asya Romanov

Series: Asian Political, Economic and Social Issues

Book Description: The first chapter examines Russia's 2018 presidential election, in which Russian President Vladimir Putin was widely expected to secure reelection (and since then, has won).

Hardcover ISBN: 978-1-53614-266-2
Retail Price: $160

Thailand: Environmental Resources, Social Issues and Related Policies

Editors: Yongyut Trisurat, Rajendra Prasad Shrestha and Palle Havmoller

Series: Asian Political, Economic and Social Issues

Book Description: Thailand has been recognized as having rich natural resources, the natural capital to support the country's economic development and the livelihood of Thai people. Tapping on its vast fertile area, the country has been one of the players in global food production for last four decades. However, these achievements have also had negative consequences on biodiversity, ecosystem functions, and human health both in rural and urban areas.

Hardcover ISBN: 978-1-53614-466-6
Retail Price: $270

Development-Induced Displacement and Resettlement in Bangladesh: Case Studies and Practices. Second Edition

Author: Mohammad Zaman, Ph.D. and Hafiza Khatun

Series: Asian Political, Economic and Social Issues

Book Description: A very first for Bangladesh, this edited book examines the complex issues of development-induced displacement and resettlement using case studies with "good practice" examples from a wide range of ongoing projects. The authors, who are largely "practitioners" in the field of resettlement studies, are well-known in the country and internationally for their expert knowledge.

Hardcover ISBN: 978-1-53612-595-5
Retail Price: $230

Central Asia: Perspectives and Present Challenges

Editor: Bárbara Beyer

Series: Asian Political, Economic and Social Issues

Book Description: Located on the Silk Road, blue domes are one of the most significant shapes in the architecture of Central Asia. The opening chapter of Central Asia: Perspectives and Present Challenges aims to identify and address the unique features of conical and pointed domes, which topped a majority of distinct buildings in the cities of Merv, Samarkand, Bukhara, and Khiva from the Parthian to the Shaybanids era.

Hardcover ISBN: 978-1-53614-635-6
Retail Price: $160